The Marine Corps
Book of Lists

Books by Albert A. Nofi

COMBINED PUBLISHING TITLES:
The Gettysburg Campaign
The Spanish-American War, 1898
American Military History
(with Maurice Matloff)
A Civil War Journal
The War Against Hitler: Military Strategy in the West
Eyewitness to the Civil War: The Opening Guns
The Waterloo Campaign
The Civil War Book of Lists
(with John Cannan and David G. Martin)
A Civil War Notebook
A Civil War Treasury
The Alamo and the Texas War for Independence, 1835-1836
James Longstreet: The Man, the Soldier, the Controversy
(with R.L. DiNardo)

With James F. Dunnigan:
TheWar in the Pacific Encyclopedia
Victory at Sea
Victory and Deceit: The Art of Deception in Warfare
Dirty Little Secrets of World War II
Shooting Blanks: Warmaking that Doesn't Work
Dirty Little Secrets: Military Information You're Not Supposed to Know

With Bela K. Kiraly:
East Central European War Leaders, Civil and Military, 1740-1920

With Bela K. Kiraly and Nandor Dreisziger:
War and Society in East Central Europe in the Era of World War I

The Marine Corps
Book of Lists

Albert A. Nofi

DA CAPO PRESS

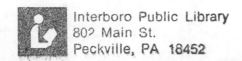

Originally Published by Combined Publishing in 2001

Library of Congress Cataloging-in-Publication Data.
Nofi, Albert A.
  Marine Corps book of lists / Nofi, Albert
    p.   cm.
  ISBN 0-938289-89-6 (pbk.)
  1. United States. Marine Corps--Miscellanea   I. Title.
  VE23.N64   1997   97-16681
  359.9′6′0973—dc21   CIP

Printed in the United States of America.

First DaCapo Edition 2001

01 02 03 04 05 EBC 8 7 6 5 4 3

For
Marilyn J.Spencer
and
Lori Fawcett
In Loving Memory

Contents

Author's Note and Acknowledgments

Data on the contemporary Marine Corps in this work is as accurate as could be established as of early 1997. In the case of some statistics rounding has been used to simplify calculations. Note that the term "list" has been interpreted rather liberally, to include occasional tables and even a few songs and poems,as well as lists. And remember that a list can have just one item.

Although care has been taken to ensure accuracy, errors and omissions are inevitable in any work of this nature. A number of omissions are obvious, notably the absence of information on several important foreign marine corps, due to a lack of available resources. If you believe you've spotted an error, or can fill in a gap, please feel free to drop the author a note, at the publishers or via e-mail at *ANOFI@AOL.COM*. When doing so, please cite a reference. Suggestions for additional items or lists for possible incorporation in future revised editions of this work are also welcome.

Please note that in lists asserting the "best" or "worst," the determination was made by means of an informal poll of Marines and students of the history of the Marine Corps.

Throughout, military stylistic conventions have been adopted. Dates are in military fashion. The designation "3/2nd" Marines stands for "3rd Battalion, 2nd Marines."

A good many people were very helpful in the preparation of this volume. Particular thanks go to Kenneth Gallagher of Combined Books, who came up with the idea for it, as well as to Dennis Casey, Brian Sullivan, Kelly Richter, C.V. Lynn, COL George Pappas, USA, Ret, COL Frederick Peck, USMC, MAJ Gene Duncan, USMC, Ret, Doyle Sanders, COL Thomas G. Cleland, NYG, CPT Juan Martinez-Esparza, *Infanteria de Marina Española*, Ruud G. Manning, Scott Slauson, Mark Stuempfig, James Eric Olson, Doyle Sanders, James Dingman, CPT Hector A Tebaldi, *ARA*, Steve Zaloga, John Prados, Martin Gordon of White Mane Publishing, Ewerton Luiz Silva de Oliveira, Kathryn C. Agel, Dick Garczynski, and Robert Mangieri, as well as several who wish to remain anonymous.

Institutions which were of considerable help include The United States Military Academy Archives, The Marine Corps Historical Center, The Navy Historical Center, The United States Army Center of Military History, and The New York Public Library.

As always, special thanks must go to my wife, Mary Spencer Nofi, who has to suffer through these projects.

Albert A. Nofi
1 July 1996-2 January 1997
Brooklyn-Acuña-Brooklyn

## CHAPTER 1

The Marine Corps Today

The smallest of the nation's armed forces (barring the Coast Guard), the Marine Corps is arguably the readiest of them all for any service that may be required, and is certainly the one with the greatest proportion of its personnel in operating forces.

The Marine Corps within the Armed Forces

Service	Active 1996	Projected 2000
Air Force	384,997	375,000
Army	485,831	475,000
Marine Corps	174,883	174,800
Navy	411,850	399,000
Total	1,457,623	1,418,800

All figures are approximate.

The Marine Corps Ranked Among the Services by Highest Enlisted-to-Officer Ratio

Service	Ratio	Rank
Air Force	4.0	4th
Army	5.0	3rd
Marine Corps	8.8	1st
Navy	6.3	2nd
Overall	5.3	

Key: *Ratio* indicates the number of active duty enlisted personnel to each active duty officer; *Rank* is the ranking of the services from that with the highest enlisted-to-officer ratio to that with the lowest. The high ranking of the Marine Corps is somewhat overstated, since the Navy provides medical, religious, and certain other technically skilled officers. However, since the enlisted-to-officer ratio in the Navy is itself relatively low, the sea services as a whole have an excellent showing in this regard. For the record, the ratio for the Coast Guard is 3.8 (28,400 enlisted persons and 7,475 officers).

Mission Assignments of Marine Corps Personnel

Mission	Number	Percent
Marine Expeditionary Forces	c. 117,000	66.9
Security Forces *	4,565	2.6
Other **	c. 52,000	29.7
Total	174,883	

* Comprise details aboard warships, at naval bases and installations, and U.S.diplomatic missions worldwide.

** Command, administration, logistics, training cadres, and personnel in training, recruiting, R&D, and miscellaneous assignments, such as those serving on diplomatic missions.

Marine Corps Personnel Allocations

Active	Reserve	Total	Select	Other	Total
Total	174,883	106,627	42,077	64,550	281,510
Officers	17,931	16,472	4,821	11,651	34,403
	(10.3%)	(15.4%)	(11.5%)	(18.0%)	(12.2%)
Enlisted	157,952	89,155	36,256	52,899	247,107
	(89.7%)	(84.4%)	(88.5%)	(82.0%)	(87.8%)

Key: Active, personnel on permanent active duty; Reserve, all personnel with some reserve obligation to the Marine Corps; Select, reserve pesonnel in organized elements of the Marine Corps Reserve; Other, personnel in the Individual Replacement Reserve and other branches of the Marine Corps Reserve. Some reservists are on "full time" duty. Percent figures refer to the summary figure at the top of each column.

Distrbution of Active Marine Corps Personnel by Rank

Enlisted Personnel		Number	% EP	% Marines
E-1	Private	13,346	8.5%	7.6%
E-2	Private First Class	19,375	12.3%	11.1%
E-3	Lance Corporal	45,838	29.2%	26.2%
E-4	Corporal	29,620	18.9%	16.9%
E-5	Sergeant	22,293	14.2%	12.7%
E-6	Staff Sergeant	13,275	8.5%	7.6%
E-7	Gunnery Sergeant	8,532	5.4%	4.9%
E-8	First Sergeant & Master Sergeant	3,333	2.1%	1.9%
E-9	Sergeant Major & Master Gunnery Sergeant	1,340	0.9%	0.8%
	Total Enlisted Personnel	156,952		

THE MARINE CORPS TODAY

Warrant Officers	Number	% WO	% Marines
W-1 Warrant Officer 1	194	10.2%	0.1%
W-2 Chief Warrant Officer 2	867	45.7%	0.5%
W-3 Chief Warrant Officer 3	513	27.0%	0.3%
W-4 Chief Warrant Officer 4	255	13.4%	0.1%
W-5 Chief Warrant Officer 5	68	3.6%	0.0%
Total Warrant Officers	**1,897**		

Commissioned Officers	Number	% Off	% Marines
O1 Second Lieutenant	2,419	15.1%	1.4%
O2 First Lieutenant	2,695	16.8%	1.5%
O3 Captain	5,424	33.8%	3.1%
O4 Major	3,167	19.8%	1.8%
O5 Lieutenant Colonel	1,634	10.2%	0.9%
O6 Colonel	627	3.9%	0.4%
O7-O10 Generals	68	0.4%	0.0%
Total Officers	**16,034**		
Grand Total	**174,883**		

Key: The first percentage column takes personnel of the indicated grade as a proportion of all personnel of their category (i.e., Enlist, Warrant, or Commissioned), the % Marines figure takes personnel of that grade as a proportion of the entire Marine Corps.

Marines by Race and Sex

	Total	Whites Men	Whites Women	Whites Total	Whites %	Blacks Men	Blacks Women	Blacks Total	Blacks %
E1	12,205	8,000	325	8,325	68.2%	1,800	80	1,880	23.5%
E2	20,745	13,650	675	14,325	69.1%	2,875	210	3,085	22.6%
E3	47,435	32,525	1,200	33,725	71.1%	6,250	375	6,625	20.4%
E4	32,225	22,525	800	23,325	72.4%	4,125	350	4,475	19.9%
E5	22,470	13,875	600	14,475	64.4%	4,850	410	5,260	37.9%
E6	14,650	8,675	375	9,050	61.8%	3,875	275	4,150	47.8%
E7	9,195	5,525	245	5,770	62.8%	2,275	150	2,425	43.9%
E8	3,445	2,150	75	2,225	64.6%	800	30	830	38.6%
E9	1,427	925	10	935	65.5%	350	10	360	38.9%
WOs	2,025	1,550	80	1,630	80.5%	225	20	245	15.8%
O1	2,244	1,725	120	1,845	82.2%	175	15	190	11.0%
O2	2,968	2,450	90	2,540	85.6%	180	10	190	7.8%
O3	5,603	4,875	135	5,010	89.4%	250	10	260	5.3%
O4	3,265	2,925	100	3,025	92.6%	110	5	115	3.9%
O5	1,691	1,525	45	1,570	92.8%	75	5	80	5.2%
O6	643	600	10	610	94.9%	18	0	18	3.0%
O7+	69	67	1	68	98.6%	1	0	1	1.5%
	182,305	123,567	4,886	128,453	70.5%	28,234	1,955	30,189	24.4%

Hispanics Men	Women	Total	%	Others Men	Women	Other	%	Gender Summaries Men	%	Women	%
1,525	50	1,500	12.3%	475	25	500	4.1%	11,800	96.7%	480	3.9%
2,400	110	2,510	12.1%	750	75	825	4.0%	19,675	94.8%	1,070	5.2%
5,010	225	5,235	11.0%	1,750"	100	1,850"	3.9%	45,535	96.0%	1,900	4.0%
3,050	175	3,225	10.0%	1,100"	100	1,200"	3.7%	30,800	95.6%	1,425	4.4%
1,850	125	1,975	8.8%	710	50	760	3.4%	21,285	94.7%	1,185	5.3%
1,025	50	1,075	7.3%	350	25	375	2.6%	13,925	95.1%	725	4.9%
700	40	740	8.0%	250	10	260	2.8%	8,750	95.2%	445	4.8%
275	10	285	8.3%	100	5	105	3.0%	3,325	96.5%	120	3.5%
90	2	92	6.4%	40	0	40	2.8%	1,405	98.5%	22	1.5%
100	15	115	5.7%	30	5	35	1.7%	1,905	94.1%	120	5.9%
130	10	140	6.2%	65	4	69	3.1%	2,095	93.4%	149	6.6%
120	5	125	4.2%	110	3	113	3.8%	2,860	96.4%	108	3.6%
175	4	179	3.2%	150	4	154	2.7%	5,450	97.3%	153	2.7%
75	0	75	2.3%	50	0	50	1.5%	3,160	96.8%	105	3.2%
25	1	26	1.5%	15	0	15	0.9%	1,640	97.0%	51	3.0%
10	0	10	1.6%	5	0	5	0.8%	633	98.4%	10	1.6%
0	0	0	0.0%	0	0	0	0.0%	68	98.6%	1	1.4%
16,560	822	17,307	9.5%	5,950	406	6,356	3.5%	174,311	95.6%	8,069	4.4%

Key to page 14: *Percent* figures are for personnel in each pay grade, as indicated.

When broken down by race, the totals for personnel on active duty in the Marine Corps are sightly *lower* than those found in the preceeding tables, by 181 Marines. This is less than one percent, compared with the official number of Marines on active duty at the end of fiscal 1996, 174,883. The difference is due to variations in basis of calcuation. Note that statistics on race and ethnicity are extremely unreliable. *White*, for example, can be applied to some Asian and African peoples, as well as to Europeans and their descendants. *Black*, in the U.S. includes persons who in many other societies would be classed as *White*. *Hispanic* is essentially a cultural rather than a racial designation, and can include persons of white, black, Native American, or even Asian or Pacific Island race (the use of *Latino* is even more confusing, since it includes not only Hispanics, but also Italians, Romanians, French, Brazilians, Portuguese, and some others, who are not Hispanic). *Other* includes Native Americans as well as persons of Asian or Pacific Island descent (both latter categories also essentially geographic rather than racial).

Authorized Organization of Marine Operational Forces

Four Duty Marine Expeditionary Forces (one in reserve), each of:
      One Marine Expeditionary Division
      One Marine Air Wing
      One Force Service Support Group

Authorized Organization of Marine Fixed-Wing Aviation Squadrons

Squadrons	Type	<————Aircraft————>			Mission
		Type	PerSqn	Total	
8	Active	F/A-18	12	96	Multirole
6	Active	F/A-18D	12	72	Multirole
7	Active	AV8B	20	140	Close Air Support
4	Reserve	F/A-18	12	48	Multirole
Totals			25	356	

Total Operational Aircraft Inventory: *
      F/A-18   144
      F/A-18D   72
      AV8B   140

* Excludes spares and training aircraft, c.300.

Major Marine Commands and Operating Forces

Commandant of the Marine Corps, Washington D.C.
    Marine Forces Atlantic, Norfolk, VA
        II Marine Expeditionary Force, MCB Camp Lejeune, NC
            2nd Marine Division, MCB Camp Lejeune, NC
            2nd Marine Aircraft Wing, MCAS Cherry Point, NC
            2nd Force Service Support Group, MCB Camp Lejeune, NC

Marine Forces Pacific, Camp Smith, HI
    I Marine Expeditionary Force, MCB Camp Pendleton, CA
        1st Marine Division, MCB Camp Pendleton, CA
        3rd Marine Aircraft Wing, MCB Camp Butler, Okinawa, Japan
        1st Force Service Support Group, MCAS El Toro, CA
    III Marine Expeditionary Force, MCB Camp Courtney, Okinawa, Japan
        3rd Marine Division MCB Camp Smedley D.Butler, Okinawa, Japan
        1st Marine Aircraft Wing, MCB Camp Pendleton, CA
        3rd Force Service Support Group, Camp Kinser, Okinawa, Japan
Marine Reserve Forces
    IV Marine Expeditionary Force, New Orleans, LA
        4th Marine Division, New Orleans, LA
        4th Marine Aircraft Wing, New Orleans, LA
        4th Force Service Support Group, New Orleans, LA

Key: MCB, Marine Corps Base; *MCAS*, Marine Corps Air Station.

Locations of Active Marine Ground Combat Operating Forces

Active Marine Infantry Battalions

Organization	Location
1/1st Marines	California
2/1st Marines	California
3/1st Marines	California
1/2nd Marines,	North Carolina
2/2nd Marines	North Carolina
3/2nd Marines	North Carolina
1/3rd Marines	Hawaii
2/3rd Marines	Hawaii .
3/3rd Marines	Hawaii
1/4th Marines	California
2/4th Marines	California
3/4th Marines	California
1/5th Marines	California
2/5th Marines	California
3/5th Marines	California
1/6th Marines	North Carolina
2/6th Marines	North Carolina
3/6th Marines	North Carolina
1/7th Marines	California
2/7th Marines	California
3/7th Marines	California
1/8th Marines	North Carolina
2/8th Marines	North Carolina
3/8th Marines	North Carolina

Active Marine Artillery Battalions

1/10th Marines	North Carolina
2/10th Marines	North Carolina
3/10th Marines	North Carolina
5/10th Marines	North Carolina
1/11th Marines	California
2/11th Marines	California
3/11th Marines	California
4/11th Marines	California
5/11th Marines	California
1/12th Marines	Hawaii

Active Marine Specialized Combat Battalions

2nd Amphibious Assault Battalion	North Carolina
3rd Amphibious Assault Battalion	California
1st Combat Assault Battalion	Okinawa
1st Combat Engineer Battalion	California
2nd Combat Engineer Battalion	North Carolina
1st Light Armored Reconnaissance Battalion	California
2nd Light Armored Reconnaissance Battalion	North Carolina
3rd Light Armored Reconnaissance Battalion	California
1st Tank Battalion	California
2nd Tank Battalion	North Carolina

Active Marine Combat Support Organizations

Combat Service Support Group-1	California
1st Force Service Support Group	California
2nd Force Service Support Group	North Carolina
3rd Force Service Support Group (Reinforced)	Okinawa

Active Marine Expeditionary Force Headquarters

I Marine Expeditionary Force Command Element	California
II Marine Expeditionary Force Command Element	North Carolina
III Marine Expeditionary Force	Okinawa

Key: The expression *"1/3rd Marines"* indicates the 1st Battalion, 3rd Marines. Note that the locations, and indeed, even designations of individual units are subject to change. In normal circustances several battalions are regularly stationed on Okinawa, while individual battalions rotate assignments to various MEUs.

Marine Expeditionary Units

MEU	Base
11th	California
13th	California
15th	California
22nd	North Carolina
24th	North Carolina
26th	North Carolina
31st	North Carolina

Formerly designated Marine Amphibious Units (MAUs), Marine Expeditionary Units are operational task forces. Three or four are serving afloat at any given time, with the others either returning from sea duty or working up to it. MEUs are more or less configured in the same way, though each varies considerably in detail.

Element	Description	Personnel
Command	Headquarters	c. 210
Ground Combat	Reinforced infantry battalion	1,200
Aviation Combat	Helicopter/Harrier squadron	800
Combat Service Support	Logistics & Service company	250
Total		c.2,500

Although their command and combat service support elements are organic, MEUs draw their infantry and aviation elements from the available pool of Marine units.

Summary of Active Ground Combat Units in the Marine Corps

Type	Number
Artillery Battalions	11*
Assault Amphibian Battalions	2
Combat Assault Battalions	1
Combat Engineer Battalions	2
Infantry Battalions	24
Tank Battalions	2

*There are, in addition, three Marine anti-aircraft battalions, plus an independent AA battery, which are listed with aviation units.

Active Marine Aviation Unit Organization

1st Marine Aircraft Wing
    Marine Aircraft Group-36 (MAG-36) (Japan)
        Marine Aviation Logistics Squadron-36 (MALS-36)
        Marine Medium Helicopter Squadron-262 (HMM-262)
        Marine Heavy Helicopter Squadron-Pacific (HMH-PAC)
        Marine Medium Helicopter Squadron-265 (HMM-265)
        Marine Light Attack Helicopter Squadron-Pacific (HMLA-PAC)
        Marine Aerial Refueler/Transport Squadron-152 (VMGR-152)
        Marine Air Control Group-18 (MACG-18)
        Marine Tactical Air Command Squadron-18 (MTACS-18)
        Air Traffic Control Detachment (ATC DET)
        Marine Wing Communications Squadron-18,Reinforced (MWCS-18(-))
        Marine Air Control Squadron-4 (MACS-4)
        Marine Air Support Squadron-2 (MASS-2)
        1st Stinger Battery
    Marine Aircraft Group-12 (MAG-12) (Japan)
        Marine Aviation Logistics Squadron-12 (MALS-12)
        Marine All Weather Fighter Attack Squadron-Pacific (VMFA(AW)-PAC)
        Marine Fighter Attack Squadron-212 (VMFA-212)

Marine Fighter Attack Squadron-Atlantic/Pacific (VMFA-LANT/PAC)
Marine Electronic Warfare Squadron-Atlantic (VMAQ-LANT)
Marine Wing Support Squadron-171 (MWSS-171)
Marine Attack Squadron-311 Detachment (VMA-311)
Air Traffic Control Detachment (ATC DET)
1st Marine Aircraft Wing (1st MAW) Aviation Support Element (Hawaii)
Marine Aviation Logistics Support Element (MALSE)
Marine Heavy Helicopter Squadron-463 (HMH-463)
Marine Heavy Helicopter Squadron-366 (HMH-366)
Marine Heavy Helicopter Squadron-363 (HMH-363)
Marine Heavy Helicopter Squadron-362 (HMH-362)
Marine Helicopter Training Squadron-301 (HMT-301)
2nd Marine Aircraft Wing(East Coast)
Marine Aircraft Group-14 (MAG-14)
Marine Aviation Logistics Squadron-14 (MALS-14)
Marine Electronic Warfare Squadron-1 (VMAQ-1)
Marine Electronic Warfare Squadron-2 (VMAQ-2)
Marine Electronic Warfare Squadron-3 (VMAQ-3)
Marine Electronic Warfare Squadron-4 (VMAQ-4)
Marine Attack Squadron-223 (VMA-223)
Marine Attack Squadron-231 (VMA-231)
Marine Attack Squadron-542 (VMA-542)
Marine Attack Training Squadron-203 (VMAT-203)
Marine Aerial Refueler/Transport Squadron-252 (VMGR-252)
Marine Aerial Refueler/Transport Training Squadron-253 (VMGR(T)-253)
Marine Unmanned Aerial Vehicle Squadron-2 (VMU-2)
Marine Air Control Group-28 (MACG-28)
Marine Tactical Air Command Squadron-28 (MTACS-28)
Marine Wing Communications Squadron-28 (MWCS-28)
Marine Air Control Squadron-6 (MACS-6)
Marine Air Support Squadron-1 (MASS-1)
2nd Low Altitude Air Defense Battalion (2nd LAAD Bn.)
Marine Wing Support Group-27 (MWSG-27)
Marine Wing Support Squadron-274 (MWSS-274)
Marine Wing Support Squadron-271 (MWSS-271)
Air Traffic Control Detachments (ATC DET)
Marine Aircraft Group-26 (MAG-26)
Marine Aviation Logistics Squadron-26 (MALS-26)
Marine Medium Helicopter Squadron-261 (HMM-261)
Marine Medium Helicopter Squadron-264 (HMM-264)
Marine Medium Helicopter Squadron-266 (HMM-266)
Marine Heavy Helicopter Squadron-461 (HMH-461)
Marine Light Attack Helicopter Squadron-167 (HMLA-167)
Marine Helicopter Training Squadron-204 (HMT-204)
Air Traffic Control Detachment (ATC DET)
Marine Aircraft Group-29 (MAG-29)
Marine Aviation Logistics Squadron-29 (MALS-29)

        Marine Medium Helicopter Squadron-162 (HMM-162)
        Marine Medium Helicopter Squadron-263 (HMM-263)
        Marine Medium Helicopter Squadron-365 (HMM-365)
        Marine Heavy Helicopter Squadron-464 (HMH-464)
        Marine Light Attack Helicopter Squadron-269 (HMLA-269)
        Marine Helicopter Training Squadron-302 (HMT-302)
        Marine Wing Support Squadron-272 (MWSS-272)
    Marine Aircraft Group-31 (MAG-31)
        Marine Aviation Logistics Squadron-31 (MALS-31)
        Marine Fighter Attack Squadron-115 (VMFA-115)
        Marine Fighter Attack Squadron-122 (VMFA-122)
        Marine Fighter Attack Squadron-251 (VMFA-251)
        Marine Fighter Attack Squadron-312 (VMFA-312)
        Marine All Weather Fighter Attack Squadron-224 (VMFA(AW)-224)
        Marine All Weather Fighter Attack Squadron-332 (VMFA(AW)-332)
        Marine All Weather Fighter Attack Squadron-533 (VMFA(AW)-533)
        Marine Wing Support Squadron-273 (MWSS-273)
        Marine Air Control Squadron-2 (MACS-2)
        Air Traffic Control Detachment (ATC DET)
3rd Marine Aircraft Wing (West Coast)
    Marine Aircraft Group-13 (MAG-13)
        Marine Aviation Logistics Squadron-13 (MALS-13)
        Marine Attack Squadron-214 (VMA-214)
        Marine Attack Squadron-311 (VMA-311)
        Marine Attack Squadron-513 (VMA-513)
        Marine Attack Squadron-211 (VMA-211)
        Marine Wing Support Squadron-371 (MWSS-371)
        1st Light Anti aircraft Missile Battalion (1st LAAM Bn.)
        Marine Air Control Squadron-7 (MACS-7)
        Air Traffic Control Detachment (ATC DET)
    Marine Aircraft Group-11 (MAG-11)
        Marine Aviation Logistics Squadron-11 (MALS-11)
        Marine All Weather Fighter Training Squadron-101 (VMFAT-101)
        Marine Aerial Refueler/Transport Squadron-352 (VMGR-352)
        Marine Air Control Group-38 (MACG-38)
        Marine Wing Communications Squadron-38 (MWCS-38)
        Marine Tactical Air Command Squadron-38 (MTACS-38)
        Air Traffic Control Detachment (ATC DET)
    Marine Wing Support Group-37 (MWSG-37)
        Marine Wing Support Squadron-172 (MWSS-172)
    Marine Aircraft Group-16 (MAG-16)
        Marine Aviation Logistics Squadron-16 (MALS-16)
        Marine Medium Helicopter Squadron-364 (HMM-364)
        Marine Medium Helicopter Squadron-161 (HMM-161)
        Marine Medium Helicopter Squadron-163 (HMM-163)
        Marine Medium Helicopter Squadron-164 (HMM-164)
        Marine Medium Helicopter Squadron-165 (HMM-165)

Marine Medium Helicopter Squadron-166 (HMM-166)
Marine Medium Helicopter Squadron-268 (HMM-268)
Air Ground Support Element
Marine Unmanned Aerial Vehicle Squadron-1 (VMU-1)
Marine Aircraft Group-39 (MAG-39)
Marine Aviation Logistics Squadron-39 (MALS-39)
Marine Light Attack Helicopter Squadron-169 (HMLA-169)
Marine Light Attack Helicopter Squadron-267 (HMLA-267)
Marine Light Attack Helicopter Squadron-367 (HMLA-367)
Marine Light Attack Helicopter Squadron-369 (HMLA-369)
Marine Helicopter Training Squadron-303 (HMT-303)
Marine Wing Support Squadron-372 (MWSS-372)
Marine Air Control Squadron-1 (MACS-1)
Marine Air Support Squadron-3 (MASS-3)
Air Traffic Control Detachment (ATC DET)
3rd Light Antiaircraft Defense Battalion (3rd LAAD Bn.)
Marine Aircraft Group-16 (MAG-16)
Marine Aviation Logistics Squadron-16 (MALS-16)
Marine Heavy Helicopter Squadron-465 (HMH-465)
Marine Heavy Helicopter Squadron-361 (HMH-361)
Marine Heavy Helicopter Squadron-462 (HMH-462)
Marine Heavy Helicopter Squadron-466 (HMH-466)
Marine Wing Support Squadron-374 (MWSS-374)
Air Traffic Control Detachment (ATC DET)
Marine Aircraft Group-11, Forward (MAG-11 FWD)
Marine Aviation Logistics Squadron-11 Detachment (MALS-11 DET)
Marine Fighter Attack Squadron-232 (VMFA-232)
Marine Fighter Attack Squadron-314 (VMFA-314)
Marine Fighter Attack Squadron-323 (VMFA-323)
Marine All Weather Fighter Attack Squadron-121 (VMFA(AW)-121)
Marine All Weather Fighter Attack Squadron-225 (VMFA(AW)-225)
Marine All Weather Fighter Attack Squadron-242 (VMFA(AW)-242)

Marine Reconnaissance Battalions ("Recon")

Although descended from the Scout units of World War II, the training and combat role of current Marine Recon battalions developed out of the long-range reconnaissance platoons in Vietnam. All members of the Recon battalions are airborne-qualified and can also be inserted by helicopter or small boats. They are adept with all standard USMC firearms, but may also carry the Hechler & Koch MP5 and other foreign weapons as required. Current dispositions are:

1st Reconnaissance Battalion	1st Marine Division (Camp Pendleton, CA)
2nd Reconnaissance Battalion	2nd Marine Division (Camp Lejeune, NC)
3rd Reconnaissance Battalion	3nd Marine Division (Okinawa)

Marine Corps Security Forces

Marine Corps Security Forces are details of Marines assigned to major warships, naval bases and installations, and U.S. diplomatic missions worldwide.

Element	Personnel
Marine Barracks	1,604
Marine Corps Security Forces Battalion	2,766
Marine Detachments Afloat	286
Total	4,565

Marine Corps Security Forces Battalion

	Location	Personnel
HQ,MC Security Forces Battalion	Norfolk, VA	165
FAST Co.,Atlantic	Norfolk, Va	321
Training Co	Chesapeake, VA	183
MCSF Co.	Yorktown, VA	242
MCSF Co.	Patuxent River, MD	67
MCSF Co.	Kings Bay, GA	369
MCSF Co.	Bangor, WA	462
MCSF Co.	North Island, CA	234
MCSF Co.	Bahrain	125
MCSF Co.	London, U.K.	80
MCSF Co.	Naples, Italy	119
MCSF Co.	Roosevelt Roads, PR	44
MCSF Detachment	Suda Bay, Greece	53
MCSF Co.	Rota, Spain	62
MCSF Co.	Keflavik, Iceland	79
MCSF Cadres	77 Locations *	161
Total		2,766

*Includes 18 ouside the U.S.

Marine Barracks

Location	Personnel
Guantanamo Bay, Cuba	342
Yokosuka, Japan	174
Washington, DC	1,088
Total	1,604

Marine Detachments Afloat

Ship	Personnel
USS *Abraham Lincoln* (CVAN-72)	26
USS *Carl Vinson* (CVAN-70)	26
USS *Constellation* (CVA-64)	26
USS *Enterprise* (CVAN-65)	26
USS *George Washington* (CVAN-73)	26

USS *Independence* (CVA-62)	26
USS *John F. Kennedy* (CVA-67)	26
USS *Kitty Hawk* (CVA-63)	26
USS *Nimitz* (CVAN-68)	26
USS *John C. Stennis* (CVAN-74)	26
USS *Theodore Roosevelt* (CVAN-71)	26
Total	286

Marine Corps Reserve Headquarters Locations

4th Marine Division, New Orleans, LA
    14th Marines, NAS Dallas, CA
    23rd Marines, San Rafael, CA
    24th Marines, Kansas City, MO
    25th Marines, Worcester, MA
4th Marine Air Wing,New Orleans, LA
    MACG-48, NAS Glenview, IL
    MAG-41, NAS Dallas, TX
    MAG-42, Marietta, GA
    MAG-46, MCAS Miramar, CA
    MAG-49, Willow Grove, PA
    MWSG-47, Selfridge, MI
4th Force Service Support Group, New Orleans, LA

The Military Background of Current Marine Corps Generals

Commisioned from	Number	Notes
Air National Guard	1	
Annapolis	16	A
The Citadel	2	B
Marine Corps Enlisted Service	12	C
Navy Enlisted Service	1	D
OCS/PLC	35	E
ROTC	21	
Unknown	6	F
Total Active	84	

Notes: Figures include active and reserve officers (82), but exclude two Navy officers effectively serving as generals in the Marine Corps. Two of the Marine officers have been counted double due to unusual circumstances.

A   One had prior enlisted service in the Navy
B   Including one who went through OCS after graduation from The Citadel.
C   Most passed through OCS or similar programs,but are not listed separately in
       that category.
D   Subsequently attended Annapolis.
E   Includes one who had previously graduated from the Citadel.
F   Could not be readily determined.

Annual Marine Corps Officer Commissioning Sources

The Marine Corps requires about 1,200-1,300 new commissioned officers each year. These officers receive their commissions from a variety of sources, as can be seen from these figures for officer accessions in Fiscal 1996. During Fiscal '96 1,268 new officers entered the Corps, a year which also saw 196 new warrant officers added to the Marine Corps.

Percent	Number	Source
12.9	164	United States Naval Academy
16.2	206	Naval Reserve Officer Training Course (NROTC)
31.3	397	Platoon Leadership Class (PLC)
10.6	135	Enlisted Commissioning Program (ECP)
28.3	359	Officers Candidacy Course (OCC)
0.6	7	Other Programs

Regulations permit up to 16.6% of each year's Annapolis graduates to choose to be commissioned in the Marine Corps. NROTC programs operate on college campuses. OCC is a training program for college graduates. PLC is a training program for persons in college who have no access to NROTC. ECP is a special program for promising enlisted personnel. All other programs include direct commissions (relatively rare in peacetime) and specialized programs for technical personnel. Aviation Officer Candidates are not listed separately, as they are included under OCC.

The Marine Corps Ranked Among the Services by Retention Rates

1. Overall Retention Rates

	Officers	Warrants	Enlisted	Total *
Air Force	91 (1-tie)	-	85 (1)	86 (1)
Army	90 (3)	89 (2)	81 (4)	83 (2-tie)
Marines	91 (1-tie)	94 (1)	82 (2-tie)	83 (2-tie)
Navy	88 (4)	82 (3)	82 (2-tie)	83 (2-tie)

* Figures in each column indicate percent of personnel in each category who remained in service throughout Fiscal Year 1995, as more recent figures were not available at the time of writing. The figure in parentheses is the relative rank of each service in terms of its success in retaining personnel. Note that there are no warrant officers in the Air Force.

2. Retention Rates for Male Personnel

	Officers	Warrants	Enlisted	Total *
Air Force	91 (1-tie)	-	85 (1)	86 (1)
Army	90 (3)	89 (2)	81 (4)	83 (2-tie)
Marines	91 (1-tie)	94 (1)	82 (2-tie)	83 (2-tie)
Navy	88 (4)	82 (3)	82 (2-tie)	83 (2-tie)

Note that for all the services the retention rate for men is the same as the overall retention rate.

3. Retention Rates for Female Personnel

Officers	Warrants	Enlisted	Total *
Air Force 89 (3)	-	84 (1)	85 (1)
Army 88 (4)	93 (2)	81 (3-tie)	83 (3)
Marines 91 (1)	84 (3)	83 (2)	84 (2)
Navy 90 (2)	97 (1)	81 (3-tie)	82 (4)

The Marine Corps Average Recruit Requirement Compared with that of the Other Services

Service	Annual Recruits Required	
	Active	Reserve Components
Air Force	30,000	16,000
Army	90,000	110,000
Marines	33,000	10,000
Navy	57,000	16,000

Key: Figures are approximate. Reserve Component figures for the Army and Air Force include the National Guard.

Marine Corps Rank Among the Services by Recruits with High School Diplomas, 1995-1996

Service	Non-Prior Service Recruits Taken in for:			
	Active Duty Forces		Reserve Components	
	%	Rank	%	Rank
Air Force	99	1st	94 (Res)	3rd -tie
			94 (NG)	3rd -tie
Army	96	2nd -tie	95 (Res)	2nd
			82 (NG)	4th
Marines	96	2nd -tie	98	1st
Navy	95	4th	*	

Key: Figures are approximate; those for the Navy were not available at the time of this writing. *Res*, Reserve; *NG*, National Guard

Marine Corps Accident Rates, Fiscal 1995

On Duty:

Type	Fatalities	Injuries
Aviation	26	6
Industrial	0	219
Motor Vehicle,Government Owned		
Tactical (Tanks,etc)	2	15
Other	2	27

Type	Fatalities	Injuries
Operations & Training	6	156
Other	2	126
Sub Total	38	549

Off Duty:

Motor Vehicle,Privately Owned		
Four Wheel	46	178
Motorcycle	7	51
Pedestrian	4	8
Sports & Recreation	9	153
Other	7	93
Sub Total	73	483
Grand Total	111	1,032

Summary: In the course of Fiscal Year 1996,

1 in every 317 Marines On Duty was injured in an accident, as was
1 in every 360 Off Duty Marines, while
1 in every 4,579 Marines injured in an On Duty accident died, and
1 in every 2,384 injured in an Off Duty accident died.

Principal Marine Corps Agencies and Installations

Marine Corps Districts

First Marine Corps District, Garden City, NY
Fourth Marine Corps District, New Cumberland, PA
Sixth Marine Corps District, Atlanta, GA
Eighth Marine Corps District, New Orleans, LA
Ninth Marine Corps District, Kansas City, MO
Twelfth Marine Corps District, San Diego, CA
Marine Corps Reserve District, San Diego, CA

Marine Corps Experimental and Doctrinal Facilities

Commandant's Warfighting Lab, Quantico, VA
Marine Corps Combat Development Command, Quantico, VA
Marine Corps Historical Center, Washington, DC
Modeling and Simulation Management Office, Newport News, VA

Marine Corps Schools and Training Establishments

Marine Corps Air/Ground Combat Center, Twentynine Palms, CA
Marine Corps Communication-Electronics School, Twentynine Palms, CA
Marine Corps Detachment, Lackland Air Force Base, TX
Marine Corps Detachment, U.S. Army Anti-Aircraft School, Ft. Bliss, TX
Marine Corps Detachment, U.S. Army Artillery School, Ft. Sill, OK
Marine Corps Expeditionary Warfare Training Group, Atlantic, Norfolk, VA
Marine Corps Mountain Warfare Training Center, MCB Camp Pendleton, CA
Marine Corps Recruit Depot, Parris Island, NC

Marine Corps Recruit Depot, San Diego, CA
Marine Corps University, Quantico, VA

Marine Corps Administrative and Support Establishments

Fleet Marine Force Meteorology, Corona, CA
Marine Corps Logistics Base, Albany, GA
Marine Corps Logistics Base, Barstow, CA
Marine Corps Morale, Welfare, and Recreation Center, Norfolk, VA
Marine Corps Recruiting Command, Arlington, VA
Marine Corps Reserve Support Command, Kansas City, MO
Marine Corps Support Activity, Kansas City, MO
Marine Corps Systems Command, Arlington, VA
Marine Corps Tactical System Support, Camp Pendleton, CA
MCRD San Diego Command Museum, San Diego, CA

Marine Corps Air Stations

Marine Corps Air Station, Cherry Point, GA
Marine Corps Air Station, El Toro, CA
Marine Corps Air Station, Futeman, Okinawa, Japan
Marine Corps Air Station, Iwakuni, Japan
Marine Corps Air Station, New River, GA
Marine Corps Air Station, Tustin, CA
Marine Corps Air Station, Yuma, AZ
Naval Air Station, Miramar, CA

Marine Corps Bases

Marine Barracks, Guantanamo Bay, Cuba
Marine Corps Base, Camp Butler, Okinawa, Japan
Marine Corps Base, Camp Courtney, Okinawa, Japan
Marine Corps Base, Camp Foster, Okinawa, Japan
Marine Corps Base, Camp Hansen, Okinawa, Japan
Marine Corps Base, Camp Kinsie, Okinawa, Japan
Marine Corps Base, Camp Lejeune, NC
Marine Corps Base, Camp Lester, Okinawa, Japan
Marine Corps Base, Camp Pendleton, CA
Marine Corps Base, Camp Schwab, Okinawa, Japan
Marine Corps Base, Kaneohe, HI

States With Marine Detachments in Their Naval Militia

1. Alaska
2. New York

In the early part of the twentieth century about a third of the states had a Naval Militia, essentially a maritime version of the National Guard. Naval militiamen played important roles in the Spanish-American War and World War I. However, by World War II many states had abandoned their naval militias, which included both naval and marine personnel. During the postwar period only New York still possessed a naval militia, to be joined by Alaska some years ago.

Major Current New Procurement Programs for the Marine Corps

Item	Planned Buy	Completion Date	Cost '96-'98
Advanced Amphibious Assault Vehicle (AAAV)	1,013	2013	$135,000,000
Light Weight 155mm Howitzer (LWH155)	598	2006	55,000,000
Predator ShRAW	21,012	2001	65,000,000
V-22A "Osprey" Tilt-Rotor Air Transport	523	2023	1,170,000,000

Key: *Planned Buy*, is the total number the Marine Corps expects to buy; *Completion Date*, is the anticipated year in which the final copies will enter service; *Cost, '96-'98* is the planned expenditure over the three indicated fiscal years. The actual total cost of each project will be considerably higher.

## CHAPTER 2

History of the Corps: General

In many ways the history of the Marine Corps is the history of the United States. It was born during the Revolutionary War, and has served in every one of the nation's conflicts since, often undertaking some of the most arduous of the nation's military tasks.

Battle Honors of the Marine Corps

1. Presidential Unit Citation (Navy) Streamer, with six silver and two bronze stars
2. Presidential Unit Citation (Army) Streamer, with one silver oak leaf cluster
3. Joint Meritorious Unit Award
4. Navy Unit Commendation Streamer, with 25 silver stars
5. Valorous Unit Award (Army)
6. Meritorious Unit Commendation (Navy-Marine Corps) Streamer
7. Meritorious Unit Commendation (Army) Streamer
8. Revolutionary War Streamer
9. Quasi-War with France Streamer
10. Barbary Wars Streamer
11. War of 1812 Streamer
12. African Slave Trade Streamer
13. Operations Against West Indian Pirates Streamer
14. Indian Wars Streamer
15. Mexican War Streamer
16. Civil War Streamer
17. Marine Corps Expeditionary Streamer, with 12 silver stars, one bronze star, and the silver "W" device
18. Spanish American War Streamer
19. Philippine Campaign Streamer
20. China Relief Expedition Streamer
21. Cuban Pacification Streamer
22. Nicaraguan Campaign Streamer
23. Mexican Service Streamer
24. Haitian Campaign Streamer, with one bronze star
25. Dominican Campaign Streamer
26. World War I Victory Streamer, with one silver and one bronze star, one Maltese Cross, and the "Siberia" and "West Indies" clasps
27. Army of Occupation of Germany Streamer
28. Second Nicaraguan Campaign Streamer

29. Yangtze Service Streamer
30. China Service Streamer, with one bronze star
31. American Defense Streamer, with one bronze star
32. American Campaign Streamer
33. European-African-Middle Eastern Campaign Streamer, with one silver and four bronze stars
34. Asiatic-Pacific Campaign Streamer, with eight silver, and two bronze stars
35. World War II Victory Streamer
36. Navy Occupation Service Streamer, with the "Europe" and "Asia" clasps
37. National Defense Service Streamer, with two bronze stars
38. Korean Service Streamer, with two silver stars
39. Armed Forces Expeditionary Streamer, with four silver stars and two bronze stars
40. Vietnam Service Streamer, with three silver and two bronze stars
41. Southwest Asia Service Streamer, with three bronze stars
42. Philippine Defense Streamer, with one bronze star
43. Philippine Liberation Streamer, with two bronze stars
44. Philippine Independence Streamer
45. French *Croix de Guerre* Streamer, with two palms and one gold star
46. Philippine Presidential Unit Citation Streamer, with two bronze stars
47. Korean Presidential Unit Citation Streamer
48. Republic of Vietnam Armed Forces Meritorious Unit Citation of the Gallantry Cross, with palm
49. Republic of Vietnam Meritorious Unit Citation Civil Actions Streamer, with palm

Streamers 1 through 7 are decorations, and thus take precedence over campaign honors, numbers 8 through 41. Streamers 42 through 49 were awarded by foreign nations, and thus take precedence after U.S. awards. A few of the honors may require some explanation. On U.S. and Philippine streamers, a bronze star indicates an additional campaign, a silver star is for five additional campaigns. Thus, the Marine Corps has earned the right to display the Expeditionary Streamer 23 times, and the streamer also bears a special "W" device, to indicate Wake Island. On French and Vietnamese streamers palms and stars indicate special honors. Number 12, the African Slave Trade Streamer, was awarded for service with the fleet on anti-slavery patrol off the coast of Africa, 1808-1861. Number 21, the Cuban Pacification Streamer, refers to occupation duty in Cuba, 1906-1909. Number 23, the Mexican Service Streamer, is for the Vera Cruz Campaign of 1914. Number 25, the Dominican Republic Streamer was awarded for the Dominican Campaign, 1916-1924. Number 27, the Army of Occupation of Germany Streamer was awarded for the post-World War I occupation of the Rhineland; the World War II occupation of Germany is commemorated in streamer Number 36.

Phases in the History of the Marine Corps

1. Traditional Marines, 1775-1898
2. Colonial Fire Brigade, 1898-1934
3. Amphibious Assault Force, 1934-1945
4. Rapid Deployment Force, 1945-date

Each of the phases is characterized by a particular type of mission in which the Marine Corps spent most of its time. In the period of the "Traditional Marines" the mission of the Marine Corps was primarily aboard ship and in landing parties. During the "Colonial Fire Brigade" phase, the Marine Corps found itself frequently occupied in protracted pacification campaigns in the Caribbean. The "Amphibious Assault Force" period found the Marine Corps polishing and then practicing amphibious assaults in the Pacific. The "Rapid Deployment Force" phase has seen the Marine Corps responding to crises quite literally as "first to fight," in many quarters of the globe. In each period, of course, the Marine Corps had many missions, but one tended to overshadow the others.

Strength of the Corps, 1775-1997

Year	Officers	Enlisted	Total	EP/Officer
1775	11	220	231	20.0
1776	25	500	525	20.0
1777	40	900	940	22.5
1778	50	1,300	1,350	26.0
1779	45	1,100	1,145	24.4
1780	25	600	625	24.0
1781	15	320	335	21.3
1782	6	80	86	13.3
1783	0	25	25	*
1798	25	58	83	2.3
1799	25	343	368	13.7
1800	38	487	525	12.8
1801	38	319	357	8.4
1802	29	330	359	11.4
1803	25	317	342	12.7
1804	25	364	389	14.6
1805	22	556	578	25.3
1806	11	307	318	27.9
1807	11	392	403	35.6
1808	11	861	872	78.3
1809	10	513	523	51.3
1810	9	440	449	48.9
1811	14	542	556	38.7
1812	10	483	493	48.3
1813	12	579	591	48.3
1814	11	637	648	57.9
1815	8	680	688	85.0
1816	21	451	472	21.5
1817	14	652	666	46.6
1818	24	536	560	22.3
1819	21	664	685	31.6

Year	Officers	Enlisted	Total	EP/Officer
1820	19	552	571	29.1
1821	35	844	879	24.1
1822	23	708	731	30.8
1823	20	681	701	34.1
1824	50	890	940	17.8
1825	35	746	781	21.3
1826	39	796	835	20.4
1827	43	903	946	21.0
1828	40	892	932	22.3
1829	43	852	895	19.8
1830	37	854	891	23.1
1831	35	780	815	22.3
1832	38	830	868	21.8
1833	43	853	896	19.8
1834	46	869	915	18.9
1835	68	1,349	1,417	19.8
1836	43	1,298	1,341	30.2
1837	37	1,524	1,561	41.2
1838	28	1,067	1,095	38.1
1839	34	916	950	26.9
1840	46	1,223	1,269	26.6
1841	44	1,156	1,200	26.3
1842	46	1,243	1,289	27.0
1843	43	1,041	1,084	24.2
1844	40	1,046	1,086	26.2
1845	42	986	1,028	23.5
1846	41	1,126	1,167	27.5
1847	75	1,757	1,832	23.4
1848	42	1,709	1,751	40.7
1849	46	1,030	1,076	22.4
1850	46	1,055	1,101	22.9
1851	43	1,150	1,193	26.7
1852	47	1,121	1,168	23.9
1853	49	1,205	1,254	24.6
1854	43	1,312	1,355	30.5
1855	52	1,552	1,604	29.8
1856	57	1,414	1,471	24.8
1857	57	1,694	1,751	29.7
1858	52	1,555	1,607	29.9
1859	47	1,804	1,851	38.4
1860	46	1,755	1,801	38.2

Year	Officers	Enlisted	Total	EP/Officer
1861	48	2,338	2,386	48.7
1862	51	2,355	2,406	46.2
1863	69	2,931	3,000	42.5
1864	64	3,075	3,139	48.0
1865	87	3,773	3,860	43.4
1866	79	3,258	3,337	41.2
1867	73	3,438	3,511	47.1
1868	81	2,997	3,078	37.0
1869	70	2,314	2,384	33.1
1870	77	2,469	2,546	32.1
1871	74	2,439	2,513	33.0
1872	77	2,126	2,203	27.6
1873	87	2,675	2,762	30.7
1874	85	2,184	2,269	25.7
1875	76	2,037	2,113	26.8
1876	76	1,904	1,980	25.1
1877	73	1,824	1,897	25.0
1878	77	2,257	2,334	29.3
1879	62	1,906	1,968	30.7
1880	69	1,870	1,939	27.1
1881	70	1,832	1,902	26.2
1882	63	1,806	1,869	28.7
1883	60	1,724	1,784	28.7
1884	66	1,822	1,888	27.6
1885	65	1,819	1,884	28.0
1886	66	1,934	2,000	29.3
1887	61	1,870	1,931	30.7
1888	72	1,829	1,901	25.4
1889	54	1,718	1,772	31.8
1890	61	1,986	2,047	32.6
1891	66	2,092	2,158	31.7
1892	66	1,973	2,039	29.9
1893	63	2,070	2,133	32.9
1894	67	2,309	2,376	34.5
1895	71	2,914	2,985	41.0
1896	72	2,145	2,217	29.8
1897	71	3,735	3,806	52.6
1898	98	3,481	3,579	35.5
1899	76	3,066	3,142	40.3
1900	174	5,240	5,414	30.1
1901	171	5,694	5,865	33.3

Year	Officers	Enlisted	Total	EP/Officer
1902	191	6,031	6,222	31.6
1903	213	6,445	6,658	30.3
1904	255	7,329	7,584	28.7
1905	270	6,741	7,011	25.0
1906	278	7,940	8,218	28.6
1907	279	7,807	8,086	28.0
1908	283	8,953	9,236	31.6
1909	328	9,368	9,696	28.6
1910	328	9,232	9,560	28.1
1911	328	9,292	9,620	28.3
1912	337	9,359	9,696	27.8
1913	331	9,625	9,956	29.1
1914	336	10,050	10,386	29.9
1915	338	9,948	10,286	29.4
1916	348	10,253	10,601	29.5
1917	776	26,973	27,749	34.8
1918	1,503	51,316	52,819	34.1
1919	2,270	46,564	48,834	20.5
1920	1,104	16,061	17,165	14.5
1921	1,087	21,903	22,990	20.1
1922	1,135	20,098	21,233	17.7
1923	1,141	18,533	19,674	16.2
1924	1,157	19,175	20,332	16.6
1925	1,168	18,310	19,478	15.7
1926	1,178	17,976	19,154	15.3
1927	1,198	18,000	19,198	15.0
1928	1,198	17,822	19,020	14.9
1929	1,181	17,615	18,796	14.9
1930	1,208	18,172	19,380	15.0
1931	1,196	17,586	18,782	14.7
1932	1,196	15,365	16,561	12.8
1933	1,192	14,876	16,068	12.5
1934	1,187	15,174	16,361	12.8
1935	1,163	16,097	17,260	13.8
1936	1,208	16,040	17,248	13.3
1937	1,312	16,911	18,223	12.9
1938	1,359	16,997	18,356	12.5
1939	1,380	18,052	19,432	13.1
1940	1,800	26,545	28,345	14.7
1941	3,339	51,020	54,359	15.3
1942	7,138	135,475	142,613	19.0

Year	Officers	Enlisted	Total	EP/Officer
1943	21,384	287,139	308,523	13.4
1944	32,788	442,816	475,604	13.5
1945	37,067	437,613	474,680	11.8**
1946	14,208	141,471	155,679	10.0
1947	7,506	85,547	93,053	11.4
1948	6,907	78,081	84,988	11.3
1949	7,250	78,715	85,965	10.9
1950	7,254	67,025	74,279	9.2
1951	15,150	177,770	192,920	11.7
1952	16,413	215,544	231,957	13.1
1953	18,731	230,488	249,219	12.3
1954	18,593	205,275	223,868	11.0
1955	18,417	186,753	205,170	10.1
1956	17,809	182,971	200,780	10.3
1957	17,434	183,427	200,861	10.5
1958	16,471	172,754	189,225	10.5
1959	16,065	189,506	205,571	11.8
1960	16,203	154,418	170,621	9.5
1961	16,132	160,777	176,909	10.0
1962	16,861	174,101	190,962	10.3
1963	16,737	172,946	189,683	10.3
1964	16,843	172,934	189,777	10.3
1965	17,258	172,955	190,213	10.0
1966	20,512	241,204	261,716	11.8
1967	23,592	261,677	285,269	11.1
1968	24,555	282,697	307,252	11.5
1969	25,698	284,073	309,771	11.1
1970	24,941	234,796	259,737	9.4
1971	21,765	190,604	212,369	8.8
1972	19,843	178,395	198,238	9.0
1973	19,282	176,816	196,098	9.2
1974	18,740	170,062	188,802	9.1
1975	18,591	177,360	195,951	9.5
1976	18,882	183,517	202,399	9.7
1977	18,650	173,057	191,707	9.3
1978	18,388	172,427	190,815	9.4
1979	18,229	167,021	185,250	9.2
1980	18,198	170,271	188,469	9.4
1981	18,363	172,257	190,620	9.4
1982	18,975	173,405	192,380	9.1
1983	19,983	174,106	194,089	8.7

Year	Officers	Enlisted	Total	EP/Officer
1984	20,366	196,214	216,580	9.6
1985	20,175	177,850	198,025	8.8
1986	20,199	178,615	198,814	8.8
1987	20,047	179,478	199,525	9.0
1988	20,079	177,271	197,350	8.8
1989	20,099	176,857	196,956	8.8
1990	19,958	176,694	196,652	8.9
1991	19,753	174,287	194,040	8.8
1992	19,132	165,397	184,529	8.6
1993	18,430	159,949	178,379	8.7
1994	17,823	156,335	174,158	8.8
1995	17,831	156,808	174,639	8.8
1996	17,931	156,952	174,883	8.8

Figures are "Fiscal Year End Strengths" where applicable. EP/Officer stands for Enlisted Persons-per -Officer, which has been rounded to the nearest tenth. Figures for the Continental Marines are estimated,based on partial data, and omit men in state marine corps and on privateers. Note that post-World War I figures omit the Marine Corps Reserve, currently over 100,000 men and women, of whom approximately 42,000 are in organized units, and 6,700 are on "full time" status.

* The last Continental Marine officer was discharged in September 1783; the last enlisted man seems to been discharged in early 1784.

** The all time peak strength of the Marine Corps, August 1945; 485,113 officers and enlisted personnel.

Marine Wars and Expeditions, with Combat Casualties, 1775-1997

Operation	Dates	KIA/MW	Wounded	Total	Ratio
1. Revolutionary War	19 Apr 1775-18 Nov 1783	47	70	117	1.5
2. Quasi-War with France	1798-1800	6	11	17	1.8
3. Caribbean Pirates Campaign	1798-1826	?	?	?	?
4. Barbary Wars	14 May 1801-4 Jun 1805	4	10	14	2.5
5. *Leopard-Chesapeake* Affair	22 Jun 1807	?	?	?	?
6. West African Anti-Slavery Patrol	1808-1861	?	?	?	?
7. Battle of 12 Mile Swamp, Florida	11 Sept 1812	?	?	?	?
8. War of 1812	1812-1815	46	33	79	0.7
9. Nukahiva, Marquesas	Dec 1813	-	—	-	
10. *Seringapatam* Mutiny, Nukahiva	7 May 1814	-	-	-	-
11. Gamble's Landing, Marquesas	1814	2	-	2	-
12. Barataria, Louisiana	16 Sept 1814	?	?	?	?
13. Second Barbary War	3 Mar-9 Aug 1815	?	?	?	?
14. Mexican Gulf Pirates Campaign	1815-1819	?	?	?	?
15. Aegean Pirates Campaign	1822-1827	?	?	?	?
16. Falkland Islands	28 Dec 1831-22 Jan 1832	-	-	-	-

Operation	Dates	KIA/MW	Wounded	Total	Ratio
17. Quallah Batoo, Sumatra	6-9 Feb 1832	2	2	4	1.0
18. Buenos Aires, Argentina	31 Oct-15 Nov 1833	-	-	-	-
19. Callao & Lima, Peru	10 Dec 1834-24 Jan 1835	-	-	-	-
20. *Potomac* Mutiny, Puerto Mahon	1836	-	-	-	-
21. Florida War	1836-1842	8	1	9	0.1
22. Quallah Batoo, Sumatra	25 Dec 1838	-	-	-	-
23. Mukee, Sumatra	1 Jan 1839	-	-	-	-
24. Monterey, California	Jun 1840	-	-	-	-
25. Mololo, Fiji	12-27 Dec 1840	-	-	-	-
26. Upola, Samoa	24 Feb 1841	-	-	-	-
27. Drummond I, South Pacific	6-8 Apr 1841	-	-	-	-
28. Monterey, California	19 Oct 1842	-	-	-	-
29. Montevideo, Uruguay	29 Sept 1844	-	-	-	-
30. War with Mexico	1846-1848	11	47	58	4.3
31. Buenos Aires, Argentina	3-12 Feb 1852	-	-	-	-
32. Buenos Aires, Argentina	17 Sept 1852-c.15 Apr 1853	-	-	-	-
33. San Juan del Sur, Nicaragua	11-13 Mar 1853	-	-	-	-
34. Perry's Expedition to Japan	1853-1854	-	-	-	-
35. Shanghai, China	4 Apr 1854	2	0	2	-
36. Tumai, Ryukyu Is.	6-7 Jul 1854	-	-	-	-
37. San Juan del Sur, Nicaragua	2-15 Jul 1854	-	-	-	-
38. Naha, Okinawa	17 Nov 1854	-	-	-	-
39. Shanghai, China	19-21 May 1855	-	-	-	-
40. Ty-Ho Bay, Hong Kong	4 Aug 1855	2	0	2	-
41. Ovolou, Fiji	28-30 Sept 1855	-	-	-	-
42. Montevideo, Uruguay	25-30 Nov 1855	-	-	-	-
43. Indian Battle, Seattle	26 Jan 1856	-	-	-	-
44. Panama	20 Sept 1856	-	-	-	-
45. Barrier Forts, Canton, China	16-23 Nov 1856	-	-	-	-
46. Arrest of William Walker	8 Dec 1857	-	-	-	-
47. Waya, Fiji	6-10 Oct 1858	-	-	-	-
48. Montevideo, Uruguay	2-27 Jan 1858	-	-	-	-
49. Paraguay Expedition	17 Oct 1858-Feb 1859	-	-	-	-
50. Peiho, China	25 Jun 1859	-	-	-	-
51. Shanghai, China	31 Jul-2 Aug 1859	-	-	-	-
52. John Brown's Raid	18 Oct 1859	1	1	2	1.0
53. Kisembo, Angola	1-4 Mar 1860	-	-	-	-
54. Panama	27 Jul-8 Oct 1860	-	-	-	-
55. Civil War	12 Apr 1861-Jun 1865	148	131	279	0.9
56. *Wyoming* at Shimonoseki	16 Jul 1863	?	?	?	-
57. New Chwang, China	20 Jun-14 Jul 1866	-	-	-	-
58. Taka, Formosa	13 Jun 1867	-	-	-	-
59. Osaka, Japan	4-8 Feb 1868	-	-	-	-
60. Montevideo, Uruguay	7-27 Feb 1868	-	-	-	-

Operation	Dates	KIA/MW	Wounded	Total	Ratio
61. Yokohama, Japan	4 Apr-12 May 1868	-	-	-	-
62. Yokohama, Japan	12-13 Jul 1868	-	-	-	-
63. Boca Tecagua, Mexico	17-18 Jun 1868	0	2	2	-
64. Khang Forts, Korea	10-12 Jun 1871	2	6	8	3.0
65. Panama	7-12 May 1873	-	-	-	-
66. Panama	23 Sept- 9 Oct 1873	-	-	-	-
67. Honolulu, Hawaii	12-20 Feb 1874	-	-	-	-
68. Alexandria, Egypt	10 Jun-29 Aug 1882	-	-	-	-
69. Panama	18-19 Jan 1885	-	-	-	-
70. Panama	16 Mar-25 May 1885	-	-	-	-
71. Seoul, Korea	19-30 Jun 1888	-	-	-	-
72. Apia, Samoa	14 Nov 1888-30 Mar 1889	-	-	-	-
73. Honolulu, Hawaii	30-31 Jul 1889	-	-	-	-
74. Buenos Aires, Argentina	15-30 Jul 1890	-	-	-	-
75. Valparaiso, Chile	28-30 Aug 1891	-	-	-	-
76. Novassa I, East Indies	2-20 Jun 1891	-	-	-	-
77. Honolulu, Hawaii	16 Jun-1 Apr 1893	-	-	-	-
78. Seoul, Korea	24 Jul 1894-3 Apr 1896	-	-	-	-
79. Chefoo & Taku, China	4 Dec 1894-10 May 1895	?	?	?	?
80. Bluefields, Nicaragua	6 Jul-7 Aug 1894	-	-	-	-
81. Panama	8-9 Mar 1895	-	-	-	-
82. Corinto, Nicaragua	2-4 May 1896	-	-	-	-
83. Bluefields, Nicaragua	7-8 Feb 1898	-	-	-	-
84. Spanish-American War	21 April-13 August 1898	7	20	27	2.9
85. Tientsin & Peking, China	4 Nov 1898-15 Mar 1899	-	-	-	-
86. Philippine Insurrection	30 Jun 98-4 July 1902	?	?	?	?
87. San Juan del Sur, Nicaragua	24-28 Feb 1899	-	-	-	-
88. Samoa Campaign	13 Mar-14 May 1899	0	2	2	-
89. Boxer Rebellion	24 May-28 Sept 1900	9	17	26	1.9
90. Panama	24 Nov-4 Dec 1901	-	-	-	-
91. Panama	16-22 Apr 1902	-	-	-	-
92. Panama	17 Sept -18 Nov 1902	-	-	-	-
93. Puerto Cortez, Honduras	28 Feb-10 Apr 1903	-	-	-	-
94. Santo Domingo	1-19 Apr 1903	-	-	-	-
95. Beirut, Syria	7-12 Sept t 1903	-	-	-	-
96. Panama	3 Nov 1903-21 Jun 1914	-	-	-	-
97. Abyssinian Mission	21 Nov 1903-18 Jan 1904	-	-	-	-
98. Puerto Playa, Santo Domingo	3 Jan-11 Feb 1904	-	-	-	-
99. Tangier, Morocco	30 May-26 Jun 1904	-	-	-	-
100. Seoul, Korea	5 Jan 1904-11 Nov 1905	-	-	-	-
101. Cuban Pacification Campaign	13 Sept 1906-23 Jun 1909	-	-	-	-
102. Puerto Cortez, Honduras	28 Apr-23 May 1907	-	-	-	-
103. Corinto, Nicaragua	22 Feb 1910	-	-	-	-

Operation	Dates	KIA/MW	Wounded	Total	Ratio
104. Bluefields, Nicaragua	19 May-4 Sept 1910	-	-	-	-
105. Philippine Moro War	1911	-	-	-	-
106. Shanghai, China	10 Oct 1911-19 Jan 1914	-	-	-	-
107. Cuban Electoral Disorders	8 Jun-5 Aug 1912	-	-	-	-
108. First Nicaraguan Campaign	17 Aug 1912-9 Jun 1913	5	16	21	3.2
109. Shanghai, China	24-30 Aug 1912	-	-	-	-
110. Shanghai, China	28-29 Jul 1913	-	-	-	-
111. Shanghai, China	14-17 Aug 1913	-	-	-	-
112. Estero Cloris, Mexico	6-7 Sept 1913	-	-	-	-
113. Port-au-Prince, Haiti	29 Jan-2 Feb 1914	-	-	-	-
114. Vera Cruz Expedition	21 Apr-23 Nov 1914	5	13	18	2.6
115. Haitian Campaign	27 Jul 1915-15 Aug 1934	10	26	36	2.6
116. Dominican Campaign	5 May 1916-15 Feb 1922	17	50	67	2.9
117. Cuban Electoral Disorders	1 Mar-11 Apr 1917	-	-	-	-
118. World War I	7 Apr 1917-11 Nov 1918	2,457	8,894	11,351	3.6
119. Cuban Occupation	24 Oct 1917-15 Feb 1922	-	-	-	-
120. Siberian Expedition	29 Jan 1918—24 Aug 1922	-	-	-	-
121. Panama	30 Aug-15Sept 1921	-	-	-	-
122. Nicaragua	25 Jan-11 Feb 1922	-	-	-	-
123. Taku & Shanghai, China	5-11 May 1922	-	-	-	-
124. Canton, China	20 Jan 1924	-	-	-	-
125. Honduras	28 Feb-13 Mar 1924	-	-	-	-
126. Honduras	7-15 Sept 1924	-	-	-	-
127. Tientsin, China	6 Oct 1924-8 Feb 1925	-	-	-	-
128. Shanghai, China	15 Jan-9 Feb 1925	-	-	-	-
129. Honduras	20-21 Apr 1925	-	-	-	-
130. Shanghai, China	9 Jun-29 Aug 1925	-	-	-	-
131. Tientsin, China	9 Nov 1925-9 Jun 1926	-	-	-	-
132. Shanghai, China	30 Dec 1925-12 Mar 1926	-	-	-	-
133. Shanghai, China	12 Nov 1926-1 Dec 1941	?	?	?	-
134. Second Nicaraguan Campaign	6 Jan 1927-3 Jan 1933	47	66	113	1.4
135. Occupation of Iceland	7 Jul 1941-Mar 1942	-	-	-	-
136. World War II	7 Dec 1941-2 Sept 1945	19,733	67,207	86,940	3.4
137. Occupation of North China	30 Sept 1945-26 May 1949	10	33	43	3.3
138. Palestine Security Details	1948	0	2	2	-
139. Korean War	27 Jun 1950-27 Jul 1953	4,267	23,744	8,011	5.6
140. Alexandria, Egypt	1-2 Nov 1956	-	-	-	-
141. Lebanon Operation	15 Jul-30 Sept 1958	-	-	-	-
142. Congo UN Mission Support	1960	-	-	-	-
143. Congo Evacuation Mission	1-8 Feb 1961	-	-	-	-
144. Thailand	16 May-10 Aug 1962	-	-	-	-
145. Cuban Missile Crisis	24 Oct-31 Dec 1962	-	-	-	-

Operation	Dates	KIA/MW	Wounded	Total	Ratio
146. Vietnam War	15 Mar 1962-28 Jan 1973	13,067	88,633	101,700	6.8
147. Dominican Peacekeeping	28 Apr 1965-6 Jan 1966	9	25	34	2.8
148. Cyprus Evacuation	Jul 1974	-	-	-	-
149. Evacuation of Phnom Penh	3-12 Apr 1975	-	-	-	-
150. Evacuation of Saigon	28-29 Apr 1975	5	0	5	-
151. *Mayaguez* Operation	12-15 May 1975	14	41	55	2.9
152. Iranian Rescue Mission	24-25 Apr 1980	3	2	5	0.7
153. Beirut Evacuation	17-24 June 1982	-	-	-	-
154. Beirut Evacuation	15 Aug-10 Sept 1982	-	-	-	-
155. Beirut Peacekeeping Mission	25 Sept 1982-27 Feb 1984	240	151	391	0.6
156. Grenada Campaign	25 Oct-1 Nov 1983	3	15	18	5.0
157. Persian Gulf Oil Well Campaign	1988	2	0	2	-
158. Panama Campaign	20-28 Dec 1989	2	3	5	1.5
159. Evacuation of Monrovia	5 Aug-30 Nov 1990	-	-	-	-
160. Evacuation of Mogadischiu	4-5 Jan 1991	-	-	-	-
161. Desert Shield/Desert Storm	14 Aug 1990-Apr 1991	24	92	116	3.8
162. Kurdish Security Zone	Apr 1991-present	-	-	-	-
163. Iraq No-Fly Zone	1991-present	-	-	-	-
164. Bosnian Peacekeeping Oper.	1991-present	-	-	-	
165. Somalia Relief Operation	1992-1993	?	?	?	-
166. Haitian Operation	1994-1996	-	-	-	-
167. Rwanda Evacuation	Apr 1994	-	-	-	-
168. Somalia Evacuation	3-5 Mar 1995	-	-	-	-
169. Persian Gulf Deployment	Nov 1995-May 1996	-	-	-	-
170. Albanian Evacuation Mission	early 1997	-	-	-	-
171. Sierra Leone Evacuation Mission	30-31 May 1997	-	-	-	-
Grand Totals		40,217	189,364	229,579	4.7

Key: This table attempts to list all distinct Marine Corps wars and expeditions since 1775. It does not include operations that are part of larger operations (*e.g.,* the Defense of Curacao in 1800 is included under the Quasi-War with France, while the several overlapping missions in Bosnia are included together). Similarly, it does not include domestic operations in the support of civil authority (except in cases of rebellion), shipboard police duties, humanitarian expeditions, consular guards, exercises, and training missions. *Operation* can be the formal name of a war, campaign, or expedition, but is often just the name of the location at which a landing or other action took place. *Dates* are those of the operation, though occasionally only a year or month is shown. *KIA/MW* indicates the number of Marines killed in action or mortally wounded in each operation. *Wounded* is the number of Marines who received non-mortal wounds. *Total* is the sum of the two preceding figures. *Ratio* is the number of Marines wounded for each one killed: Thus, in the history of the Marine Corps, approximately 4.7 Marines have suffered non-fatal wounds for every one who died as a result of combat. Where a ? appears, the number of killed and wounded is not clear; a - indicates either none or none reported. Note that the *Grand Totals* omit a number of Marines killed or injured by hostile forces while engaged in duties not listed, such as on training missions, serving as embassy, legation guards and the like.

The Twenty-Five Most Important Actions in the History of the Marine Corps

1. New Providence, Nassau, the Bahamas, 3 March 1776: first action by the Marine Corps
2. USS *Cabot* vs HMS *Glasgow*, 6 April 1776: first casualties among US Marines.
3. Second Battle of Trenton (Assunpink Creek), 2 January 1777: first combat by Marines alongside the army.
4. John Paul Jones' Whitehaven Raid, 27-28 April 1778: First Marine landing in the Old World.
5. Banks Island, Penobscot, Maine, 26 July 1779: First opposed amphibious landing by U.S.Marines.
6. The Advance from Alexandria to Derna, 8 March-25 April 1805: The longest overland wartime march in Marine Corps history—nearly 600 miles in fifty days.
7. Derna, 25 April, 1805: First storming of a fortress in the Old World.
8. Bladensburg, 24 August 1814: With the sailors of the Naval Brigade, the Marines are the only American troops who did not flee during the battle.
9. Cape Fajardo, Puerto Rico, 12 November 1824: First intervention in Latin America, as Marines go ashore to enforce respect for the American flag.
10. Chapultepec, Mexico, 13-14 September 1847: A battalion of Marines takes part in the storming of the Mexican Military Academy.
11. Guantanamo, Cuba, 8-12 June 1898: First Marine seizure of an advanced base in a foreign war.
12. Peking, 20 June-14 August 1900: Defense of the Legation Quarter.
13. Samar, October-December 1901: "Stand, gentlemen, he served on Samar."
14. Belleau Wood, 2 June-1 July 1918: First large scale US attack on the Western Front breaks German defensive lines.
15. Quilali, Nicaragua, 1-8 January 1928: First successful aerial resupply of a besieged garrison.
16. Wake Island, 8-23 December 1941: Unprecedented defense against a Japanese assault.
17. Guadalcanal, 7 August 1942-1 Feb 1943: First counter offensive against the Japanese Empire, initiating the most protracted battle in Marine Corps history.
18. Tarawa, Gilbert Islands, 28 November-1 December 1943: First amphibious assault against a Japanese occupied coral atoll.
19. Peleliu, 15 September-15 October, 1944: First assault against Japanese defense in depth tactics.
20. Iwo Jima, 19 February-26 March 1945: "The most desperate battle in Marine Corps history," a place "Where uncommon valor was a common virtue."
21. Okinawa, 1 April-2 July 1945: The largest Marine Campaign of World War II.
22. Chosin Reservoir, 27 November-9 December 1950: The attack "in another direction."
23. Khe Sanh, 21 January-30 March 1968: Longest defensive battle in Marine Corps history.
24. Hue City, 30 January-25 February 1968: Most protracted house-to-house battle in Marine history.
25. The Gulf War (Operation Desert Shield), 26 January-2 March 1991, the largest operation in Marine Corps history.

Arguably the Four Toughest Battles in the History of the Marine Corps

1. "Reorganization Battle" of 1829-1834. The anomalous situation of the Marine Corps, governed by Naval regulations when at sea, but Army regulations while on land, led to some debatable practices (such as higher pay for shore based officers, rather than seagoing ones). A resulting series of Congressional investigations, partially prompted by President Andrew Jackson, who favored abolition of the Corps, went on for several years, until its status was regularized as part of the Navy in Marine Corps Act of 1834.
2. "Abolition Battle" of 1867-1868. Congressional economizers proposed abolition of the Corps, leading to a surprisingly strong show of support from war-hero Rear Admiral David Dixon Porter, which put the "fiscal conservatives" to rout.
3. "The Amalgamation Battle" of 1906-1909. In what many viewed as the opening round in the "amalgamation" of the Marine Corps into the Army—advocated by some senior army and naval officers—President Theodore Roosevelt ordered the removal of Marines from the principal ships of the fleet. During the ensuing bureaucratic and legislative battle the Marine Corps was supported by Admiral of the Navy George Dewey, and emerged with its shipboard mission intact.
4. "Unification Battle" of 1945-1952. From the end of World War II through the passage of the Douglas-Mansfield Act (PL 416, 82nd Congress) in 1952, the role—and indeed the very existence—of the Marine Corps as part of the defense establishment was under siege from many quarters.

Nine Notable Places Where the Marines Have Raised the "Old Glory"

1. Fortress Derna, North Africa, 24 April 1805
2. Customs House, Monterey, California, 7 July 1846
3. The Palacio Nacional, Mexico City, 13 September 1847
4. Customs House, Cavite, Luzon, Philippine Islands, 3 May 1898
5. Mt. Suribachi, Iwo Jima, 23 February 1945
6. Shuri Castle, Okinawa, 28 May 1945
7. U.S.Embassy, Seoul, Korea, 27 September 1950
8. The Citadel, Hue City, Vietnam, 19 February 1968
9. U.S.Embassy, Kuwait City, 28 February 1991

One Occasion on Which the USMC Left the Field Precipitously

1. The Battle of Bull Run, 21 July 1861

Trying to put the best "spin" on this unfortunate incident, Alexander Vandegrift remarked "Surely the Marines were the last to leave the field." In fact, he did not have to do so. During the battle the battalion initially did quite well, even taking some cannon fire without wavering. It then helped form battle line in support of an artillery battery, alongside two militia regiments. With these troops it held under fairly heavy fire delivered from about 400 yards, until they were struck by a surprise cavalry attack. Only at that point did the battalion begin to falter. Even then, the handful of veteran Marines present managed to rally the battalion three times before it finally collapsed, a predictable outcome given that only 15 of the 339 men present had seen more than three weeks' service.

Occasions on Which a USMC Amphibious Assault Has Failed

None.

The Dozen Occasions on Which Contingents of Marines Have Become Prisoners of War

1. Charleston, S.C., 12 May 1780: A battalion of some 200 Marines were among the approximately 7,000 American troops under MG Benjamin Lincoln who surrendered to the British after a hard siege.
2. Tripoli, 31 October 1803: The USS *Philadelphia* went aground on a reef and, after strenuous efforts failed to get her off, her captain surrendered to the Tripolitanians, a company of about 40 Marines became prisoners.
3. Pensacola, FL, 12 April 1861: A company of 40 Marines was included when the Pensacola Navy Yard was surrendered to Confederate forces by the superannuated Commodore James Armstrong.
4. SS *Ariel,* at sea off Cuba, 7 December 1862: A demi-battalion of approximately 112 Marines were among some 700 military and civilian personnel aboard the steamer when it was captured by the Confederate cruiser *Alabama*.
5. Fort Sumter, S.C., 8 September 1863: An attempt to storm Fort Sumter, in Charleston Harbor, resulted in heavy losses among the attacking parties of sailors and Marines, 104 of whom became prisoners, a quarter of the attacking force, including 41 Marines.
6. Chingwangtao, China, 8-9 December 1941: Despite an expressed willingness to go down fighting, nearly 200 Marines of the U.S. Legation Guard from Peking and Tientsin were ordered to surrender to the Japanese by U.S. diplomatic personnel.
7. Guam, 10 December 1941: 151 Marines surrendered after a two day battle against overwhelming Japanese forces.
8. Wake Island, 23 December 1941: Approximately 400 Marines surrendered after an epic resistance against overwhelming forces that lasted more than two weeks.
9. Java Sea, 1 March 1942: After the heavy cruiser USS *Houston* sunk in "one of the most gallant" fights in the history of the Navy, some 24 Marines were among the more than 300 survivors captured by the Japanese.
10. Bataan, 7 April 1942: Approximately 105 Marines are among the more than 70,000 U.S.and Philippine troops who surrendered to the Japanese after a protracted siege.
11. Corregidor, 6 May 1942: The 4th Marines (1,283 Marines, plus many U.S.Navy and Philippine Navy personnel attached to the regiment) passed into Japanese captivity when MG Jonathan Wainwright IV surrendered the island fortress.
12. Hell Fire Valley, near Hagaru, Korea, 30 November 1950: Approximately 42 Marines from the ill-fated "Task Force Drysdale" were part of a contingent of about 100 Allied personnel

who surrendered to Chinese forces after a spirited defense of more than 24 hours, with heavy casualties, having run out of all means to resist.

In each instance it can hardly be said that the Marines in question became prisoners of war under circumstances that were dishonorable.

Five Occasions on which the USMC Fielded "Horse Marines"

1. Florida, 1836-1839, a company of Marines served mounted during the First Seminole War.
2. Peking, a detail of the Legation Guard served mounted from 1907 into the early 1930s
3. Haiti, several companies or parts of companies served mounted from 1915 until the end of U.S.intervention.
4. France, during the final Allied drive to the Meuse River in early November 1918 Marines mounted the horses of fallen French cavalrymen in order to better chase the Germans.
5. Nicaragua, 1927-1928, several detachments of Marines served mounted during the Sandino War.

In addition to "Horse Marines," the USMC also has the distinction of having once deployed a contingent of "Camel Marines," 1LT Presley N. O'Bannon and his men during the Derna Expedition in 1805.

Ten Notable Occasions on Which Marines Were Employed in Support of the Civil Authority

1. Massachusetts State Prison Riot, 1824
2. Washington Riot, 1831
3. Nat Turner's Rebellion, Southampton County, Virginia, 1831
4. Plug Ugly Riot, Washington, 1 June 1857
5. Staten Island Anti-Quarantine Riot, 1-2 September 1858
6. John Brown's Raid, 18 October 1859
7. Gardiner's Island, New York, arrest of Cuban filibusters, 1869
8. Security details, US Mails, 1921
9. Security details, US Mails, 1926
10. Alcatraz Prison Riot, 1946

Six Occasions on Which the Marine Corps Aided the Civil Authority in Brooklyn

1. 16 February 1870
2. 28 March 1870
3. 2-3 November 1870
4. 12-14 July 1871
5. 15 September 1871
6. 17 October 1871

When the local police, Internal Revenue Agents ("The Revenooers"), and Federal Marshals all proved incapable of suppressing illegal distilleries in the "Irishtown" section, not far from the Brooklyn Navy Yard, the IRS decided to call in the USMC for assistance. The series of clashes between the Marines and bootleggers resulted in a complete victory for the former. Actually, Marines took part in 9 anti-moonshining operations in Brooklyn between 1867 and 1871, the six listed qualifying as "major civil disorders."

A Score of Occasions on Which the Marines Have Rendered Aid in a Disaster

1. Treasury Building Fire, Washington, 1833
2. Great Fire of New York, 1835
3. Fire at San Juan del Sur, Nicaragua, 1852
4. Fire at Portland, Maine, 1866
5. Fire at Boston, 1872
6. Fire at Boston, 1873
7. Fire at Yokohama, Japan, 1890
8. Fire at Port-of-Spain, Trinidad, British West Indies, 1896
9. San Francisco Earthquake and Fire, 1906
10. Messina Earthquake, 1908
11. Great Tokyo Earthquake, 1923
12. Ionian Islands Earthquake, Greece, 1953
13. Tampico Flood, Mexico, 1955
14. Flood, Valencia, Spain, 1957
15. Peruvian Earthquake, 1970
16. Earthquake in Soviet Georgia, 1989
17. Philippine Earthquake, 1990
18. Bangladesh Cyclone, 1991
19. Kobe Earthquake, 1991
20. Western forest fires, 1996

There are literally hundreds of occasions on which the Marine Corps has been called upon to render aid in times of natural disaster.

Eight Occasions on Which the Marines Have Helped Put Down Mutinies Aboard Ship

1. An incipient mutiny aboard the USS *Congress* was foiled with the assistance of the ship's Marine Guard, 1800.
2. The ship's Marine Guard helped foil a threatened mutiny aboard the USS *President*, 1803.
3. The ship's Marine detachment foiled a mutiny aboard the USS *Constitution*, 1807.
4. Mutinous conduct aboard the ketch USS *Dispatch* ended when the ship's Marines subdued the principal miscreant, 1812.
5. Marines from several ships quelled a mutiny aboard the USS *Potomac* at Puerto Mahon, the Balearic Islands, Spain, 1836.
6. A threatened mutiny aboard the USS *Somers* was put down with the aid of Marine SGT Michael H. Garty, 1842.

7. A detail of Marines from the USS *Dale* helped suppress a mutiny aboard the bark *Paulina* in the Comoro Islands, 1851.

8. A detail of Marines assisted the skipper of a Siamese ship in suppressing a mutiny aboard his vessel at Canton, China, 1863.

Marine Corps Base Monthly Pay Since 1775

Grade	1775	1798	←The Civil War→ 1861-US	1861-CS	Spain 1898	WWI 1918	WWII 1942	Korea 1951	Vietnam 1969	Today 1996
E1	$6.66	$6.00	$13.00	$11.00	$13.80	$15.00	$50.00	$75.00	$115.28	$833.40
E2						18.00	53.33	80.00	127.80	1,010.10
E3									155.10	1,049.70
E4	7.33	8.00	13.00	13.00	15.85	21.00	66.00	90.00	209.20	1,113.60
E5	8.00	9.00	17.00	17.00	18.00	30.00	78.00	100.00	254.70	1,194.30
E6					20.00	20.00	96.00	115.00	294.90	1,360.80
E7		10.00	21.00	21.00	25.00	45.00	114.00	135.00	342.30	1,581.90
E8							114.00	135.00	544.50	2,265.60
E9		10.00	21.00	21.00	32.35	45.00	138.00	165.00	648.90	2,701.80
W1							150.00	210.98	378.90	1,540.20
W2							175.00	254.63	454.80	1,848.60
W3							200.00	291.00	519.30	2,110.80
W4							250.00	320.10	571.20	2,322.30
W5										3,963.60
O1	13.35	25.00	105.50	80.00	116.65	141.67	150.00	213.75	363.40	1,725.90
O2	13.35	25.00	105.50	90.00	125.00	166.67	166.67	249.38	449.70	1,987.80
O3	30.00	40.00	115.00	130.00	150.00	200.00	200.00	313.50	561.00	2,279.40
O4		50.00	169.00	150.00	208.33	250.00	250.00	384.75	603.60	2,452.80
O5		60.00	181.00	170.00	250.00	291.67	291.67	456.00	715.50	2,910.30
O6			212.00	195.00	291.67	333.33	333.33	570.00	894.60	3,638.40
O7						500.00	500.00	769.50	1,207.20	4,909.20
O8						666.67	666.67	926.25	1,453.20	5,908.20
O9							666.67	926.25	1,604.40	6,522.90
O10								926.25	1,810.20	7,360.20

Figures are for base pay, upon attainment of the indicated grade, without longevity or other allowances. Rather than use actual titles of rank, modern pay grade equivalents have been used. Enlisted ranks from earlier times are not directly comparable to those in use today, if only because some ranks have risen or fallen in status relative to others, while some have passed from the scene entirely. In cases where differing pay grades are shown as receiving the same pay, higher ranking personnel were usually the beneficiaries of additional allowances for rations, quarters, and so forth. In addition, the CMC was usually given a special allowance above his regular pay through most of the nineteenth century.

Note how much better paid officers were in earlier times, relatively speaking, than today. In 1898 a second lieutenant was making more than eight times what a private made, while today the difference is less than twice that of a private. Of course in earlier times not only did officers have to provide their own uniforms, but all their other equipment as well, including weapons and, in theory, ammunition.

It is not possible to draw a neat comparison between the purchasing power of the pay of a Marine in earlier times and that of his modern counterparts, since there is no way of accurately equating the value of money over so many generations. By way of example, a laborer who was making $150 a year in George Washington's day was doing rather well, as was his grandson if he was taking in $300 a year in Lincoln's time. In Washington's time $1,000 a year would have enabled someone to have a house and a couple of servants.

As is the case today, Marines in earlier times received allowances for rations, quarters, and other expenses, which varied depending upon type of service, longevity, and so forth. These benefits are relatively greater today, though perhaps the beer and spirits rations provided Marines in earlier generations helped compensate for the differences. For example, in1798 a first lieutenant received not only his $25 a month and his standard allotments for a batman, quarters, firewood, and even a horse, should his duties require him to have one, but also an extra ration of food, plus a pint of rum or brandy, and two quarts of beer a day.

* In 1862 Confederate enlisted Marines were given a monthly raise of $4.00, which put them slightly ahead of their Union counterparts. Union enlisted Marines received an additional $3.00 a month in June 1864. Morcover, their raise was in greenbacks, by then worth about 18 times what Confederate money was worth.

Principal Muskets and Rifles of the Marine Corps, 1775-1997

Year	Weapon	Weight	Bore	Magazine	RPM	Notes
1775	Tower Musket Mk III	11.00	18.7 (.74)	1	2-3	A
1776	Charleville Musket '63	10.60	17.2 (.68)	1	2-4	B
1816	US Musket 1816	9.50	17.5 (.69)	1	2-3	C
1861	US Rifled Musket (Springfield)	9.75	14.7 (.58)	1	2-3	
1871	Remington	9.60	11.0 (.43)	1	5-8	
1884	Springfield '84	9.50	11.4 (.45)	1	5-8	
1896	Winchester-Lee	8.50	6.0 (.236)	5	20	
1898	Krag-Jorgenson	9.30	7.62 (.30)	5	20	
1903	Springfield .30	8.50	7.62 (.30)	5	30	
1942	M1 Garand	9.50	7.62 (.30)	8	30-40	
1959	M14	8.70	7.62 (.30)	20	750	*
1965	M16	8.80	5.56 (.22)	30	800	* D

Only weapons in common issue have been shown. In fact, many other muskets and rifles have been used from time to time, such as the French *fusil* Maugbuege 1777, which was toted by the Marines aboard John Paul Jones' *Bon Homme Richard* in 1779. *Key: Year* is that of adoption; *Weapon*, is the common name; *Weight* is given in pounds, unloaded and without bayonet, except as indicated; *Bore* is given in both mm and calibers; *Magazine* is the maximum number of rounds the piece could *hold; RPM*, rounds per minute. Note that range has not bcen indicated, since the difference between effective range and maximum range is frequently considerable. For the smoothbore pieces (those issued 1775-1842), effective range was only about 100-150 yards, and even then accuracy was problematic. Early rifles (1861 Springfield) were effective and accurate out to about 450 yards. Most subsequent weapons could be accurate at considerably greater ranges.

A. "Old Brown Bess," standard British infantry musket until about 1830, used extensively by American forces during the Revolutionary War.

B. The standard French musket, issued to American forces during the French Alliance.

C. There were numerous variants of this, which remained in production for over 30 years, until the U.S. began issuing rifles in the mid-1850s.

D. Weight is with 30-round magazine, all other pieces are given unloaded.

* Cyclic rate, both weapons can fire c.40 rounds on semiautomatic.

Principal Machine Guns of the Marine Corps, 1896-1997

Year	Weapon	Weight	Bore	Feed	RPM *	Notes
1866	Gatling	1,100	11.43 (.45)	Hopper	600	A
1896	Colt	101	7.62 (.30)	Belt	500	
1909	Benet-Mercie M1909	22	7.62 (.30)	Strip	600	B
1917	Berthier, M1916	50	7.62 (.30)	Mag	400	C
1917	Browning M1919A1 Heavy	86	7.62 (.30)	Belt	600	
1917	Chauchat, M1915	20	7.62 (.30)	Mag	250	D
1917	Lewis, M1917	25	7.69 (.303)	Drum	550	
1917	Hotchkiss M1914	108	7.62 (.30)	Belt	500	E
1919	Browning M1919A4 Light	41	7.62 (.30)	Belt	450	
1919	Browning M1917 AR	19.5	7.62 (.30)	Mag	550	
1919	Browning M1919 Heavy	121	12.7 (.50)	Belt	550	
1957	M60 Light	18.75	7.62 (.30)	Belt	550	
1985	M249 Squad Automatic Weapon	15.2	5.56 (.223)	Belt	725	F
1989	M240G Light	24.2	7.62 (.30)	Belt	950	

Only machine guns in regular issue have been listed, and minor variations in model and make have been ignored, as have light automatic cannon. *Key*: *Year* is that of adoption; *Weapon* is the common name; *Weight* is given in pounds, normally unloaded but with bipod or tripod, as applicable, and water for water cooled models; *Bore* is given in both mm and calibers; *Feed* is the means by which ammunition can be fed to the piece, magazine, belt, or drum; *RPM* is maximum rounds per minute the weapon can fire, this is usually a theoretical "Cyclic Rate," which is generally much higher than the practical sustainable rate of fire on the battlefield.

A. Strictly, the Gatling was not a machine gun. Loading and firing was the result of cranking the handle, and constant cranking was required to keep it firing. A proper machine gun uses the physical recoil or the gas blowback from the discharge of one round to load and fire another.

B. Despite its name the Benet-Mercie was an American weapon. Weight is without the bipod mount, which was later replaced by a sturdier tripod. Feed was by means of a 30 round metallic strip. Although not as good as some others, it was cheap and made in the U.S. It remained in use into World War I.

C. A French design, specially chambered for U.S. .30 ammunition.

D. A French design, manufactured for use with U.S. .30 ammunition, it was in practical terms a rather poor automatic rifle, rather than a proper machine gun.

E. A French designed-weapon, was specially manufactured to take US .30 ammunition. It was fed using either an articulated metal belt or a metallic "strip."

F. A Belgian design.

Principal Tanks Used by the Marine Corps, 1926-1997

Tank	Used	Weight	Crew	Gun	Armor	HP	HP/WT	Speed	Notes
US 6-Ton	1925-1929	7.0	2	37	25	35	5.0	4.5	A
M3A1 Stuart	1941-1944	14.2	4	37	45	250	27.6	35	B
M4A2 Sherman	1942-1950	34.8	5	75	95	375	10.8	20	C
M26 Pershing	1950-1960	46.0	5	90	100	500	10.9	30	D
M103A2	1960s-1970s	62.5	5	120	194	810	13.0	20	E
M48A2 Patton	1960s-1970s	51.9	5	90	120	825	15.9	30	F
M60A1	1970s-1992	52.9	5	105	>110	750	14.2	35	G
M1A1 Abrams	1985-	62.6	5	120	>700	1500	24.0	45	H

Only formally adopted tanks have been listed. In fact, the Marine Corps tested many other tanks, such as the British Marmon-Harrington Tankette, which was extensively field tested in the early 1930s. Minor variations in make and model have been omitted, as have machine guns.

Key: *Tank* is the model and name of the vehicle; *Used* indicates the dates it was employed in line units; *Weight* is in tons; *Crew* is the normal complement; *Gun* the main gun, in millimeters; *Armor* is the maximum thickness, in millimeters, with > indicating that the vehicle uses appliqué or composite armor that has an effective thickness that is greater than the figure shown; *HP* is horsepower; *HP/Wt*, horsepower to weight ratio (HP per ton, in effect, the higher the figure indicating the "livelier" the vehicle); *Spd*, miles per hour, maximum.

Notes:

A. The American version of the French Renault FT-17, first introduced in 1917. It was used operationally in China in 1927-1927.

B. First used in combat on Guadalcanal, it was later replaced by the substantially similar M5A1 in 1944.

C. First used in combat on Tarawa in late 1943, and continued in use into the early part of the Korean War.

D. First used in Korea.

E. Some in use in the late 1950s.

F. Replaced the somewhat similar M46, used extensively in Vietnam.

G. The versions used in combat during Operation Desert Storm had reactive armor.

H. First used in Operation Desert Storm.

## CHAPTER 3

The Medal of Honor and Other Decorations

The Medal of Honor was instituted in 1862, during the Civil War, in two versions, one for the Navy and one for the Army. Subsequently an Air Force version was created as well. Although regulations instituting the Army Medal of Honor in 1863 allowed for its award to officers as well as enlisted men, the Navy Medal of Honor was limited to enlisted men of the Navy and Marine Corps. The Navy Medal of Honor also differed from the Army's in that it could be awarded for non-combat heroism.

In 1916 regulations outlining the circumstances under which the Medal of Honor could be awarded were tightened. All previous awards were reviewed, and a considerable number rescinded. In addition, regulations for the Navy Medal of Honor were revised, to permit its award to officers and to members of the Coast Guard. One result of this was that there was something of a disgraceful "rush" of nominations—and awards—for officers who had participated in the Vera Cruz Operation.

In 1917 the Navy instituted a new version of its Medal of Honor, a cross patee, quite similar in appearance to Britain's Victoria Cross. This was to be awarded for combat heroism, while the "Old" version continued to be awarded for non-combat related valor. This dual award arrangement prevailed for about 25 years. On 7 August 1942—Guadalcanal Day—a slightly modified version of the "Old" Navy Medal of Honor was instituted for both combat and non-combat heroism, although in fact there has been only one non-combat related award since then.

Marines Who Have Been Awarded the Medal of Honor, 1862-1970

War	# Rank & Name	Born-Died/Birthplace	Unit	Action Date	Action or Location
CW	1 CPL John F.Mackie	1835-1910 NY	USS *Galena*	15 May 1862	Reconnaissance at Drewry's Bluff,VA
CW	2 SGT Pinkerton R.Vaughn	1839-1866 PA	USS *Mississippi*	14 Apr 1863	Scuttling of USS *Mississippi*,Port Hudson,LA
CW	3 OrdSGT Christopher Nugent	1838-1898 Ireland	USS *Fort Henry*	15 Jun & 30 Jul 1863	Cutting out parties, Crystal City and Depot Key,FL
CW	4 CPL Miles M.Oviatt	1840-1880 NY	USS *Brooklyn*	5 Aug 1864	Mobile Bay
CW	5 CPL Willard M.Smith	1840-1918 NY	USS *Brooklyn*	5 Aug 1864	Mobile Bay
CW	6 OrdSgt David Sprowle (Sprowls)	1811-???? NY	USS *Richmond*	5 Aug 1864	Mobile Bay
CW	7 SGT James S.Roantree	1835-1873 Ireland	USS *Oneida*	5 Aug 1864	Mobile Bay
CW	8 SGT Henry Denig	1839-???? PA	USS *Brooklyn*	5 Aug 1864	Mobile Bay
CW	9 SGT Michael Hudson	1834-1891 Ireland	USS *Brooklyn*	5 Aug 1864	Mobile Bay
CW	10 SGT James Martin	1826-1895 Ireland	USS *Richmond*	5 Aug 1864	Mobile Bay
CW	11 SGT Andrew Miller	1836-???? Germany	USS *Richmond*	5 Aug 1864	Mobile Bay

THE MEDAL OF HONOR AND OTHER DECORATIONS

War	# Rank & Name	Born-Died/Birthplace	Unit	Action Date	Action or Location
CW	12 SGT Richard Binder(Bigle)	1839-1912 Germany	USS *Ticonderoga*	24-25 Dec 1864 13-15 Jan 1865	Ft Fisher,NC
CW	13 CPL John Rannahan	1836-???? Ireland	USS *Minnesota*	24-25 Dec 1864	Ft Fisher,NC
CW	14 OrdSGT Isaac N.Fry	????-???? PA	USS *Ticonderoga*	13-15 Jan 1865	Ft Fisher,NC
CW	15 CPL Andrew J.Tomlin	1845-1905 NJ	USS *Wabash*	15 Jan 1865	Ft Fisher,NC
CW	16 PVT Henry A.Thompson (Roderick P.Connelly)	1841-1889 England	USS *Minnesota*	15 Jan 1865	Ft Fisher,NC
CW	17 PVT John Shivers	1830-???? Canada	USS *Minnesota*	15 Jan 1865	Ft Fisher,NC
KKF	18 CPL Charles Brown	????-???? NY	USS *Colorado*	11 Jun 1871	Kanghwa Forts
KKF	19 PVT Hugh Purvis	1846-1922 PA	USS *Alaska*	11 Jun 1871	Kanghwa Forts
KKF	20 PVT John Coleman	1847-???? Ireland	USS *Colorado*	11 Jun 1871	Kanghwa Forts
KKF	21 PVT James Dougherty	1839-1897 Ireland	USS *Benicia*,serving in USS *Carondolet*	11 Jun 1871	Kanghwa Forts
KKF	22 PVT Michael McNamara	1841-???? Ireland	USS *Benicia*	11 Jun 1871	Kanghwa Forts
KKF	23 PVT Michael Owens	1837-1890 NY	USS *Colorado*	11 Jun 1871	Kanghwa Forts
-	24 CPL James A.Stewart	1839-???? PA	USS *Plymouth*	1 Feb 1872	Life saving, Villefranche,France
-	25 CPL John Morris	1855-???? NY	USS *Lancaster*	25 Dec 1881	Life saving, Villefranche,France
SAW	26 PVT James Meredith (Patrick Ford,Jr.)	1872-1915 NB	USS *Marblehead*	11 May 1898	Cable Cutting Party, Cienfuegos,Cuba
SAW	27 PVT Oscar Field	1873-1912 NJ	USS *Nashville*	11 May 1898	Cable Cutting Party, Cienfuegos,Cuba
SAW	28 PVT Joseph J.Franklin	1870-1940 NY	USS *Nashville*	11 May 1898	Cable Cutting Party, Cienfuegos, Cuba
SAW	29 PVT Michael Kearny	1874-1937 Ireland	USS *Nashville*	11 May 1898	Cable Cutting Party, Cienfuegos,Cuba
SAW	30 PVT Hermann W.Kuchneister	1877-1923 Germany	USS *Marblehead*	11 May 1898	Cable Cutting Party, Cienfuegos,Cuba
SAW	31 PVT Joseph F.Scott	1866-1941 MA	USS *Nashville*	11 May 1898	Cable Cutting Party Cienfuegos,Cuba
SAW	32 PVT Edward Sullivan	1870-1955 Ireland	USS *Marblehead*	11 May 1898	Cable Cutting Party, Cienfuegos,Cuba
SAW	33 PVT Daniel J.Campbell	1874-1955 Canada	USS *Marblehead*	11 May 1898	Cable Cutting Party, Cienfuegos,Cuba
SAW	34 PVT Frank Hill	1864-???? CT	USS *Nashville*	11 May 1898	Cable Cutting Party, Cienfuegos,Cuba
SAW	35 PVT Pomeroy Parker	1874-1946 NC	USS *Marblehead*	11 May 1898	Cable Cutting Party, Cienfuegos,Cuba
SAW	36 PVT Walter Scott West	1872-1943 NH	USS *Marblehead*	11 May 1898	Cable Cutting Party, Cienfuegos,Cuba
SAW	37 SGT Philip Gaughan	1865-1913 Ireland	USS *Nashville*	11 May 1898	Cable Cutting Party, Cienfuegos,Cuba
SAW	38 PVT John Fitgerald	1873-1948 Ireland	1st Marine Bn	14 Jun 1898	Cuzco,Cuba
SAW	39 SGT John Henry Quick	1870-1922 WV	1st Marine Bn	14 Jun 1898	Cuzco,Cuba
SAW	40 PVT Harry L.MacNeal	1879-1950 PA	USS *Brooklyn*	3 Jul 1898	Naval Battle of Santiago de Cuba
PI	41 CPL Thomas F.Prendergast	1871-1913 Ireland	1st Marine Bde	25,27,& 29 Mar, & 4 Apr 1899	Service with VIII Corps
PI	42 PVT Howard M.Buckley	1862-1941 NY	1st Marine Bde	25,27,& 29 Mar, & 4 Apr 1899	Service with VIII Corps
PI	43 PVT Joseph H.Leonard	1876-1946 NY	1st Marine Bde	25,27,& 29 Mar, & 4 Apr 1899	Service with VIII Corps
Sam	44 PVT Henry L.Hulbert	1867-1918 England	USS *Philadelphia*	1 Apr 1899	Tagalli
Sam	45 SGT Bruno A.Forsterer	1869-1957 Germany	??	1 Apr 1899	Tagalli
Sam	46 SGT Michael J.McNally	1860-???? NY	??	1 Apr 1899	Tagalli
PI	47 SGT Harry Harvey	1873-1929 NY	1st Marine Bde	16 Feb 1900	Benefictican
Box	48 CPL Reuben J.Phillips	1874-1936 CA	??	13,20-22 Jun 1900	Tientsin
Box	49 GySGT Peter Stewart	1858-1914 Scotland	USS *Newark*	13,20-22 Jun 1900	Tientsin
Box	50 PVT Harry W.Orndoff	1875-1938 OH	??	13,20-22 Jun 1900	Tientsin
Box	51 CPL Edwin N.Appleton	1877-1937 NY	Legation Guard	20 Jun 1900	Action near Tientsin

War	# Rank & Name	Born-Died Birthplace	Unit	Action Date	Action or Location
Box	52 PVT James Burnes	1870-???? MA	Legation Guard	20 Jun 1900	Tientsin
Box	53 PVT Albert R.Campbell	1875-1925 PA	Legation Guard	20 Jun 1900	Tientsin
Box	54 PVT Henry W.Heisch	1872-1941 Germany	Legation Guard	20 Jun 1900	Tientsin
Box	55 PVT Martin Hunt	1873-1938 Ireland	USS Oregon	20 Jun-16 Jul 1900	Peking
Box	56 PVT John O.Dahlgren	1872-1963 Sweden	Legation Guard	20 Jun-16 Jul 1900	Peking
Box	57 PVT Frank A.Young	1876-1941 WI	Legation Guard	20 Jun-16 Jul 1900	Peking
Box	58 PVT Harry Fisher	1874-1900* PA	Legation Guard	20 Jun-16 Jul 1900	Peking
	First posthumous award to a Marine				
Box	59 SGT Edward A.Walker	1864-1946 Scotland	Legation Guard	20 Jun-16 Jul 1900	Peking
Box	60 PVT Alexander J.Foley	1866-1910 PA	USS Monadock	21 Jun 1900	Tientsin
Box	61 PVT Charles R.Francis	1875-1946 PA	Relief Force	21 Jun 1900	Tientsin
Box	62 PVT Thomas W.Kates	1865-???? NY	Relief Force	21 Jun 1900	Tientsin
Box	63 PVT France Silva	1876-1951 CA	Legation Guard	21 Jun-17 Aug 1900	Peking
Box	64 CPL Harry C.Adriance	1864-1934 NY	Relief Force	13 Jul 1900	Tientsin
Box	65 PVT Clarence E.Mathias	1876-1935 PA	Relief Force	13 Jul 1900	Tientsin
Box	66 SGT John M.Adams	1871-1921 MA	Relief Force	13 Jul 1900	Tientsin
Box	67 SGT Clarence E.Sutton	1871-1916 VA	Relief Force	13 Jul 1900	Tientsin
Box	68 PVT Henry W.Davis	1876-1923 NY	Legation Guard	21 Jul-17 Aug 1900	Peking
	(William Henry Murray)				
Box	69 PVT John A.Murphy	1881-1935 NY	Legation Guard	21 Jul-17 Aug 1900	Peking
Box	70 PVT Erwin J.Boydston	1875-1957 CO	Legation Guard	21 Jul-17 Aug 1900	Peking
Box	71 PVT William L.Carr	1878-1921 MA	Legation Guard	21 Jul-17 Aug 1900	Peking
Box	72 PVT James Cooney	1860-1903 Ireland	Legation Guard	21 Jul-17 Aug 1900	Peking
Box	73 PVT Louis R.Gaienne	1878-1942 MO	Legation Guard	21 Jul-17 Aug 1900	Peking
Box	74 PVT William M.C.Horton	1876-1969 IL	Legation Guard	21 Jul-17 Aug 1900	Peking
Box	75 PVT Albert Moore	1862-1916 CA	Legation Guard	21 Jul-17 Aug 1900	Peking
Box	76 PVT Herbert I.Preston	1876-???? NJ	Legation Guard	21 Jul-17 Aug 1900	Peking
Box	77 PVT David J.Scannel	1875-1923 MA	Legation Guard	21 Jul-17 Aug 1900	Peking
Box	78 PVT Oscar J.Upham	1871-1949 OH	Legation Guard	21 Jul-17 Aug 1900	Peking
Box	79 PVT William F.Zion	1872-1919 IN	Legation Guard	21 Jul-17 Aug 1900	Peking
Box	80 PVT Daniel J.Daly	1873-1937 NY	Legation Guard	14 Aug 1900	Peking
	First award,see also 24 Oct 1915				
-	81 SGT John H.Helms	1874-1919 IL	USS Chicago	10 Jan 1901	Lifesaving,Montevideo, Uruguay
-	82 PVT Louis F.Pfeifer	1876-???? PA	USS Petrel	31 Mar 1901	Lifesaving,shipboard explosion.
PI	83 COL Hiram I.Bearss	1875-1938 IN	1st Marine Bde	17 Nov 1911	Samar,Philippines
PI	84 CPT David Dixon Porter	1877-1944 DC	1st Marine Bde	17 Nov 1911	Samar,Philippines
VC	85 CPT Jessee F.Dyer	1873-1955 MN	??	21-22 Apr 1914	Vera Cruz landing
VC	86 CPT Eli T.Fryer	1878-1963 NJ	2nd Advanced Base Regt	21-22 Apr 1914	Vera Cruz landing
VC	87 CPT Walter N.Hill	1881-1955 MA	??	21-22 Apr 1914	Vera Cruz landing
VC	88 CPT John A.Hughes	1880-1942 NY	??	21-22 Apr 1914	Vera Cruz landing
VC	89 LTC Wendell C.Neville	1870-1930 VA	2nd Regt, Marines & Sailors	21-22 Apr 1914	Vera Cruz landing
VC	90 MAJ George G.Reid	1876-1861 OK	??	21-22 Apr 1914	Vera Cruz landing
VC	91 MAJ Randolph C.Berkely	1875-1960 VA	2nd Advanced Base Regt	21-22 Apr 1914	Vera Cruz landing
VC	92 MAJ Smedley D.Butler	1881-1940 PA	2nd Advanced Base Regt	21-22 Apr 1914	Vera Cruz landing
	First award,see also 17 Nov 1915				
VC	93 MAJ Albertus W.Caitlin	1868-1933 NY	3rd Marines	21-22 Apr 1914	Vera Cruz landing
Hai	94 1LT Edward A.Osterman	1882-1969 OH	2nd Marines	24 Oct 1915	Ft.Dipitie
Hai	95 CPT William P.Upshur	1881-1943 VA	2nd Marines	24 Oct 1915	Ft.Dipitie
Hai	96 GySGT Daniel J.Daly	1873-1937 NY	2nd Marines	24 Oct 1915	Ft.Dipitie
	Second award,see also 14 Aug 190l				
Hai	97 MAJ Smedley D.Butler	1881-1940 PA	Provisional Bn	17 Nov 1915	Ft.Riviere
	Second award,see also 21-22 Apr 1914				
Hai	98 PVT Samuel Gross (Marguilies)	1891-1934 PA	Provisional Bn	17 Nov 1915	Ft.Riviere
Hai	99 SGT Ross L.Iams	1881-1952 PA	Provisional Bn	17 Nov 1915	Ft.Riviere
DR	100 1SGT Roswell Winans	1887-1968 IN	??	2 Jul 1916	Guayacanas

War	# Rank & Name	Born-Died Birthplace	Unit	Action Date	Action or Location
DR	101 CPL Joseph A.Glowin	1892-1952 MI	??	3 Jul 1916	Guayacanas
DR	102 1LT Ernest C.Williams	1887-1940 IL	??	29 Nov 1916	San Francisco de Macoris
WW1	103 GySGT Charles Hoffman	1878-1940 NY	2nd Div,5th Marines	6 Jun 1918	Chateau-Thierry,France
	Double awadree (Ernest August Jameson)				
WW1	104 GySGT Fred W.Stockham	1881-1918* MI	2nd Div,6th Marines	13 Jun 1918	Belleau Wood,France
	Only Marine winner in the 2nd Div who did not also receive the Navy Medal as well				
WW1	105 SGT Louis Cukela	1888-1956 Croatia	2nd Div,5th Marines	18 Jul 1918	Villers-Cotterets, France
	Double awardee				
WW1	106 PVT John J.Kelly	1898-1957 IL	2nd Div,6th Marines	3 Oct 1918	Mont Blanc Ridge,France
	Double awardee				
WW1	107 CPL John H.Pruitt	1896-1918* AR	2nd Div,6th Marines	4 Oct 1918	Mont Blanc Ridge, France
	Double awardee				
WW1	108SGT Matej Kocak	1882-1918* Slovakia	2nd Div,5th Marines	8 Oct 1918	Soissons,France
	Double awardee				
WW1	109 2LT Ralph Talbot	1897-1918* MA	1st Mar Aviation Force, Sqn C	8 & 14 Oct 1918	Pittham,Belgium
WW1	110 GySGT Robert G.Robinson	1896-1974 NY	1st Mar Aviation Force	14 Oct 1918	Pittham,Belgium
Hai	111 2LT Herman H.Hanneken	1893-1986 MO	Garde d'Haiti	31 Oct- 1 Nov 1919	Grand Riviere
Hai	112 CPL William R.Button	1895-1921 MO	Garde d'Haiti	31 Oct- 1 Nov 1919	Grand Riviere
-	113 PVT Albert J.Smith	1898-1973 MI	Marine Barracks, Pensacola	11 Feb 1921	NAS Pensacola,Fl
Nic	1141LT Christian F.Schilt	1895-1987 IL	VMO 7	6-8 Jan 1928	Quilali
Nic	115 CPL Donald L.Truesdell	1906-1993 SC	Guardia Nacional	24 Apr 1932	Constancia
WW2	116 1LT George H.Cannon	1915-1941* MO	6th Defense Bn	7 Dec 1941	Midway
WW2	117 CPT Henry T.Elrod	1905-1941* GA	VMF 211	8-23 Dec 1941	Wake Island
WW2	118 LTC Harold W.Bauer	1908-1942* KS	VMF 212	10 May 14 Nov 1942	SW Pacific & Guadalcanal
WW2	119 CPT Richard E.Fleming	1917-1942* MN	VMS 241	4-5 Jun 1942	Midway
WW2	120 MAJ John L.Smith	1914-1972 OK	VMF 223	1 Aug-30 Sep 1942	Guadalcanal
WW2	121 MG Alexander A.Vandegrift	1887-1973 VA	1st Marine Div	7 Aug- 9 Dec 1942	Guadalcanal
WW2	122 SGT Clyde A.Thomason	1914-1942*GA	2nd Raider Bn	17-18 Aug 1942	Makin I
WW2	123 MAJ Kenneth D.Bailey	1910-1942*OK	1st Raider Bn	12 Sep 1942	Guadalcanal
WW2	124 LTC Merritt A.Edson	1897-1955 VT	1st Raider Bn	13-14 Sep Aug 1942	Guadalcanal
WW2	125 MAJ Robert E.Galer	1913- WA	VMF 244	1 Oct 1942	Guadalcanal
WW2	126 CPT Joseph J.Foss	1915- SD	VMF 121	9 Oct-19 Nov 1942 & 15,23 Jan 1943	Solomon Islands
WW2	127 SGT John Basilone	1916-1945 NY	1st Marine Div, 7th Marine	24 Oct 1942	Guadalcanal
WW2	128 SGT Mitchell Paige	1918- PA	1st Marine Div, 7th Marines	26 Oct 1942	Guadalcanal
WW2	129 CPL Anthony Casamento	1920-1987NY	1st Marine Div, 5th Marines	1 Nov 1942	Guadalcanal
	(Most belated Marine award of World War II,not issued until 1980.)				
WW2	130 CPT Jefferson J.DeBlanc	1921- LA	VMF 112	31 Jan 1943	Kolombangara
WW2	131 1LT James E.Swett	1920- WA	VMF 221	7 Apr 1943	Guadalcanal
WW2	132 1LT Kenneth A.Walsh	1916- NY	VMF 124	15 & 30 Aug 1943	Vella LaVella
WW2	133 MAJ Gregory Boyington	1912-1988 ID	VMF 214	12 Sep 1943- 3 Jan 44	Central Solomons
	Awarded partially for courage while P/W,from mid-1943.				
WW2	134 1LT Robert M.Hanson	1904-1944 India	VMF 315	Nov 1943- 1 Jan 44	Bougainville
	KIA,3 February 1944				
WW2	135 SGT Robert A.Owens	1920-1943*SC	3rd Marine Div	1 Nov 1943	Bougainville
WW2	136 SGT Herbert J.Thomas	1918-1943*OH	3rd Marine Div, 3rd Marines	7 Nov 1943	Bougainville
WW2	137 PFC Henry Gurke	1922-1943*ND	3rd Raider Bn	9 Nov 1942	Bougainville
WW2	138 1LT William D.Hawkins	1914-1943*KS	2nd Marine Div, 2nd Marines	20-21 Nov 1943	Tarawa
WW2	139 1LT Alexander Bonnyman,Jr.	1910-1943*GA	2nd Marine Div, 8th Marines	20-22 Nov 1943	Tarawa
WW2	140 COL David M.Shoup	1904-1983 IN	2nd Marine Div, 2nd Marines	20-22 Nov 1943	Tarawa

THE MEDAL OF HONOR AND OTHER DECORATIONS

War	# Rank & Name	Born-Died Birthplace	Unit	Action Date	Action or Location
WW2	141 SSG William J.Bordeleon	1920-1943*TX	2nd Marine Div, 18th Marines	20 Nov 1934	Tarawa
WW2	142 1LT John V.Power	1918-1944 MA	4th Marine Div	1 Feb 1944	Kwajelein (Namur)
WW2	143 LTC Aquilla J.Dyess	1909-1944 GA	4th Marine Div, 24th Marines	1-2 Feb 1944	Kwajelein (Namur)
WW2	144 PFC Richard B.Anderson	1921-1944*WA	4th Marine Div, 23rd Marines	1 Feb 1944	Kwajelein (Roi)
WW2	145 PVT Richard K.Sorenson	1924- MN	4th Marine Div, 24th Marines	1-2 Feb 1944	Kwajelein (Namur)
WW2	146 CPL Anthony P.D'Amato	1922-1944*PA	??	19-20 Feb 1944	Eniwetok (Engebi)
WW2	147 GySGT Robert H.McCard	1918-1944*NY	4th Marine Dn, 4th Tank Bn	16 Jun 1944	Saipan
WW2	148 PFC Harold G.Epperson	1923-1944*OK	2nd Marine Div, 6th Marines	25 Jun 1944	Saipan
WW2	149 PFC Harold C.Agerholm	1925-1944*WI	2nd Marine Div, 10th Marines	7 Jul 1944	Saipan
WW2	150 SGT Grant F.Timmerman	1919-1944*KS	2nd Marine Div, 6th Marines	8 Jul 1944	Saipan
WW2	151 PFC Luther Skaggs,Jr.	1923-1976 KY	3rd Marine Div, 3rd Marines	21-22 Jul 1944	Guam
WW2	152 PFC Leonard F.Mason	1920-1944*NY	3rd Marine Div, 3rd Marines	22 Jul 1944	Guam
WW2	153 PFC Frank P.Witek	1921-1944*CT	3rd Marine Div, 9th Marines	3 Aug 1944	Guam
WW2	154 PFC Robert Lee Wilson	1921-1944*IL	2nd Marine Div, 6th Marines	4 Aug 1944	Tinian
WW2	155 CPT Louis H.Wilson,Jr.	1920- MS	3rd Marine Div, 9th Marines	25-26 Aug 1944	Guam
WW2	156 PVT Joseph W.Ozbourn	1919-1944*IL	4th Marine Div, 23rd Marines	28 Aug 1944	Tinian
WW2	157 1LT Carlton R.Rouh	1919-1977 NH	1st Marine Div, 5th Marines	15 Sep 1944	Peleliu
WW2	158 CPL Lewis K.Bausell	1924-1944*VA	1st Marine Div, 5th Marines	15 Sep 1944	Peleliu
WW2	159 CPT Everett P.Pope	1919- MA	1st Marine Div, 1st Marines	16 Sep 1944	Peleliu
WW2	160 PFC Arthur Jackson,Jr.	1924- OK	1st Marine Div, 7th Marines	18 Sep 1944	Peleliu
WW2	161 PFC Charles H.Roan	1923-1944*TX	1st Marine Div, 7th Marines	18 Sep 1944	Peleliu
WW2	162 PFC John D.New	1924-1944*AL	1st Marine Div, 7th Marines	25 Sep 1944	Peleliu
WW2	163 PVT Wesley Phelps	1923-1944*KY	1st Marine Div, 7th Marines	4 Oct 1944	Peleliu
WW2	164 PFC Richard E.Kraus	1925-1944*IL	8th Amphtrac Bn	5 Oct 1944	Peleliu
WW2	165 CPL Tony Stein KIA,Iwo Jima,1 March 1945.	1921-1945OK	5th Marine Div, 28th Marines	19 Feb 1945	Iwo Jima
WW2	166 LTC Justice M.Chambers	1908-1982 WV	4th Marine Div, 25th Marines	19-22 Feb 1945	Iwo Jima
WW2	167 PFC Donald J.Ruhl	1923-1945*MT	5th Marine Div, 28th Marines	19-21 Feb 1945	Iwo Jima
WW2	168 SGT Daril S.Cole	1920-1945*MO	4th Marine Div, 23rd Marines	19 Feb 1945	Iwo Jima
WW2	169 CPT Robert H.Dunlap	1920- IL	5th Marine Div, 26th Marines	20-21 Feb 1945	Iwo Jima
WW2	170 PFC Jacklyn H.Lucas	1928- NC	5th Marine Div, 26th Marines	20 Feb 1945	Iwo Jima
WW2	171 CPT Joseph J.McCarthy	1911- IL	4th Marine Div, 24th Marines	12 Feb 1945	Iwo Jima
WW2	172 CPL Hershel W.Williams	1923- WV	3rd Marine Div, 21st Marines	23 Feb 1945	Iwo Jima

War	# Rank & Name	Born-Died Birthplace	Unit	Action Date	Action or Location
WW2	173 PFC Douglas T.Jacobson	1925- NY	4th Marine Div, 24th Marines	26 Feb 1945	Iwo Jima
WW2	174 PVT Wilson D.Watson	1922-1994 AL	3rd Marine Div, 9th Marines	26-27 Feb 1945	Iwo Jima
WW2	175 GySGT William G.Walsh	1922-1945*MA	5th Marine Div 27th Marines	27 Feb 1945	Iwo Jima
WW2	176 SGT Ross F.Gray	1920-1945*AL	4th Marine Div 25th Marines	27 Feb 1945	Iwo Jima
WW2	177 CPL Charles J.Berry	1923-1945*OK	5th Marine Div 26th Marines	3 Mar 1945	Iwo Jima
WW2	178 PFC William R.Caddy	1922-1945*MA	5th Marine Div 26th Marines	3 Mar 1945	Iwo Jima
WW2	179 SGT William G.Harrell	1922-1964 TX	5th Marine Div 28th Marines	3 Mar 1945	Iwo Jima
WW2	180 2LT John H.Leims	1921-1985 IL	3rd Marine Div 9th Marines	7 Mar 1945	Iwo Jima
WW2	181 1LT Jack Lummus	1915-1945*TX	5th Marine Div 27th Marines	8 Mar 1945	Iwo Jima
WW2	182 PFC James D.La Belle	1925-1945*MN	5th Marine Div 27th Marines	8 Mar 1945	Iwo Jima
WW2	183 SGT Joseph R.Julian	1918-1945*MA	5th Marine Div 27th Marines	9 Mar 1945	Iwo Jima
WW2	184 PVT Franklin E.Sigler	1924-1995 NJ	5th Marine Div 26th Marines	14 Mar 1945	Iwo Jima
WW2	185 PVT George Phillips	1926-1945 MO	5th Marine Div 28th Marines	14 Mar 1945	Iwo Jima
WW2	186 1LT Harry L.Martin	1911-1945*OH	5th Marine Div 5th Pion Bn	26 Mar 1945	Iwo Jima
WW2	187 PFC Harold Gonsalves	1926-1945*CA	6th Marine Div 15th Marines	4 Apr 1945	Okinawa
WW2	188 CPL Richard E.Bush	1923- KY	6th Marine Div 4th Marines	16 Apr 1945	Okinawa
WW2	189 SGT Elbert L.Kinser	1922-1945*TN	1st Marine Div 1st Marines	4 May 1945	Okinawa
WW2	190 PFC Wiliam A.Foster	1915-1945*OH	1st Marine Div 1st Marines	5 May 1945	Okinawa
WW2	191 CPL John P.Fardy	1922-1945*IL	1st Marine Div 1st Marines	7 May 1945	Okinawa
WW2	192 PFC Albert E.Schwab	1920-1945*DC	1st Marine Div 5th Marines	7 May 1945	Okinawa
WW2	193 PVT Dale M.Hansen	1922-1945*NB	1st Marine Div 1st Marines	7 May 1945	Okinawa
WW2	194 CPL Louis J.Hauge,Jr	1924-1945*MN	1st Marine Div 1st Marines	14 May 1945	Okinawa
WW2	195 MAJ Henry A.Courtney,Jr.	1916-1945*MN	6th Marine Div, 22nd Marines	14-15 May 1945	Okinawa
WW2	196 PVT Robert M.McTureous,Jr.	1924-1945*FL	6th Marine Dn, 29th Marines	11 Jun 1945	Okinawa
Kor	197 1LT Baldomero Lopez	1925-1950*FL	1st Marine Div 5th Marines	15 Sep 1950	Inchon
Kor	198 PFC Walter C.Monegan,Jr.	1930-1950*MA	1st Marine Div 1st Marines	17-20 Sep 1950	Sosa-ri
Kor	199 2LT Henry A.Commisky,Sr.	1927-1971 MS	1st Marine Div 1st Marines	20 Sep 1950	Yongdungp'o
Kor	200 PFC Eugene A.Obregon	1930-1950*CA	1st Marine Div 5th Marines	26 Sep 1950	Seoul
Kor	201 PFC Stanley R.Christianson	1925-1950*WI	1st Marine Div 1st Marines	29 Sep 1950	Seoul
Kor	202 SSG Archie Van Winkle	1925-1986 AK	1st Marine Div 7th Marines	2 Nov 1950	Sudong

War	# Rank & Name	Born-Died Birthplace	Unit	Action Date	Action or Location
Kor	203 CPL Lee H.Phillips MIA from 27 Nov 1950, presumed killed	1930-1950 CA	1st Marine Div 7th Marines	4 Nov 1950	Sudong
Kor	204 SGT James I.Poynter	1916-1950*IL	1st Marine Div 7th Marines	4 Nov 1950	Sudong
Kor	205 2LT Robert D.Reem	1925-1950*PA	1st Marine Div 7th Marines	6 Nov 1950	Shinhng-ni
Kor	206 1LT Frank N.Mitchell	1921-1950*TX	1st Marine Div 7th Marines	26 Nov 1950	Hanson-ni
Kor	207 SSG Robert S.Kennemore	1920-1989 SC	1st Marine Div 7th Marines	27-28 Nov 1950	Yudam-ni
Kor	208 PVT Hector A.Cafferata,Jr.	1929- NY	1st Marine Div 7th Marines	28 Nov 1950	Toktong Pass
Kor	209 CPT Carl L.Sitter	1922- MO	1st Marine Div 1st Marines	29 Nov 1950	Hagaru-ri
Kor	210 MAJ Reginald R.Myers	1919- ID	1st Marine Div 1st Marines	29 Nov 1950	Hagaru-ri
Kor	211 PFC William B.Baugh	1930-1950*KY	1st Marine Div 1st Marines	29 Nov 1950	Koto-ri/Hagaru-ri Road
Kor	212 LTC Raymond G.Davis	1915- GA	1st Marine Div 7th Marines	1-4 Dec 1950	Hararu-ri
Kor	213 CPT William E.Barber	1919- KY	1st Marine Div 7th Marines	2 Dec 1950	Chosin Reservoir
Kor	214 SSG William G.Windrich	1921-1950*IL	1st Marine Div 5th Marines	2 Dec 1950	Yudam-ni
Kor	215 SGT James E.Johnson P/W,died 2 November 1953	1926-1953*ID	1st Marine Div 7th Marines	2 Dec 1950	Yundam-ni
Kor	216 PFC Herbert A.Littleton	1930-1951*AR	1st Marine Div 7th Marines	22 Apr 1951	Chungchon
Kor	217 TSG Harold E.Wilson	1921- AL	1st Marine Div 7th Marines	23-24 Apr 1951	??
Kor	218 PFC Whitt L.Moreland	1930-1951*TX	1st Marine Div 5th Marines	29 May 1951	Kwangch'i-dong
Kor	219 CPL Charles G.Abrell	1931-1951*IN	1st Marine Div 1st Marines	10 Jun 1951	Hangnyong
Kor	220 2LT George H.Ramer	1927-1951*PA	1st Marine Div 7th Marines	12 Sep 1951	??
Kor	221 SGT Frederick W.Mausert III	1931-1951*NY	1st Marine Div 7th Marines	12 Sep 1951	Songnap-yong
Kor	222 PFC Edward Gomez	1932-1951*NB	1st Marine Div 1st Marines	14 Sep 1951	Hill 749
Kor	223 CPL Joseph Vittori	1929-1951*MA	1st Marine Div 1st Marines	16 Oct 1951	Hill 749
Kor	224 CPL Jack A.Davenport	1931-1951*MO	1st Marine Div 5th Marines	21 Oct 1951	Songnae-dong
Kor	225 CPL Duane E.Dewey	1931- MI	1st Marine Div 5th Marines	16 May 1952	Panmunjom
Kor	226 CPL David B.Champagne	1932-1952*ME	1st Marine Div 7th Marines	20 May 1952	??
Kor	227 PFC John D.Kelly	1928-1952*OH	1st Marine Div 7th Marines	28 May 1952	??
Kor	228 SSG Wiliam E.Shuck,Jr.	1926-1952*MD	1st Marine Div 7th Marines	3 Jul 1952	??
Kor	229 PFC Robert E.Simanek	1930- MI	1st Marine Div 5th Marines	17 Aug 1952	Outpost Irene
Kor	230 PFC Alford L.McLaughlin	1928-1977 AL	1st Marine Div 5th Marines	4-5 Sep 1952	Outpost Bruce
Kor	231 PFC Fernando L.Garcia	1929-1952*PR	1st Marine Div 5th Marines	5 Sep 1952	??
Kor	232 PFC Jack W.Kelso	1934-1952*CA	1st Marine Div 7th Marines	2 Oct 1952	??

War	# Rank & Name	Born-Died Birthplace	Unit	Action Date	Action or Location
Kor	233 SSG Lewis G.Watkins	1925-1952* SC	1st Marine Div 7th Marines	7 Oct 1952	??
Kor	234 2LT Sherrod E.Skinner,Jr.	1929-1952* CT	1st Marine Div 11th Marines	26 Oct 1952	??
Kor	235 2LT George H.O'Brien,Jr	1926- TX	1st Marine Div 7th Marines	27 Oct 1952	The Hook
Kor	236 2LT Raymond G.Murphy	1930- CO	1st Marine Div 5th Marines	3 Feb 1953	Ungok Hill
Kor	237 SGT Daniel P.Matthews	1931-1953*CA	1st Marine Div 7th Marines	20 Mar 1953	Vegas Hill
Kor	238 SSG Ambrosio Guillen	1929-1953*CO	1st Marine Div 7th Marines	26 Jul 1953	Songuch-on
Vtn	239 CPT Donald G.Cook Cited for actions while a P/W	1934-1967*NY	Naval Advisor Group, MAC	31 Dec 1964- 8 Dec 1967	Phout Tuy (Binh Gia)
Vtn	240 1LT Frank S.Reasoner	1937-1965*WA	3rd Marine Div 3rd Recon Bn	12 Aug 1965	Quang Nam (Da Nang)
Vtn	241 CPL Robert Emmett O'Malley	1943- NY	3rd Marine Div 3rd Marines	18 Aug 1965	An Cu'ong 2
Vtn	242 LCPL Joe C.Paul	1946-1965*KY	3rd Marine Div 4th Marines	19 Aug 1965	Chu Lai
Vtn	243 1LT Harvey C.Barnum,Jr.	1940- CT	3rd Marine Div 9th Marines	18 Dec 1965	Quang Tin (Ky Phu No)
Vtn	244 SSG Peter S.Connor	1932-1966*NJ	1st Marine Div 3rd Marines	8 Mar 1966	Quang Nai
Vtn	245 SSG Jimmie E.Howard	1929- IO	1st Marine Div 1st Recon Bn	16 Jun 1966	Hill 488,Chu Lai
Vtn	246 CPT Howard V.Lee	1933- NY	3rd Marine Div 4th Marines	8-9 Aug 1966	Cam Lo
Vtn	247 CPT Robert J.Modrzejewski 1934-WI		3rd Marine Div 4th Marines	15-18 Jul 1966	Quang Tri
Vtn	248 SGT John J.McGinty III	1940- MA	3rd Marine Div 4th Marines	18 Jul 1966	Quang Tri
Vtn	249 LCPL Richard A.Pittman	1945- CA	1st Marine Div 5th Marines	24 Aug 1966	DMZ
Vtn	250 PFC James Anderson.Jr.	1947-1967* CA	3rd Marine Div 3rd Marines	28 Feb 1967	Quang Tri (Cam Lo)
Vtn	251 SGT Walter K.Singleton	1944-1967* TN	3rd Marine Div 9th Marines	24 Mar 1967	Quang Tri (Gio Linh)
Vtn	252 PFC Douglas E.Dickey	1946-1967* OH	3rd Marine Div 4th Marines	26 Mar 1967	Quang Tri (Gio An)
Vtn	253 2LT John Paul Bobo	1943-1967* NY	3rd Marine Div 9th Marines	30 Mar 1967	Quang Tri
Vtn	254 PFC Gary W.Martini	1948-1967* VA	1st Marine Div 1st Marines	21 Apr 1967	Binh Son
Vtn	255 CPT James A.Graham	1940-1967* PA	1st Marine Div 5th Marines	2 Jun 1967	Quang Tri
Vtn	256 PFC Melvin E.Newlin	1948-1967* OH	1st Marine Div 5th Marines	3-4 Jul 1967	Quang Nam
Vtn	257 LCPL Roy M.Wheat	1947-1967* MS	1st Marine Div 7th Marines	11 Aug 1967	Quang Nam (Dien Ban)
Vtn	258 CPT Stephen W.Pless	1939- GA	1st MAW,MAG 36, VMO 6	19 Aug 1967	Quang Nai
Vtn	259 SGT Lawrence D.Peters	1946-1967* NY	1st Marine Div 5th Marines	4 Sep 1967	Quang Tri
Vtn	260 SGT Rodney M.Davis	1942-1967* GA	1st Marine Div 5th Marines	6 Sep 1967	Quang Nam
Vtn	261 LCPL Jedh C.Barker	1945-1967* NH	3rd Marine Div 4th Marines	21 Sep 1967	Quang Tri (Con Thein)
Vtn	262 CPL William T.Perkins,Jr.	1947-1967* NY	1st Marine Div 1st Marines	12 Oct 1967	Quang Tri

THE MEDAL OF HONOR AND OTHER DECORATIONS

War	# Rank & Name	Born-Died Birthplace	Unit	Action Date	Action or Location
Vtn	263 SGT Paul H.Foster	1939-1967* CA	3rd Marine Div 4th Marines	14 Oct 1967	Quang Tri (Con Thien)
Vtn	264 CPL Larry E.Smedley	1949-1967* VA	1st Marine Div 7th Marines	20-21 Dec 1967	Quang Nam (Phouc Ninh)
Vtn	265 CPL Larry L.Maxam	1948-1968* CA	3rd Marine Div 4th Marines	2 Feb 1968	Quang Tri (Cam Lo)
Vtn	266 SGT Alfredo Gonzalez	1946-1968* TX	1st Marine Div 1st Marines	4 Feb 1968	Thua Thien
Vtn	267 2LT Terrance C.Graves	1945-1968* TX	3rd Marine Div 3rd Recon Bn	17 Feb 1968	Quang Tri
Vtn	268 CPT Jay R.Vargas	1937- AZ	3rd Marine Div 4th Marines	30 Apr 1968	Quang Tri (Dai Do)
Vtn	269 CPT James E.Livingston Rose to MG	1940- GA	3rd Marine Div 4th Marines	2 May 1968	Quang Tri (Dai Do)
Vtn	270 PFC Robert C.Burke	1949-1968* IL	1st Marine Div 27th Marines	17 May 1968	Quang Nam (Go Nai Island
Vtn	271 LCPL Kenneth L.Worley	1948-1968* NM	1st Marine Div 7th Marines	8 Aug 1968	Quang Nam (Bo Ban)
Vtn	272 PFC DeWayne T.Williams	1949-1968* MI	1st Marine Div 1st Marines	18 Sep 1968	Quang Nam
Vtn	273 SSG Karl G.Taylor,Sr.	1939-1968* MD	3rd Marine Div 26th Marines	8 Dec 1968	??
Vtn	274 LCPL Thomas P.Noonan,Jr.	1943-1969* NY	3rd Marine Div 9th Marines	5 Feb 1969	Quang Tri (Firebase Vandegrift)
Vtn	275 LCPL William R.Prom	1948-1969* PA	3rd Marine Div 3rd Marnies	9 Feb 1969	Quang Nam (An Hoa)
Vtn	276 LCPL Thomas E.Creek	1950-1969* MO	3rd Marine Div 9th Marines	13 Feb 1969	Quang Tri (Cam Lo)
Vtn	277 1LT Wesley L.Fox	1931- VA	3rd Marine Div 9th Marines	22 Feb 1969	Quang Tri (A Shau Valley)
Vtn	278 LCPL Lester W.Weber	1948-1969* IL	1st Marine Div 7th Marines	23 Feb 1969	Quang Nam (Bo Ban)
Vtn	279 PFC Oscar P.Austin	1948-1969* TX	1st Marine Div 7th Marines	23 Feb 1969	Quang Nam (Da Nang)
Vtn	280 CPL William D.Morgan	1947-1969* PA	3rd Marine Div 9th Marines	25 Feb 1969	Quang Tri (Firebase Vandegrift)
Vtn	281 PFC Daniel D.Bruce	1950-1969* IN	1st Marine Div 5th Marines	1 Mar 1969	Quang Nam (Firebase Tomahawk)
Vtn	282 PFC Alfred M.Wilson	1948-1969* IL	3rd Marine Div 9th Marines	3 Mar 1969	Quang Tri (Firebase Cunningham)
Vtn	283 PFC Robert H.Jenkins,Jr.	1948-1969* FL	3rd Marine Div 3rd Recon Bn	5 Mar 1969	DMZ (Firebase Argonne)
Vtn	284 PFC Ralph H.Johnson	1949-1969* SC	1st Marine Div 1st Recon Bn	5 Mar 1969	Quan Duc Valley (Hill 146)
Vtn	285 PFC Ronald L.Coker	1947-1969* NB	3rd Marine Div 3rd Marines	24 Mar 1969	Quang Tri
Vtn	286 PFC Jimmy W.Phipps	1950-1969* CA	1st Marine Div 1st Eng Bn	27 May 1969	Quang Nam (An Hoa)
Vtn	287 PFC Bruce Wayne Carter	1950-1969* NY	3rd Marine Div 3rd Marines	7 Aug 1969	Quang Tri
Vtn	288 LCPL Richard A.Anderson	1948-1969* DC	3rd Marine Div 3rd Recon Bn	24 Aug 1969	Quang Tri
Vtn	289 LCPL Jose F.Jimenez	1946-1969* Mexico	1st Marine Div 7th Marines	28 Aug 1969	Quang Nam (Da Nang)
Vtn	290 PFC Ralph E.Dias	1950-1969* PA	1st Marine Div 7th Marines	12 Nov 1969	Khe Son
Vtn	291 PFC Raymond M.Clausen,Jr.	1947- LA	MAG 16,HHM 263	31 Jan 1970	??
Vtn	292 SSG Allan Jay Kellogg,Jr.	1943- CT	1st Marine Div 5th Marines	11 Mar 1970	Quang Nam
Vtn	293 LCPL Emilio A.De la Garza,Jr.	1949-1970* IN	1st Marine Div 1st Marines	11 Apr 1970	Quang Nam (Da Nang)

War	# Rank & Name	Born-Died Birthplace	Unit	Action Date	Action or Location
Vtn	294 LCPL James D.Howe	1948-1970* SC	1st Marine Div 7th Marines	6 May 1970	??
Vtn	295 LCPL Miguel Keith	1951-1970 TX	III 'Phib,CAPltn 1-2-3 8	May 1970	Quang Ngai

Key: *War* indicated by abbreviation: CW, the Civil War; KKF, Korean, Kangwah Forts, 1871; SAW, Spanish-American War; Sam, Samoan Campaign of 1899; PI, Philippine Insurrection; Box, the Boxer Rebellion (China Relief Expedition); VC, Vera Cruz Expedition; Hai, Haitian Campaigns; DR, Domincian Republic Campaign; WW1, World War I; Nic, Nicaraguan Campaign: WW2, World War II; Kor, Korean War; Vtn, Vietnam; - indicates a non-combat award. # indicates the order of awardees, from the first to the most recent. *Rank* is that at the time of the deed. *Name* is that borne at the time, with any different names used at other times in parentheses. *Born-Died* indicates the years of birth and death, where known, with a * indicating one of the 120 Marines who were killed or mortally wounded in the course of earning the Medal of Honor: Awardees killed in combat subsequent to the events for which they were decorated are indicated in notes. *Birthplace* shows state or country. *Unit* is that to which the man was assigned or attached at the time of the deed, which, surprisingly, is not always clear. *Action Date* gives the date or dates for which the man was cited. *Action* gives the location or name of battle in which the man earned his Medal of Honor.

The phrase "Double Award" indicates Marines given both the Army and Navy Medal of Honor for the same deed during World War I. Marines awarded a second Medal of Honor for a separate deed (Smedley D. Butler and Daniel Daly) are listed separately.

Note that though the awardees are listed by the date of their earning the Medal of Honor, the order in which they were awarded it may vary considerably. Some men did not receive their decorations for years—even decades—after they were cited. In addition, not until the Navy Act of 1916 were officers eligible for the Medal of Honor. As a result, officer awardees with dates prior to 1916 often received the Medal of Honor long after the deeds for which they were decorated. For example, David Dixon Porter (grandson of the nation's second admiral, and nephew of the first) received his Medal of Honor in 1934, over 32 years after his heroism on 17 November 1901, and then only through the intervention of President Franklin D. Roosevelt.

Alphabetical Index of Marine Medal of Honor Winners

Check on the following pages if you know the name of a Marine who earned the Medal of Honor, but do not know the occasion of its award. When you have determined the "Award Number," check the chronological listing. This list includes alternative names for some of the awardees.

Name	Award	War	Name	Award	War
Abrell, Charles G.	219	Kor	Basilone, John	127	WW2
Adams, John M.	66	Box	Bauer, Harold W.	118	WW2
Adriance, Harry C.	64	Box	Baugh, William B.	211	Kor
Anderson, James, Jr.	250	Vtn	Bausell, Lewis K.	158	WW2
Anderson, Richard A.	288	Vtn	Bearss, Hiram I.	83	PI
Anderson, Richard B.	144	WW2	Berkely, Randolph C.	91	VC
Angerholm, Harold C.	149	WW2	Berry, Charles J.	177	WW2
Appleton, Edwin N.	51	Box	Bigle, Richard		
Austin, Oscar P.	279	Vtn	(Binder, Richard)		
Bailey, Kenneth D.	123	WW2	Binder, Richard	12	CW
Barber, William E.	213	Kor	Bobo, John Paul	253	Vtn
Barker, Jedh C.	261	Vtn	Bonnyman, Alexander	139	WW2
Barnum, Harvey C., Jr.	243	Vtn	Bordeleon, William J.	141	WW2
			Boydston, Erwin J.	70	Box

Name	Award	War	Name	Award	War
Boyington, Gregory	133	WW2	Dunlap, Robert H.	169	WW2
Brown, Charles	18	KKF	Dyer, Jesse, F.	85	VC
Bruce, Daniel D.	281	Vtn	Dyess, Aquilla J.	143	WW2
Buckley, Howard M.	42	PI	Edson, Merrit A.	124	WW2
Burke, Robert C.	270	Vtn	Elrod, Henry T.	117	WW2
Burnes, James	52	Box	Epperson, Harold G.	148	WW2
Bush, Richard E.	188	WW2	Fardy, John P.	191	WW2
Butler, Smedley D.	92	VC	Field, Oscar	27	SAW
Butler, Smedley D.	97	Hai	Fisher, Harry	58	Box
Button, William R.	112	Hai	Fitzgerald, John	38	SAW
Caddy, William R.	178	WW2	Fleming, Richard E.	119	WW2
Caferata, Hector A.	208	Kor	Foley, Alexander J.	60	Box
Campbell, Albert R.	53	Box	Ford, Patrick, Jr.		
Campbell, Daniel J.	33	SAW	(Meredith, James)		
Cannon, George H.	116	WW2	Forster, Bruno A.	45	Sam
Carr, William L.	71	Box	Foss, Joseph J.	126	WW2
Carter, Bruce Wayne	287	Vtn	Foster, Paul H.	263	Vtn
Casamento, Anthony	129	WW2	Foster, William A.	190	WW2
Catlin, Albertus W.	93	VC	Fox, Wesley L.	277	Vtn
Chamebrs, Justice M.	166	WW2	Francis, Charles R.	61	Box
Champagne, David B.	226	Kor	Franklin, Joseph J.	28	SAW
Christianson, Stanley R.	201	Kor	Fry, Isaac N.	14	CW
Clausen, Raymond M., Jr.	291	Vtn	Fryer, Eli T.	86	VC
Coker, Ronald L.	285	Vtn	Gaienne, Louis R.	73	Box
Cole, Daril S.	168	WW2	Galer, Robert E.	125	WW2
Coleman, John	20	KKF	Garcia, Fernando L.	231	Kor
Commisky, Henry A., Sr.	199	Kor	Gaughan, Philip	37	SAW
Connelly, Roderick P.			Glowin, Joseph A.	101	DR
(Thompson, Henry A)			Gomes, Edward	222	Kor
Connor, Peter S.	244	Vtn	Gonsalves, Harold	187	WW2
Cook, Donald G.	239	Vtn	Gonzalez, Alfredo	266	Vtn
Cooney, James	72	Box	Graham, James A.	255	Vtn
Courtney, Henry A., Jr.	195	WW2	Graves, Terrance C.	267	Vtn
Creek, Thomas E.	276	Vtn	Gray, Ross F.	176	WW2
Cukela, Louis	105	WW1	Gross, Samuel	98	Hai
Dahlgren, John O.	56	Box	Guillen, Ambrosio	238	Kor
Daly, Daniel J.	80	Box	Gurke, Henry	137	WW2
Daly, Daniel J.	96	Hai	Hanneken, Herman H.	111	Hai
D'Amato, Anthony P.	146	WW2	Hansen, Dale M.	193	WW2
Davenport, Jack A.	224	Kor	Hanson, Robert M.	134	WW2
Davis, Henry W.	68	Box	Harrell, William G.	179	WW2
Davis, Raymond G.	212	Kor	Harvey, Harry	47	PI
Davis, Rodney M.	260	Vtn	Hauge, Louis J.	194	WW2
De la Garza, Emilio A., Jr.	293	Vtn	Hawkins, William D.	138	WW2
DeBlanc, Jefferson J.	130	WW2	Heisch, Henry W.	54	Box
Denig, Henry	8	CW	Helms, John H.	81	-
Dewy, Duane E.	225	Kor	Hill, Frank	34	SAW
Dias, Ralph E.	290	Vtn	Hill, Walter N.	87	VC
Dickey, Douglas E.	252	Vtn	Hoffman, Charles	103	WW1
Dougherty, James	21	KKF	Horton, William M.C.	74	Box

THE MEDAL OF HONOR AND OTHER DECORATIONS

Name	Award	War	Name	Award	War
Howard, Jimmie E.	245	Vtn	McCarthy, Joseph J.	171	WW2
Howe, James D.	294	Vtn	McGinty, John J.	248	Vtn
Hudson, Michael	9	CW	McLaughlin, Alford L.	230	Kor
Hughes, John A.	88	VC	McNally, Michael J.	46	Sam
Hulbert, Henry L.	44	Sam	McNamara, Michael	22	KKF
Hunt, Martin	55	Box	McTureous, Robert M., Jr.	196	WW2
Iams, Ross L.	99	Hai	Meredith, James	26	SAW
Jackson, Arthur, Jr.	160	WW2	Miller, Andrew	11	CW
Jacobson, Douglas T.	173	WW2	Mitchell, Frank N.	206	Kor
Jameson, Ernest August (Hoffman, Charles)			Modrzejewski, Robert J.	247	Vtn
			Monegan, Walter C., Jr.	198	Kor
Jenkins, Robert H., Jr.	283	Vtn	Moore, Albert	75	Box
Jimenes, Jose F.	289	Vtn	Moreland, Whitt L.	218	Kor
Johnson, James E.	215	Kor	Morgan, William D.	280	Vtn
Johnson, Ralph H.	284	Vtn	Morris, John	25	-
Julian, Joseph R.	183	WW2	Murphy, John A.	69	Box
Kates, Thomas W.	62	Box	Murphy, Raymond G.	236	Kor
Kearny, Michael	29	SAW	Murray, William Henry (Davis, Henry W.)		
Keith, Miguel	295	Vtn			
Kellogg, Allan Jay, Jr.	292	Vtn	Myers, Reginald R.	210	Kor
Kelly, John D.	227	Kor	Neville, Wendell C.	89	VC
Kelly, John J.	106	WW1	New, John D.	162	WW2
Kelso, Jack W.	232	Kor	Newlin, Melvin E.	256	Vtn
Kennemore, Robert S.	207	Kor	Noonan, Thomas P., Jr.	274	Vtn
Kisner, Albert L.	189	WW2	Nugent, Christopher	3	CW
Kocak, Matej	108	WW1	Obregon, Eugene A.	200	Kor
Kraus, Richard E.	164	WW2	O'Brien, George H.	235	Kor
Kuchneister, Hermann W.	30	SAW	O'Malley, Robert Emmett	241	Vtn
La Belle, James D.	182	WW2	Orndoff, Harry W.	50	Box
Lee, Howard V.	246	Vtn	Osterman, Edward A.	94	Hai
Leims, John H.	180	WW2	Oviatt, Miles M.	4	CW
Leonard, Joseph H.	43	PI	Owens, Michael	23	KKF
Littleton, Herbert A.	216	Kor	Ownes, Robert A.	135	WW2
Livingston, James E.	269	Vtn	Ozbourn, Joseph W.	156	WW2
Lopez, Baldomero	197	Kor	Paige, Mitchell	128	WW2
Lucas, Jacklyn H.	170	WW2	Parker, Pomeroy	35	SAW
Lummus, Jack	181	WW2	Paul, Joe C.	242	Vtn
MacHeal, Harry L.	40	SAW	Perkins, William T., Jr.	262	Vtn
Mackie, John F.	1	CW	Peters, Lawrence D.	259	Vtn
Marguilies, Samuel (Gross, Samuel)			Pfeifer, Louis F.	82	-
			Phelps, Wesley	163	WW2
Martin, Harry L.	186	WW2	Phillips, George	185	WW2
Martin, James	10	CW	Phillips, Lee H.	203	Kor
Martini, Gary W.	254	Vtn	Phillips, Reuben J.	48	Box
Mason, Leonard F.	152	WW2	Phipps, Jimmy W.	286	Vtn
Mathias, Clarence E.	65	Box	Pittman, Richard A.	249	Vtn
Matthews, Daniel P.	237	Kor	Pless, Stephen W.	258	Vtn
Mausert, Frederick W.	221	Kor	Pope, Everett P	159	WW2
Maxam, Larry L.	265	Vtn	Porter, David Dixon	84	PI
McCard, Robert H.	147	WW2	Power, John V.	142	WW2
			Poynter, James I.	204	Kor

THE MEDAL OF HONOR AND OTHER DECORATIONS

Name	Award	War	Name	Award	War
Prendergast, Thomas F.	41	PI	Sutton, Clarence E.	67	Box
Preston, Herbert I.	76	Box	Swett, James E.	131	WW2
Prom, William R.	275	Vtn	Talbot, Ralph	109	WW1
Pruitt, John H.	107	WW1	Taylor, Karl G., Jr.	273	Vtn
Purvis, Hugh	19	KKF	Thomas Herbert J.	136	WW2
Quick, John Henry	39	SAW	Thomason, Clyde A.	122	WW2
Ramer, George H.	220	Kor	Thompson, Henry A.	16	CW
Rannahan, John	13	CW	Timmerman, Grant F.	150	WW2
Reasoner, Frank S.	240	Vtn	Tomlin, Andrew J.	15	CW
Reem, Robert D.	205	Kor	Truesdale, Donald L.		
Reid, George G.	90	VC	(Truesdell, Donald L.)		
Roan, Charles H.	161	WW2	Truesdell, Donald L	115	Nic
Roantree, James S.	7	CW	Upham, Oscar J.	78	Box
Robinson, Robert G.	110	WW1	Upshur, William P.	95	Hai
Rouh, Carlton R.	157	WW2	Van Winkle, Archie	202	Kor
Ruhl, Donald J.	167	WW2	Vandegrift, Alexander A.	121	WW2
Scannel, David J.	77	Box	Vargas, Jay R.	268	Vtn
Schilt, Christian F.	114	Nic	Vaughn, Pinkerton R.	2	CW
Schuck, William E.	228	Kor	Vittori, Joseph	223	Kor
Schwab, Albert E.	192	WW2	Walker, Edward A.	59	Box
Scott, James F.	31	SAW	Walsh, Kenneth A.	132	WW2
Shivers, John	17	CW	Walsh, William G	175	WW2
Shoup, David M.	140	WW2	Watkins, Lewis G.	233	Kor
Sigler, Franklin E.	184	WW2	Watson, Wilson D.	174	WW2
Silva, France	63	Box	Weber, Lester W.	278	Vtn
Simanek, Robert E.	229	Kor	West, Walter Scott	36	SAW
Singleton, Walter K.	251	Vtn	Wheat, Roy M.	257	Vtn
Sitter, Carl L.	209	Kor	Williams, DeWayne T.	272	Vtn
Skaggs, Luther, Jr.	151	WW2	Williams, Ernest C.	102	DR
Skinner, Sherrod E.	234	Kor	Williams, Hershel W.	172	WW2
Smedley, Larry E.	264	Vtn	Wilson, Alfred M.	282	Vtn
Smith, Albert J.	113	-	Wilson, Harold E.	217	Kor
Smith, John L.	120	WW2	Wilson, Louis H., Jr.	155	WW2
Smith, Willard M.	5	CW	Wilson, Robert Lee	154	WW2
Sorenson, Richard K.	145	WW2	Winans, Roswell	100	DR
Sprowle, David	6	CW	Windrich, William G.	214	Kor
Stein, Tony	165	WW2	Witek, Frank P.	153	WW2
Stewart, James A.	24	-	Worley, Kenneth L	.271	Vtn
Stewart, Peter	49	Box	Young, Frank A.	5	Box
Stockham, Fred W.	104	WW1	Zion, William F.	79	Box
Sullivan, Edward	32	SAW			

Six Occasions on Which Six or More Marines Have Earned the Medal of Honor in the Same Action

Date	Action	Awards
1. 11 May 1898	Cable Cutting Raid, Cienfuegos, Cuba	12 (#26-37)
2. 21 July 1900	Defense of the Peking Legislation	12 (#68-79) *
3. 5 August 1864	Battle of Mobile Bay	8 (#4-11)
4. 21 April 1914	Capture of Vera Cruz	8 (#85-93)
5. 15 January 1865	Storming of Fort Fisher	6 (#12-17)
6. 11 June 1871	Storming of the Kanghwa Forts, Korea	6 (#18-23)

* One man was specifically cited for heroism on 21 July, eleven others for the period from 21 July through 17 August 1900. In addition, a thirteenth award went to PVT Dan Daly for heroism on 14 August 1900 (#80).

Distribution of Marine Corps Medal of Honor Winners by Rank

Rank	Number	Note
Major General	1	
Colonel	2	
Lieutenant Colonel	6	
Major	11	A
Captain	23	
First Lieutenant	18	
Second Lieutenant	11	
Gunnery/Orderly/Staff/Tech Sergeant	22	B
Sergeant	18	
Corporal	36	
Lance Corporal	14	
Private First Class	44	
Private	62	C

The table counts one award for those Marines given both the Army and Navy Medal of Honor during World War I.

Notes:

A. Includes Smedley Butler twice.

B. Includes Dan Daly's award while a gunnery sergeant

C. Includes Dan Daly's award while a private

Two Dozen Marine Generals Who Held the Medal of Honor

	#	Name and Final Rank	Campaign
1.	83	BG Hiram I. Bearss	Samar
2.	84	MG David Dixon Porter	Samar
3.	85	BG Jessee F. Dyer	Vera Cruz
4.	86	BG Eli T. Fryer	Vera Cruz
5.	87	BG Walter N. Hill	Vera Cruz
6.	88	BG John A. Hughes	Vera Cruz
7.	89	MG Wendell C. Neville	Vera Cruz
8.	90	BG George G. Reid	Vera Cruz
9.	91	BG Randolph C. Berkely	Vera Cruz
10.	92/97	MG Smedley D. Butler	Vera Cruz & Haiti
11.	93	MG Albertus W. Catlin	Vera Cruz
12.	94	MG Edward A. Osterman	Haiti
13.	95	MG William P. Upshur	Haiti
14.	100	BG Roswell Winans	Dominican
15.	111	BG Herman H. Hanneken	Haiti
16.	114	BG Christian F. Schilt	Nicaragua
17.	121	GEN Alexander A. Vandegrift	Guadalcanal
18.	124	MG Merritt A. Edson	Guadalcanal
19.	125	BG Robert E. Galer	Guadalcanal
20.	126	BG Joseph J. Foss	Solomons
21.	140	GEN David M. Shoup	Tarawa
22.	155	GEN Louis H. Wilson, Jr.	Guam
23.	212	GEN Raymond G. Davis	Korea
24.	269	MG James E. Livingston	Vietnam

This list may not be complete, since the records of some Medal of Honor winners were not available for examination when it was compiled. Joseph I. Foss held his brigadier generalcy in the National Guard; all other officers indicated held theirs in the Marine Corps. # is the man's number in the master list of Marine Medal of Honor winners.

Living Marine Corps Medal of Honor Winners *

1. William E. Barber, #213
2. Harvey C. Barnum, Jr, #243
3. Richard E. Bush, #188
4. Hector A. Cafferata, Jr., #208
5. Raymond M. Clausen, Jr., #291
6. Raymond G. Davis, #212, retired as a general, USMC
7. Duane E. Dewey, #225
8. Robert H. Dunlap, #169

9.   Joseph Foss, #126, retired as brigadier general, Army National Guard
10. Wesley Fox, #277,
11. Robert E.Galer, #125, retired as a brigadier general, USMC
12. Arthur J.Jackson, #160, retired as a captain, USAR
13. Douglas T.Jacobson, #173
14. Allan J.Kellogg, Jr., #292
15. Howard V.Lee, #246
16. James E.Livingston, #269, retired as a major general, USMC, 14 July 1995 **
17. Jack H.Lucas, #170
18. Joseph J.McCarthy, #171
19. John J.McGinty, III, #248
20. Robert J.Modrejewski, #247
21. Raymond D.Murphy, #236
22. Reginald R.Myers, #210
23. George H.O'Brien, Jr., #235
24. Robert E.O'Malley, #241
25. Mitchell Paige, #128
26. Richard Pittman, #249
27. Everett P.Pope, #159
28. Robert E.Simanek, #229
29. Carl L.Sitter, #209
30. Richard K.Sorenson, #145
31. James E.Swett, #131
32. Jay R.Vargas, #268
33. Kenneth A.Walsh, #132
34. Hershel W.Williams, #172
35. Louis H.Wilson, Jr., #155, CMC # 26
36. Harold E.Wilson, #217

* Based on information available at the time of the compilation of this table, in mid-1996.

** MG Livingston was the last active duty Marine who held the Medal of Honor when he retired on 14 July 1995.

One Marine Medal of Honor Winner Born on the 4th of July

SGT Harry Harvey, who won his in the Philippines in 1900 (# 47).

Two Irish Marine Medal of Honor Winners Born on St.Patrick's Day

1. SGT Philip Gaughan, who earned his at Cienfuegos, Cuba in 1898 (# 37).
2. PVT John Fitzgerald, who won his in the fighting around Guantanamo Bay, in 1898 (# 38).

The Five Youngest Marine Winners of the Medal of Honor

1. PFC Jacklyn H. Lucas was the youngest Marine ever to win the Medal of Honor; born on 14 Feb 1928, he won his medal on Iwo Jima on 20 February 1945, at 17 years and 6 days old (# 170).*
2. PFC Robert C. Burke, born 7 Nov 1949, was just 18 years, 6 months, and 10 days old when he gave his life on 17 May 1968 in Vietnam, earning a Medal of Honor in the process (# 270).
3. PFC Jimmy W. Phipps, born 1 Nov 1950, earned his Medal of Honor on 27 May 1969 in Vietnam, at the age of 18 years, 6 months, and 26 days, when he was killed in action(# 286).
4. PFC Jack W. Kelso, born 23 Jan 1934, was just 18 years, 8 months, and 10 days old when he gave his life winning the Medal of Honor in Korea on 2 Oct 1952 (# 232).
5. CPL Larry E. Smedley, born 4 Mar 1949, was just 18 years, 8 months, and 16 days old when he won the Medal of Honor on 20-21 Dec 1967, in Vietnam, giving his life as he did (# 264).

* PFC Lucas had enlisted while underage, his true age not being discovered until after his heroic deeds.

The Five Oldest Marines to Win the Medal of Honor

1. MG Alexander A. Vandegrift, the oldest Marine ever to win the Medal of Honor,was born on 13 Mar 1887,and was decorated for his services while commanding the 1st Marine Division on Guadalcanal, from 7 Aug through 9 Dec 1942, which began when he was 55 years, 4 months, and 24 days (# 121).
2. Ordnance Sergeant David Sprowle, born in 1811, was at least 53 years old when he won the Medal of Honor aboard the USS *Richmond* in Mobile Bay on 5 Aug 1864 (# 6).
3. MAJ Albertus W. Catlin, born 1 Dec 1868, was 45 years,4 months, and 20 days, when he earned a Medal of Honor at Vera Cruz,Mexico, on 21-22 Apr 1914 (# 93).
4. LTC Merritt A. Edson, born 25 April 1897, was 45 years,4 months, and 18 days when he won the Medal of Honor on Guadalcanal (# 124).
5. LTC Wendell C. Neville, born 12 May 1870, was 43 years,11 months, and 9-10 days when he won the Medal of Honor at Vera Cruz,Mexico, on 21-22 Apr 1914 (# 89).

Two Marines Who Won the Medal of Honor Twice

1.MG Smedley D. Butler (1881-1940)
>   First Award: 22 April 1914, at Vera Cruz, Mexico,as a major (#92)
>   Second Award: 17 November 1915 at Ft.Riviere, Haiti, as a major (#97)

2.GySGT Daniel J. Daly (1873-1937)
>   First Award: 14 August 1900, at Peking, China, as a private (#80)
>   Second Award: 24 October 1915 at Ft.Dipitie, Haiti, as a GySGT (#96)

Occasions on which Smedley D. Butler Was Nominated for the Medal of Honor

1. Tientsin, China, 13 July 1900. Disapproved, as until 1916 Naval regulations did not permit the award of the Medal of Honor to officers, and he was given a brevet promotion.*
2. Vera Cruz, Mexico, 22 April 1914. Approved.**
3. Ft. Riviere, Haiti, 17 November 1915. Approved.

* This was the same occasion on which the Medal of Honor was awarded to CPL Harry C. Adriance (#64), PVT Clarence E. Mathias (#65), SGT John M. Adams (#66), and SGT Clarence E. Sutton (#67), who assisted Butler and 1LT Carl Cambourg-Andersen (who also received a brevet promotion in lieu of a Medal of Honor) in carrying a wounded comrade 17 miles to safety, virtually the whole time pursued by Boxers, with whom they several times were forced to skirmish.

** Butler attempted to decline the first award of the Medal of Honor, on the grounds that he hadn't done anything sufficiently courageous, writing "I ...can not remember a single achievement ...of mine that in the slightest degree warranted such a decoration, " and "The undersigned [i.e., Butler] feels that no service rendered by him at Vera Cruz, deserves such recognition."

Occasions on Which Daniel Daly Was Nominated for the Medal of Honor

1. 14 August 1900, at Peking, China, while a private. Approved.
2. 24 October 1915 at Ft. Dipitie, Haiti, while a gunnery sergeant. Approved.
3. 5-7 and 10 June 1918 for Belleau Wood. Disapproved. In lieu of a third Medal of Honor, Daly was given the Navy Cross and the Distinguished Service Cross, as well as the French *Medaille Militaire*, and an offer of a commission, which he declined.

Five Marines Who Each Received Two Medals of Honor for the Same Deed

1. GySGT Charles Hoffman, 5th Marines, on 6 June 1918 at Belleau Wood (#103).
2. SGT Louis Cukela, 5th Marines, on 18 July 1918 at Villers-Cotterets, France (#105).
3. PVT John J. Kelly, 6th Marines, on 3 October 1916, at Mont Blanc Ridge, France (#106).
4. CPL John H. Pruitt, 6th Marines, on 4 October 1918, at Mont Blanc Ridge, France, where he was killed in action (#107).
5. SGT Matej Kocak, 5th Marines, on 8 October 1918 at Soissons, France, where he was killed in action (#108).

When the Army awarded these Marines the Medal of Honor, the Navy, not to be outdone, decided to award them its Medal of Honor as well. As a result, each of these men had the right to wear both the Army and Navy medals. The only Marine Medal of Honor winner in the 2nd Division who did not receive a Navy version of the decoration as well as the Army one was Fred W. Stockham (#104), who was killed in action on 13 June 1918 in Belleau Wood; the reason for the anomaly has never been explained. Interestingly, GySGT Hoffman received one medal under his assumed name and one under his real name, Ernest August Jameson.

Five Marines Who Won the Medal of Honor for Non-Combat-Related Heroism

1. CPL James A. Stewart (#24) rescued a midshipman from drowning on 1 Feb 1872, at Villefranche, France.
2. CPL John Morris (#25) rescued a seaman from drowning on 25 Dec 1881, Villefranche, France.
3. SGT John H. Helms (#81) saved a shipmate from drowning on 10 Jan 1901, Montevideo, Uruguay.
4. PVT Louis F. Pfeifer (#82) saved a seaman from burning to death during a shipboard fire aboard USS *Petrel* on 31 Mar 1901.
5. PVT Albert J. Smith (#113) saved a machinist from burning to death in a seaplane fire on 11 Feb 1921 at NAS Pensacola, Florida.

Although primarily a combat decoration, the Navy Medal of Honor may be awarded to members of the sea services who risk their lives in non-combat emergencies. The last such award was in 1945. # indicates number in the master list of Marine Medal of Honor winners.

Four Marine Medal of Honor Winners Who Later Joined the Army

1. PVT William F. Zion, who earned a Medal of Honor at Peking in 1900, later joined the Army and rose to first lieutenant (#79).
2. CPL Edwin N. Appleton, who won a Medal of Honor at Tientsin in 1900, later became a captain in the Army (#51).
3. CPT Joseph J. Foss, who received a Medal of Honor as a fighter pilot in the Solomons in 1942, ended his military career as a brigadier general in the Army National Guard (#126).
4. PFC Arthur J. Jackson, who won the Medal of Honor on Peleliu, later went on to become a captain in the Army Reserve.(#160).

One Army Medal of Honor Winner Who Later Joined the Marines

1. CPL Ludovicus M.M.Van Iersal (1893-1987), 9th Infantry, earned a Medal of Honor in the course of a reconnaissance during which he was forced to swim the Meuse River under fire, at Mouzon, France, on 9 November 1918. After his discharge, he changed his name to Louis M.M.Van Iersal, joined the Marines, and rose to sergeant major, retiring shortly after World War II.

One Army Medal of Honor Winner Who *Almost* Became a Marine

1. COL William O. Donovan, who won the Medal of Honor in France at the head of the 165th Infantry (New York's "Fighting 69th").

Between the World Wars, Donovan, a prominent Wall Street banker, undertook a number of covert intelligence missions for several presidents. When World War II loomed on the horizon, it was proposed that Donovan be commissioned a brigadier general in the Marine Corps and placed in charge of special operations. Nothing came of this, but Donovan went on to become the head of the OSS (Office of Special Services), which conducted intelligence and covert operations missions during the war, and eventually evolved into the CIA.

Twenty-one Navy Medical Corpsmen Who Won the Medal of Honor Serving with the Marines

# Rank & Name	Born-Died	Birth Place	Unit	Action Date	Campaign
1. LT Middleton S. Elliot	1872-1952	SC	??	21-22 Apr 1914	Vera Cruz
2. LtCdr Alexander G. Lyle	1889-1955	MA	2nd Div, 5th Marines	23 Apr 1918	France
3. LT Orlando H. Petty	1874-1932	OH	2nd Div, 5th Marines	11 Jun 1918	France
4. LT Joel T. Boone	1889-1975	PA	2nd Div, 6th Marines	19 Jul 1918	France
5. PM1 John H. Balch	1896-198	OKS	2nd Div, 6th Marines	19 Jul & 5 Oct 1918	France
6. HA1 David E. Hayden	1897-1974	TX	2nd Div, 6th Marines	15 Sep 1918	France
7. PM1 John Harlan Willis	1921-1945*	TN	5th Marine Div, 27th Marines	28 Feb 1945	Iwo Jima
8. M2 George E. Wahlen	1924-	UT	5th Marine Div, 26th Marines	3 Mar 1945	Iwo Jima
9. PM3 Jack Williams	1924-1945*	AR	5th Marine Div, 28th Marines	3 Mar 1945	Iwo Jima
10. PM1 Francis Pierce, Jr.	1924-1986	IA	4th Marine Div, 24th Marines	15-16 Mar 1945	Iwo Jima
11. HA1 Robert E. Bush	1926-	WA	1st Marine Div, 5th Marines	2 May 1945	Okinawa
12. PM2 William D. Halyburton, Jr.	1924-1945*	NC	1st Marine Div, 5th Marines	18 May 1945	Okinawa
13. HA1 Fred F. Lester	1926-1945*	IL	6th Marine Dn, 22nd Marines	6 Jun 1945	Okinawa
14. HC3 Richard D. Dewert	1931-1951*	MA	1st Marine Div	5 Apr 1951	Korea
15. HC3 John E. Kilmer	1930-1952*	IL	1st Marine Div	15 Aug 1952	Korea
16. HC3 Edward C. Benfold	1931-1952*	NY	1st Marine Div	5 Sep 1952	Korea
17. HC3 Francis C. Hammond	1931-1953*	VA	1st Marine Div, 5th Marines	26 Mar 1953	Korea
18. HC3 William R. Charette	1932-	MI	1st Marine Div, 7th Marines	27 Mar 1953	Korea
19. HC2 Donald E. Ballard	1945-	MO	3rd Marine Div, 4th Marines	16 Jun 1968	Vietnam
20. HC3 Wayne M. Caron	1946-1968*	MA	1st Marine Div, 7th Marines	28 Aug 1968	Vietnam
21. HC2 David R. Ray	1945-1969*	TN	1st Marine Div, 11th Marines	19 May 1969	Vietnam

LtCdr Lyle (#2) and LT Boone (#4) rose to vice admirals in the Navy Medical Corps. PM2 Whalen (#8) and HC2 Ballard (#19) later became army officers.

# indicates the rank order of awardees in this list, from the first to the most recent. *Rank* is that held at the time of the deed. *Born-Died* indicates the years of birth and death, where known, with a * indicated killed or mortally wounded in the course of the deed which earned him the Medal of Honor.

One Navy Chaplain Who Won the Medal of Honor Serving with the Marines

1. CHAP (LT) Vincent R. Capodanno (1929-1967), from Staten Island, NY, was killed in action at Quang Tin, Republic of Vietnam, 4 Sep 1967, while serving with the 5th Marines, 1st Marine Div.

Two Naval Officers Who Won the Medal of Honor Commanding Marines in Ground Combat

1. CPT Edwin A. Anderson (1860-1933), won his commanding the 2nd Regiment of Marines and Bluejackets at Vera Cruz, 22 April 1914, for "His indifference to the heavy fire ...."
2. CPT William R. Rush (1857-1940), won his commanding the Naval Brigade at Vera Cruz, 21-22 Apr 1914.

One Coast Guardsman Who Earned a Medal of Honor Serving With the Marines

1. Signalman 1st Class Douglas A. Munro (1919-1942), who commanded a landing craft in a flotilla engaged in evacuating Marines from an unsuccessful amphibious "end run" at Point Cruz, Guadalcanal on 27 September 1942, was killed while deliberately using his boat to draw Japanese fire and thus help protect the Marine withdrawal.

Marine Corps Medal of Honor Awards by Division

Division	Marines	Navy	WW II		Korea		Vietnam		Total
			M	N	M	N	M	N	
1st	91	10	18	2	47	5	28	3	101
2nd	8		8						8
3rd ·	40	1	9				31	1	32
4th	12	1	12	1					13
5th	17	3	17	3					20
6th	2		2	1					3

Key: In the second and third columns *Marines* indicates awards to Marines in the division, *Navy,* those to Navy personnel in the division. For succeeding columns the abbreviations *M* and *N* have been used. *Total* is the sum of all awards to men of the division, Marine and Navy personnel combined. Even without the Navy awards, more men from the 1st Marine Division have earned the Medal of Honor than from any other American division, Army or Marines.

Marine Corps Medal of Honor Awards by Regiment

Regiment	Marines	Navy	Other		WWI		WWII		Korea		Vietnam		Total
			M	N	M	N	M	N	M	N	M	N	
1st	18						6		8		5		18
2nd	9		7				2						9
3rd	10		1				3				6		10
4th	12	2					1	1			11	1	14
5th	32	6			5	2	6	2	12	1	9	1	38
6th	9	3			6	3	3						12
7th	36	2					6		23	1	9	1	38
8th	1						1						1
9th	12						4				8		12
10th	1						1						1
11th	2	1							2			1	3
15th	1						1						1
18th	1						1						1
21st	1						1						1
22nd	1						1						1
23rd	3						3						3
24th	5	1					5	1					6
25th	2						2						2
26th	7						6				1		7
27th	6	1					5				1		7
28th	5	1					5	1					6
29th	1						1						1

Key: In the second and third columns *Marines* indicates awards to Marines in the regiment, *Navy*, those to Navy personnel in the regiment. For succeeding columns the abbreviations *M* and *N* have been used. *Total* is the sum of all awards to men of the division, Marine and Navy personnel combined. Under *Other* are included on 3rd Marines award for Vera Cruz, 1914, four awards to the 2nd Marines for Vera Cruz, 1914, and three for the same regiment in Haiti, 1915. Counting Marine awards alone, the 7th Marines, with 36, has more than any other comparable American military unit. Note that there may be some errors in this tabulation, since some Medal of Honor citations do not indicate the man's regiment.

The Brevet Medal

Until the practice ended early in the Twentieth Century, it was customary to recognize unusually distinguished or heroic services by officers with a "brevet" promotion. This was essentially an honorary promotion, which brought a few benefits to the bearer (for example, he could sit on courts martial in his higher rank), but no increase in seniority or pay (except for those occasions on which he was serving in his brevet rank). Since Navy Regulations did not permit the award of the Medal of Honor to officers until 1916, it was common for Marine officers to be awarded a brevet in lieu of a Medal of Honor. However, the practice of awarding brevets came to an end before World War I, and public awareness of the meaning of a brevet waned. As a result, in 1921, CMC John A. Lejeune proposed that surviving officers who held brevets be given a special decoration. This was approved, and all living brevet holders were awarded the Brevet Medal, which resembled the 1917 version of the Navy Medal of Honor, a gold cross pattee, with a red ribbon seasoned with gold stars. The Brevet Medal was second only to the Medal of Honor in precedence. The following officers were awarded the Brevet Medal.

Officer	Breveted	Effective	For
1. 1LT James Forney	CPT	24 Apr 1862	Fts Jackson & St Philip, 1862*
2. 1LT Percival C. Pope	CPT	8 Sep 1863	Ft. Sumter, 1863
3. CPT James Forney	MAJ	15 Apr 1869	Formosa, skirmish, 1867 *
4. CPT James Forney	LTC	25 May 1870	Gundpowder Bridge, 1864 *
5. 1LT Charles C. Long	CPT	11 Jun 1898	Guantanamo, Cuba, 1898
6. CPT Charles L. McCawley	MAJ	11 Jun 1898	Guantanamo, Cuba, 1898
7. 1LT Wiliam N. McKelvy, Sr	CPT	11 Jun 1898	Guantanamo, Cuba, 1898
8. 1LT Albert S. McLemore	CPT	11 Jun 1898	Guantanamo, Cuba, 1898
9. 1LT James E. Mahoney	CPT	11 Jun 1898	Guantanamo, Cuba, 1898
10. 2LT Melville J. Shaw	1LT	11 Jun 1989	Guantanamo, Cuba, 1898
11. 2Lt Philip M. Bannon	1LT	13 Jun 1898	Guantanamo, Cuba, 1898
12. 1LT Lewis C. Lucas	CPT	13 Jun 1898	Guantanamo, Cuba, 1898
13. 2LT Louis J. Magill	CPT	13 Jun 1898	Guantanamo, Cuba, 1898**
14. 1LT Wendell C. Neville	CPT	13 Jun 1898	Guantanamo, Cuba, 1898
15. CPT Allan C. Kelton	MAJ	3 Jul 1898	Guantanamo, Cuba, 1898
16. CPT Paul St. Clair Murphy	MAJ	3 Jul 1898	Naval Battle of Santiago, 1898
17. 1LT David Dixon Porter	CPT	8 Oct 1899	Novaleta, Philippines, 1899
18. 1LT George C. Thorpe	CPT	8 Oct 1899	Novaleta, Philippines, 1899
19. 1LT William G. Powell	CPT	21 Jun 1900	Tientsin, China, 1900
20. 1LT Smedley D. Butler	CPT	13 Jul 1900	Tientsin, China, 1900
21. 1LT Carl Gamborg-Andersen	CPT	13 Jul 1900	Tientsin, China, 1900
22. MAJ George Richards	LTC	13 Jul 1900	Tientsin, China, 1900
23. MAJ Littleton W.T. Waller	LTC	13 Jul 1900	Tientsin, China, 1900
24. CPT John T. Myers	MAJ	20 Jul 1900	Peking, China, 1900
25. CPT Newt H. Hall	MAJ	14 Aug 1900	Peking, China, 1900

* Held three brevets

** A double brevet, being specifically awarded a 1LT as well.

Three Marines Who Held Both the Brevet Medal and Medal of Honor

1. 1LT Smedley D. Butler, Brevet Medal for 13 Jul 1900, and Medal of Honor #92 and #97
2. 1LT Wendell C. Neville, Brevet Medal for 13 Jun 1898, and Medal of Honor #89
3. 1LT David Dixon Porter, Brevet Medal for 8 Oct 1899, and Medal of Honor #84

MG Smedley D. Butler's Decorations

1. Medal of Honor
2. Medal of Honor
3. Brevet Medal
4. Distinguished Service Medal, Navy
5. Distinguished Service Medal, Army
6. West Indian Campaign Medal
7. Spanish-American War Campaign Medal
8. China Relief Expedition Medal
9. Philippine Campaign Medal
10. Marine Corps Expeditionary Medal, with three bronze stars
11. Nicaraguan Campaign Medal
12. Mexican Service Medal
13. Haitian Campaign Medal
14. Dominican Campaign Medal
15. World War I Victory Medal, with clasp
16. Yangtze Service Medal
17. *Medaille militaire* (Haiti)
18. *Etoile noire* (France)

And two Wound Stripes, the Purple Heart not being revived until the 1930s.

SGM Dan Daly's Decorations

1. Medal of Honor
2. Medal of Honor
3. Navy Cross
4. Distinguished Service Cross
5. Good Conduct Medal, with two bronze stars
6. China Relief Expedition Medal
7. Philippine Campaign Medal
8. Marine Corps Expeditionary Medal, with one bronze star
9. Mexican Service Medal
10. Haitian Campaign Medal
11. World War I Victory Medal, with four clasps
12. *Medaille militaire* (France)
13. *Croix de guerre avec palm* (France)

As well as two Letters of Commendation and two Wound Stripes, which in World War II would have been a Silver Star, with bronze star, and the Purple Heart, with bronze star.

LG Lewis "Chesty" Puller's Decorations

1. Navy Cross, with four stars
2. Distinguished Service Cross, Army
3. Silver Star
4. Legion of Merit, with one star and the "V" device

5. Bronze Star, with the "V" device
6. Air Medal, with two stars
7. Purple Heart
8. Presidential Unit Citation with five stars
9. Good Conduct Medal with one star
10. World War I Victory Medal with one star
11. Haitian Campaign Medal
12. Nicaraguan Campaign Medal
13. Marine Corps Expeditionary Medal with one star
14. China Service Medal
15. American Defense Medal with one star
16. American Campaign Medal
17. Asiatic-Pacific Campaign Medal with four stars
18. World War II Victory Medal
19. National Defense Service Medal
20. United Nations Service Medal
21. *Medaille Militaire* (Haiti)
22. *Medalla de Merito con estrella* (Nicaragua)
23. Presidential Unit Citation (Korea)
24. Ulghi Medal with Palm (Korea)
25. Cloud and Banner (China)

The Five Occasions for Which Lewis "Chesty" Puller Was Awarded the Navy Crosses

1. Nicaragua, for actions over several weeks in June and July 1930
2. Nicaragua, for a series of six actions that took place 20-30 September 1932
3. Guadalcanal, for the night battle of 24-25 October 1942 *
4. Cape Gloucester, 2-3 January 1944
5. Chosin, Korea, for actions during the breakout from the Chosin Reservoir, November-December 1950**

*On this occasion MG Alexander M. Vandegrift nominated Puller for the Medal of Honor, which was "reduced" to a Navy Cross.

** On this occasion Puller was also awarded the DSC.

One Marine Who Was Nominated for the Victoria Cross

1LT Smedley D. Butler, Tientsin, China, 13 July 1900.

On this occasion Butler and 1LT Carl Gamborg-Andersen (Brevet Medal #21), assisted by CPL Harry C. Adriance (Medal of Honor #64), PVT Clarence E. Mathias (#65), SGT John M. Adams (#66), and SGT Clarence E. Sutton (#67) carried a wounded comrade 17 miles while hotly pursued by the enemy. British Brigadier General Arthur R.F. Dorward was so impressed by Butler's performance that he wrote a letter commending his conduct to MG Adna R. Chafee, commander of American forces in China, and also nominated Smedley for a Victoria Cross, which under British regulations could not be awarded to someone not a subject of the Crown, not that U.S. regulations would have permitted him to receive it anyway.

## CHAPTER 4

The Principal Units of the Marine Corps

Until early in the twentieth century the largest permanent organizations in the Marine Corps were companies, which were numbered sequentially, although battalions and occasionally regiments were formed on an *ad hoc* basis. The first permanent regiments were organized in 1911. Over the next few years several brigades were formed, more or less as task forces for specific missions, the most famous of which was the 4th Marine Brigade, which served in France during World War I as part of the Army's 2nd Division in 1917-1918.

After World War I several brigades remained active in the Dominican Republic, Haiti, and Nicaragua, as well as the Advanced Base Force, an amphibious task force created in 1913, and later redesignated a brigade. The expansion of the Marine Corps during the 1930s (from c.16,000 men in 1934 to c.50,000 in 1941), led to the creation of two brigades in the Fleet Marine Force, which were expanded into divisions in 1941.

Marine Amphibious Corps/Marine Expeditionary Forces

The military term "corps" has two meanings. The older meaning is that reflected in the terms "Marine Corps" or "Corps of Engineers," that is a distinct military institution. The other derives from the old term *"corps d'armee,"* which entered English as "army corps," and was finally shortened to "corps." In this sense a corps is an operational command usually consisting of two or more divisions. During the Second World War the Marines formed three "amphibious corps," the I, III, and V (given these numbers because they originally operated in the First, Third, and Fifth Fleets) to oversee landings against enemy held territories.

In Marine Corps organizational charts such command levels have long since been replaced by "Marine Expeditionary Forces." Essentially a Marine Expeditionary Force is a corps-sized command normally encompassing one Marine Division, one Marine Air Wing, and one Force Service Support Group, though it can include additional forces, as did the I Marine Expeditionary Force in the Persian Gulf in 1990-1991.

I Marine Amphibious Corps. Organized in early 1943, the corps conducted operations in the Solomon Islands beginning in early 1943, including landings on Bougainville, New Britain, and other islands. By early 1944 it had been inactivated. As the "I Marine Expeditionary Force" it served in the Gulf War.

II Marine Expeditionary Force. Created after World War II, the II Marine Expeditionary Force has never served in a theater of war, though major components of the force were in the Persian Gulf under the I Marine Expeditionary Force in 1990-1991.

III Marine Amphibious Corps. Organized in mid-1943, the Corps operated in the Central Pacific, conducted the landings on Peleliu, Guam, and Okinawa, and was scheduled to invade

Honshu in March 1946. The corps performed occupation duties in North China after the war, and, redesignated the "III Marine Amphibious Force," was the principal Marine headquarters in Vietnam, and oversees Marine units in the Pacific.

IV Marine Expeditionary Force. Essentially comprises the operational units of the Marine Corps Reserve.

V Marine Amphibious Corps. Created in mid-1943, the corps conducted operations in the Gilbert and Marshals, on Saipan and Tinian, and on Iwo Jima. Had it become necessary to invade Japan, the corps was scheduled for the Kyushu operation in November 1945, and performed occupation duties there after the war. The corps has not been active since the occupation of Japan.

The Divisions

A division is a large (c.10,000-20,000 troops in modern American practice) general purpose, all arms force (*i.e.*, composed of infantry, artillery, armor, and other types of troops in various proportions) capable of sustained combat for an extended period. Although divisions were formed in the army and militia as early as the Revolutionary War, it was not until the early Twentieth Century that the idea of forming Marine divisions was proposed. This was in consequence of the development of what eventually became "War Plan Orange," which envisioned an amphibious offensive across the Central Pacific.

During World War I the Marine Corps, with its 4th Brigade already committed to combat in France as part of the Army's 2nd Division, sent the 5th Brigade and the 10th Marines overseas as well, in the hope of forming a Marine division. The project never bore fruit, however, since GEN John J. Pershing was opposed to the idea: Not only would it have caused the breakup of the 2nd Division, probably his best, but the Army would have had to supply additional forces (two artillery regiments, an engineer regiment, a third machine gun battalion, and train units) to fill the division out to its authorized full strength, approximately 24,000 men.

Nevertheless Marine Corps interest in creating division-sized formations remained alive during the inter-war period, particularly after war became increasingly likely in the late 1930s. Soon after the outbreak of the Sino-Japanese War in 1937, serious planning for the creation of Marine divisions began. The first Marine divisions, the 1st and 2nd, were raised in early 1941.

1st Marine Division. The division was formed in 1913 as the Advanced Base Force, which was later redesignated a brigade. Various changes of designation followed, until it became the 1st Marine Brigade in the late 1930s. In February 1941 the 1st Marine Brigade was reorganized as the 1st Marine Division. It entered combat on Guadalcanal on 7 August 1942, and went on to fight in Eastern New Guinea, on New Britain, Peleliu, and Okinawa, and was training for the projected invasion of Honshu in early 1946 when the war ended. It then spent more than a year on occupation duty in northern China before returning to the U.S. in 1947. During the Korean War a brigade from the division helped stop the North Korean assault on the Pusan Perimeter, and the division then went on to make the Inchon landing, retaking Seoul; it made the long march to the Chosin Reservoir and back, and then fought on until the armistice in July 1953. The division remained on alert in South Korea for nearly two years after the armistice, and then returned to the U.S. In 1962 it briefly deployed to the Caribbean during the Cuban Missile Crisis. In May 1964 the first elements of the division began arriving in Vietnam, and it was fully committed there from mid-1966 until withdrawn in 1971. Based on the West Coast, elements of the division took part in various landings and exercises through the 1970s and 1980s, and played a major role in the 1990-1991 Gulf War, Operation Desert Shield/Desert Storm.

2nd Marine Division. Activated in February of 1941 from the 2nd Marine Brigade, the 2nd Division relieved the 1st Division on Guadalcanal during late 1942 and worked with Army troops to finish driving the Japanese out by early 1943. It then went on to mount the first genuine Marine Corps amphibious assault, at Tarawa, in 1943, and took part in the landings on Saipan and Tinian. Although available for the Okinawa Campaign, it was not committed to action. When the war ended the division was training to take part in the invasion of Kyushu, scheduled for November 1945. It served on occupation duty in Japan until early 1946, when it returned to the U.S. Although the division remained on active duty during the Cold War, deploying to the Caribbean during the Cuban Missile Crisis, and though elements of the division took part in landings in Lebanon in 1956 and the Dominican Republic in 1965, it did not see combat again until Operation Desert Shield/Desert Storm in 1990-1991.

3rd Marine Division. Formed in September 1942 from veteran personnel of the 1st and 2nd Marine Divisions, the 3rd Marine Division went into action on Bougainville in 1943, and then made landings on Guam and Iwo Jima. At the time of the Japanese surrender it was preparing for a role in the invasion of Kyushu, scheduled for November 1945. It was inactivated on Guam at the end of 1945. The division was reactivated in January 1952, the division deployed to Okinawa in mid-1953. In early 1965 elements of the division began arriving in Vietnam. The division was heavily engaged until withdrawn from Vietnam in late 1969. Since then it has been stationed on Okinawa. The division has been stationed in the continental United States for only about two of its 45 years of active service. Motto: *Fidelity, Honor, Valor*.

4th Marine Division. Formed in August 1943 by splitting up the already forming 3rd Marine Division and drawing veterans from the 1st and 2nd Divisions, the 4th Marine Division first saw action in February 1944 at Kwajelein and Roi-Namur islands, and fought on Saipan, Tinian, and Iwo Jima. At the war's end it was preparing for the invasion of Honshu scheduled for early 1946. The division was inactivated in California in November 1945. The division was subsequently reactivated in the Marine Corps Reserve, serving throughout the Cold War, with elements being activated for the Gulf War.

5th Marine Division. Formed in January 1944, incorporating men from the recently disbanded Marine parachute battalions as well as new recruits and drafts from the older divisions, the division participated in the Iwo Jima assault during February 1945 and was preparing to take part in the invasion of Kyushu scheduled for November 1945 when the war ended. After a brief tour of occupation duty in Japan, it returned to the U.S., where it was inactivated in early 1946. Reactivated during the Vietnam War, some elements saw service in southeast Asia.

6th Marine Division. Formed on Guadalcanal in August 1944 through the expansion of the 1st Provisional Marine Brigade, which fought on Guam, the 6th Marine Division fought on Okinawa in April-June 1945, and was preparing for the invasion of Honshu, scheduled for November 1945, when the war ended. The division's 4th Marines was the first U.S. unit to take up occupation duties in Japan, landing at Yokosuka on 29 August. After a short tour on occupation duty, the division was transferred to support the 1st Marine Division in China, arriving in October 1945. It was inactivated in China in April 1946. The only Marine division never to have set foot in the United States, it has remained inactive since.

The Regiments

Although the lineage of several Marine regiments reaches back to the first decade of the twentieth century, and, indeed, in one case to the end of the nineteenth, none of the regiments has had a continuous existence. Early in the twentieth century it was common to form regiments as needed, and deactivate them when the need passed, recycling numbers as they became available. Nevertheless, the present regiments are descended from these often short-lived organizations, and inherit their honors. As a result, this summary makes no mention of most of the often numerous activations and inactivations that many of the regiments experienced.

1st Marines. The regiment's origins can be traced back to 1899, and it had served in the Philippine Insurrection, the Boxer Rebellion, Panama, Cuba, Vera Cruz, and the Dominican Republic by 1925, when it returned to the US. Deactivated in 1931, the regiment was reactivated in Puerto Rico in 1941, and became part of the 1st Marine Division, with which it has served ever since.

2nd Marines. The regiment was first raised in 1900. It served in the Philippine Insurrection, 1901-1902, Panama, 1904, Cuba, 1906, Panama, 1909-1910, Cuba in 1911 and again in 1912, the Dominican Republic, 1912, Cuba, 1913, Vera Cruz, 1914, and in Haiti and the Dominican Republic, 1914-1933, generally being inactivated after each of these deployments, only to be reformed again for the next, often within weeks of having been broken up. Deactivated in 1934, it was not reformed again until 1941, and was shortly incorporated in the 2nd Marine Division, with which it served during World War II and since, in the Gulf War.

3rd Marines. Originally formed in 1911, it served at Vera Cruz in 1914, in the Dominican Republic, 1916-1922, and passed to the Marine Corps Reserve in 1925, until deactivated in 1937. Reformed in 1942, it joined the 3rd Marine Division in the South Pacific in mid-1943 and served with it through the war. Deactivated in 1947, it was reformed in 1951, and helped rebuild the 3rd Marine Division, with which it served through the Vietnam War. During the Gulf War it formed part of the 1st Marine Division.

4th Marines. Created in 1914 for the Vera Cruz operation, the regiment served in the Dominican Republic, 1916-1918, and was in Shanghai, 1927-1941. The 4th Marines is the only Marine regiment that was continuously in existence between the world wars. In November 1941, down to only 800 men (the Commander, Asiatic Fleet preferring to retain Marine replacements in the Philippines), it was transferred to the Philippines. Beefed up to about 1500 men through the assignment of Marines from Cavite and other naval installations, as well as Navy personnel and even Philippine Navy personnel, the regiment formed the backbone of the final defense of Corregidor. It fell prisoner of the Japanese when U.S. forces in the Philippines surrendered in early May 1942. The regiment was reformed in February 1944 from the old Marine Raiders, and served as an independent unit in the occupation of Emirau Island, and as part of the 1st Provisional Marine Brigade on Guam in June of 1944. It was then incorporated in the 6th Marine Division, fighting on Okinawa. At the end of World War II the regiment was the first American combat unit to land in Japan, early on 30 August 1945, to take up occupation duties. Subsequently incorporated in the 3rd Marine Division, the regiment saw action in Vietnam, and served as part of the 2nd Marine Division during the Gulf War.

5th Marines. Originally formed for the Vera Cruz expedition in 1914, the regiment later served in Haiti, and then became the first Marine unit in France, in July 1917, fighting in the 4th Marine Brigade, 2nd Division during World War I. During the early 1920s it served in the U.S., on two occasions helping to guard the mails from train robbers, and then went to Nicaragua 1927-1933, and was inactivated in 1934. Reactivated in 1941, it formed part of the 1st Marine Division during World War II, Korea, and Vietnam, but during the Gulf War saw service as a separate unit.

6th Marines. Formed in 1917, the regiment was part of the 4th Marine Brigade in World War I. During the 1920s it served in Cuba, the Dominican Republic, and China. Incorporated in the 2nd Marine Division in 1941, it was shortly sent to occupy Iceland, 1941-1942, before returning to the division in time to fight on Guadalcanal. It has remained with the 2nd Marine Division ever since.

7th Marines. Formed in 1917, the regiment spent several years in Cuba during World War I until inactivated in 1919. Altogether the regiment was deactivated and reactivated more than a dozen times during the interwar period. In 1941 it was reactivated and assigned to the 1st Marine Division, with which it has served ever since.

8th Marines. Formed during World War I, the regiment served on the Mexican border 1917-1919 and in Haiti in the early 1920s. Deactivated in 1925, it was reactivated on the eve of World War II and has formed part of the 2nd Marine Division since 1941.

9th Marines. Originally formed in 1917, the regiment saw service in Cuba and on the Mexican Border during World War I, and was deactivated in 1919. Reactivated in 1925, it served in the Marine Corps Reserve until 1937, when it was again inactivated. It was reformed in February 1942 and served in the 3rd Marine Division during World War II. Inactivated in 1945, the regiment was reformed in 1952 and has since been part of the 3rd Marine Division.

10th Marines. The oldest artillery regiment in the Marine Corps, the 10th Marines was organized as an ad hoc artillery battalion for the Vera Cruz expedition in 1914. Retained on duty after that operation, it was expanded into a regiment during World War I, and elements later served in Haiti, the Dominican Republic, and China. Reduced to a single battalion between the wars, it was reformed as a full regiment in 1940. A battalion accompanied the 6th Marines to Iceland 1941-1942, but returned to accompany the rest of the regiment into action with the 2nd Marine Division, with which it has served since 1942.

11th Marines. Formed for World War I, the regiment arrived in France in late 1918, but saw no combat. By 1941 it was serving as the artillery contingent of the 1st Marine Division, with which it has been ever since.

12th Marines. Organized as an infantry regiment in China in 1927, serving until deactivated the following year. Reactivated as an artillery regiment in 1942, and assigned to the 3rd Marine Division, to which it has been attached ever since, although inactive 1945-1946 and 1947-1951.

13th Marines. Arrived in France in late 1918, but saw no combat. Inactive between the wars, it was reactivated as an artillery regiment in January 1944 as part of the 5th Marine Division. It has since become an independent unit, seeing service in the Gulf War.

14th Marines. Activated as the artillery regiment of the 4th Marine Division in 1943, with which it still serves.

15th Marines. Formed in 1944 as the engineer contingent of the 6th Marine Division.

16th Marines. Activated in late 1943, it became the engineer contingent of the 5th Marine Division in early 1944.

17th Marines. Formed in 1941 to serve as the engineer regiment of the 1st Marine Division.

18th Marines. Formed in 1941 as the engineer contingent of the 2nd Marine Division, to which it has been attached ever since.

19th Marines. Formed in mid-1942 as the engineer contingent of the 3rd Marine Division, with which it has served ever since.

20th Marines. Formed in 1943 as the engineer regiment of the 4th Marine Division, to which it remains attached.

21st Marines. Formed in 1942, the regiment has served with the 3rd Marine Division since.

22nd Marines. Raised in early 1942, occupied Eniwetok Atoll in the Marshalls as an independent unit, in 1943, and fought on Guam in the 1st Provisional Marine Brigade, before being incorporated in the 6th Marine Division, fighting on Okinawa.

23rd Marines. Formed in 1942 as part of the 3rd Marine Division, the regiment was detached from the division in mid-1943, and became part of the 4th Marine Division, in which it continues to serve.

24th Marines. Raised in late 1942, it became part of the 4th Marine Division, with which it continues to serve.

25th Marines. Formed in late 1942 it has been part of the 4th Marine Division since 1943.

26th Marines. Formed in January 1944 as part of the 5th Marine Division, during the Vietnam War it formed part of the 3rd Marine Division.

27th Marines. Formed in January 1944 as part of the 5th Marine Division, it formed part of the 1st Marine Division during the Vietnam War.

28th Marines. Formed in February 1944 as part of the 5th Marine Division.

29th Marines. Formed in 1944, its 1st Battalion saw action on Saipan as an independent unit, the regiment was then incorporated in the 6th Marine Division, fighting on Okinawa.

The Marine Parachute Battalions

The Marine Corps began forming a parachute element in 1940. Initial plans called for assigning a battalion of parachutists to each Marine division. By April of 1943 there were four battalions of "paramarines,"* three of which were fighting in the South Pacific as part of the 1st Marine Parachute Regiment. At that point the Brass decided that "paramarines" were an unnecessary expense, since they had never been used in an airborne mode. In late 1943 the Marine parachute battalions were concentrated at San Diego, and they were disbanded in January of 1944, the men going to help form the 5th Marine Division.

1st Battalion: Organized in August 1941, it captured Gavutu-Tanambogo, fought on Guadalcanal in conjunction with the 1st Raider Battalion, raided Choiseul, and occupied Vella Lavella.

2nd Battalion: Organized in August 1941, it fought in the Central Solomons and on Vella Lavella.

3rd Battalion: Organized in 1942, it joined the other battalions on Vella Lavella.

4th Battalion: Organized in April 1943, it never left San Diego.

* The commonly used term "paramarines" was not popular with senior members of the Marine Corps, as it implied something less than a proper Marine (as in "paramilitary").

The Marine Raiders

Inspired by the Chinese use of irregular raiding forces in their resistance to the Japanese invasion that began in 1937, in 1941 Marine LTC Evans F. Carlson, a former military observer with the Chinese Communist Eighth Route Army in 1937-1938, urged President Roosevelt (whom he had met while serving as commander of the Marine security detachment at Warm Springs, Georgia) to prod the Marine Corps into forming special units designed for raiding and guerrilla warfare. As a result, the Marine Corps began to organize what became known as Marine Raider Battalions, with some 5,000 Marines being trained as raiders. Four battalions were raised, and in March 1943 these were formed into the 1st Raider Regiment, which in September 1943 was split to form a provisional 2nd Raider Regiment, comprising the 2nd and 3rd Raider Battalions.

1st Raider Battalion. Organized in February 1942, from the 1st Separate Battalion, itself redesignated from the 1st Battalion, 5th Marine Regiment in January 1942, and commanded by LTC Merritt A. Edson. It spearheaded the assault on Tulagi at the onset of the Guadalcanal Campaign, and went on to conduct many operations on Guadalcanal, usually combined with the 1st Parachute Battalion, most notably the Battle of Edson's Ridge (12-14 September 1942), an action for which Edson and one of his men were awarded the Medal of Honor. After Guadalcanal it fought on New Georgia in 1943.

2nd Raider Battalion. Organized in February 1942 from the 2nd Separate Battalion, a newly created formation, and commanded by LTC Evans F. Carlson, with CPT James Roosevelt as his

Executive Officer. Two companies helped defend Midway Island during the famous battle of 4-7 June 1942. On 17 August 1942, two companies, some 221 men, conducted a raid on Makin Island, landing from two submarines. The battalion later served on Guadalcanal, making a famous 30-day raid behind Japanese lines, 4 November-4 December 1942, and, reinforced by the 1st Marine Dog Platoon, the first American canine unit to see action in the war, supported the 3rd Marine Division landings on Bougainville late 1943. One man won the Medal of Honor.

3rd Raider Battalion. Organized in Samoa in September 1942 from individual volunteers, the 3rd Battalion took part in the unopposed occupation of the Russell Islands early in 1943, and then went on to support the 3rd Marine Division's landings on Bougainville later that year. One man won the Medal of Honor.

4th Raider Battalion. Organized from volunteers in October 1942, under MAJ James Roosevelt, the battalion fought on New Georgia in 1943.

In late 1943 Marine Corps reconsidered the concept of the Raiders. While they had performed well in combat, they had actually made only two raids, Carlson's on Makin and Guadalcanal, all their other missions being normal for Marine units. As a result, on 1 February 1944 the Raiders were reorganized as the cadre of the reactivated 4th Marine Regiment: Headquarters, 1st Raider Regiment became the Headquarters of the 4th Marines, the 1st, 3rd, and 4th Raider Battalions became the 1st, 2nd, and 3rd Battalions, 4th Marines, and the 2nd Raider Battalion became the Weapons Company, 4th Marines.

Marine Defense Battalions

Since distant island outposts had to be held against enemy attacks and invaded beachheads defended against counterinvasion, in the mid-1930s the Marine Corps began developing the concept of the "defense battalion," a self-contained unit designed to provide coast defense for critical locations. These battalions had variable tables of organization and equipment but usually included artillery and infantry, and sometimes tanks. Their formation began in late 1939, and by the time of the Japanese attack on Pearl Harbor there were six, five of them already deployed in the Pacific. By late 1943 twenty defense battalions had been formed (two of them composed primarily of black personnel), of which 18 were serving in the Pacific. By then, however, the need for defense battalions passed, and most were redesignated as anti-aircraft battalions, having the same numerical designation. Only three defense battalions were active at the end of the war.

1st Defense Battalion. Elements of the battalion were at Pearl Harbor on 7 December 1941, as well as on Johnston Island and Palmyra, but the largest contingent, about 40%, was on Wake Island under MAJ James Devereaux, where it put up an heroic defense, its 5-inch guns accounting for a Japanese destroyer. The contingents from Hawaii, Palmyra, and Johnston formed the nucleus of a rebuilt battalion, which took part in the occupation of the Marshall Islands and Eniwetok.

2nd Defense Battalion. In California at the start of the war, it held Samoa for a time, and then took part in the occupation of the Gilbert Islands in late 1943,

3rd Defense Battalion. Began the war at Pearl Harbor and then served on Midway during the famous battle in June 1942, before supporting the 1st Marine Division on Guadalcanal, and went on to fight on Bougainville.

4th Defense Battalion. At Pearl Harbor at the time of the Japanese attack, elements helped garrison Midway during the Battle of Midway, later fighting on Vella LaVella.

5th Defense Battalion. In Hawaii at the time of Pearl Harbor, it went on to support operations on Guadalcanal, helping to garrison Tulagi, and later took part in the occupation of the Gilbert Islands.

6th Defense Battalion. Was at Midway from late 1941, and with the 3rd DB helped defend the island from the Japanese air attacks during the Battle of Midway, in June 1942. It remained on Midway for the entire war. One man in the battalion won the Medal of Honor on Midway.

7th Defense Battalion. Was newly assigned to Samoa when the war broke out, where it helped organize the 1st Samoan Battalion. It later took part in the occupation of the Gilbert Islands.

8th Defense Battalion. Formed shortly after Pearl Harbor, it went on to take part in the occupation of the Gilbert Islands.

9th Defense Battalion. Joined the 3rd on Guadalcanal in late 1942, and went on to fight on Rendova, New Georgia, and Guam.

10th Defense Battalion. Served in the Solomons and in the occupation of Eniwetok.

11th Defense Battalion. Served on Guadalcanal, Rendova, and New Georgia.

12th Defense Battalion. Took part in the occupation of Woodlark Island, off New Guinea, and fought on New Britain.

13th Defense Battalion. Served in the Caribbean.

14th Defense Battalion. Formed from part of the 5th DB on Tulagi in January 1943, elements of the battalion later took part in the occupation of the Admiralty Islands, and the entire unit was on Guam.

15th Defense Battalion. Deployed to the Pacific, but was not seriously engaged.

16th Defense Battalion. Deployed to the Pacific, but was not seriously engaged.

17th Defense Battalion. Deployed to the Pacific, but was not seriously engaged.

18th Defense Battalion. Deployed to the Pacific, but was not seriously engaged.

51st Defense Battalion. Formed from mostly black personnel, the battalion performed occupation duties in the Ellice and Marianas Islands, but was not seriously engaged.

52nd Defense Battalion. Also formed mostly from African-American personnel, the battalion saw service in the Marshall and Marianas Islands, but was not seriously engaged.

Some Unusual Marine Units

The Barrage Balloon Squadrons. Barrage balloons were a passive anti-aircraft weapons system. Raised on tethers above installations and ships, even ships underway, the large balloons, from which dangled steel cables, made it hazardous for enemy aircraft to undertake low level attacks. The Marine Corps began organizing barrage balloon squadrons in late 1940. A school was opened in mid-1941, and two squadrons were formed in October of that year. Although it was eventually planned to have 20 Marine barrage balloon squadrons, only six were actually formed, all by the end of 1942. All six saw service in the Pacific, but their contribution to the war effort was difficult to determine. By early 1943 it was becoming clear that anti-aircraft artillery units were more cost-effective than the expensive, somewhat delicate barrage balloons, and the six squadrons were all disbanded by the end of 1943.

The Glider Group. The German demonstrations of the military use of gliders for the assault landing of troops and equipment in 1940-1941, stimulated Marine Corps interest in developing a glider capability of its own. In July 1941 volunteers were solicited for glider training, and plans were laid for an "Air Infantry Battalion" of 900 men, complete with light anti-tank equipment and motor vehicles, to be transported in 75 gliders, with the ultimate intention of raising one glider battalion for each Marine division. Training and experimentation proceeded rapidly, and by March 1942 the Marine Corps activated Glider Group 71. This unit, composed of a headquarters and one operational squadron, conducted more intensive training and experiments, but by early 1943 it was clear that the gliders were not as useful as had been expected. The program was terminated in mid-1943.

The Guam Insular Force Guard. A company of about 80 *Chamorros*—native Guamanians—organized and officered by Marines, the Insular Force Guard took part in the spirited, if short, defense of Guam on 10 December 1941, losing several of their number before the island was surrendered to the Japanese. Marines also provided the cadre for the Guam Territorial Militia, some 250 volunteers.

The Navaho Code Talkers. Actually not a unit at all, but essentially a "corps" or pool of some 350-400 Navaho who were trained as battlefield communications specialists, using their native language, thereby greatly saving time, since messages could be sent without the necessity of encoding and decoding them. Organized in May 1942, the Navaho code talkers were disbanded at the end of the war, after having served on numerous Pacific battlefields from early 1943 on, earning a Presidential Certificate of Appreciation.

The Samoan Battalion. With the Japanese striking all across the Pacific in a seemingly unstoppable tide of conquest, in early 1942 it was decided to bolster the defense of Samoa by raising a battalion of local volunteers. Organized by the 7th Defense Battalion, the 1st Samoan Battalion, USMCR, eventually numbered nearly a thousand men, many of whom subsequently volunteered to serve with Marine combat units.

The United Nations Guard. A detachment of c.125 Marines was organized and assigned to the newly organized United Nations in 1945, for security and ceremonial purposes, serving until disbanded by Secretary General Trygve Lic on 31 January 1947.

## CHAPTER 5

The Old Corps, 1775-1898 Wars, Expeditions, and Engagements

For more than a century after its founding in the early weeks of the Revolutionary War, the Marine Corps served primarily in the traditional role of European "soldiers of the sea." Marines served afloat in support of naval operations, essayed expeditions and landings, and protected American lives, property, and interests in all quarters of the globe. In addition, Marines served ashore in conventional campaigns alongside the Army.

The Beginning Colonial and Revolutionary Times

Colonial Marines

In 1740 COL William Gooch of Virginia raised the 43rd Foot, a Marine regiment of four battalions, in the Colonies for the British, for a total of about 3,000 men. They served under Admiral Lord Vernon ("Old Grog") during his Caribbean Campaign, only about 10% surviving the fevers and fighting to return home in 1741.

State Marine Corps in the Revolutionary War

1. Connecticut
2. Georgia
3. Maryland
4. Massachusetts
5. New Hampshire
6. New York
7. North Carolina
8. Pennsylvania
9. Rhode Island
10. South Carolina
11. Virginia

The state marine corps had varied careers. Most did little more than guard naval installations and provide security aboard state vessels. However, some state marines saw considerable service. Eight Connecticut Marines took part in the capture of Fort Ticonderoga, on 10 May 1775, arguably the earliest action by "United States Marines." The Massachusetts Marines were not formally created until July of 1775, but a contingent of 17 marines under LT John Watson was serving on the state's ship *Enterprise* from 3 May 1775. In addition to serving in the state's ships, a contingent of Massachusetts Marines helped man Benedict Arnold's squadron on Lake Champlain, in 1776, and another contingent joined Continental Marines and soldiers in the unsuccessful expedition to Penobscot, Maine, in July 1779. The South Carolina Marines saw considerable service in the state's warships, primarily in raiding British shipping. Not only did the Virginia Marines serve in the state's ships, but a company also patrolled the Ohio River, deep in the wilderness. The Maryland Marine Corps was formed after Congress created the Continental Marines, and was quite active both aboard the state's ships and in fending off British raids.

The Continental Army's Marines

The first ships to take to the waters wearing the Continental flag belonged not to the Navy, but to the Army. The crews of these ships—including Marines—were recruited from men who had enlisted as soldiers. Some of these contingents are of particular interest.

1. Benedict Arnold's Marines: The squadron with which Benedict Arnold fought the Battle of Valcour Island, on Lake Champlain on 11 October 1776, included militiamen and soldiers assigned as sailors and marines, as well as a contingent of state marines from Massachusetts.

2. George Washington's Marines: George Washington commissioned several ships to support operations of the army deployed around Boston in 1775-1776, manning them with soldiers who had formerly been fishermen and merchant seamen. Many of them were Massachusetts men from the Marblehead Regiment, which went on to save Washington's army after the Battle of Long Island, 26-27 August 1776, by ferrying the troops from Brooklyn to Manhattan.

3. The Western River Marines. In 1777 James Willing, a shady Pennsylvanian with a commission from Congress as a captain in the Navy, recruited a contingent of marines from the army garrison at Fort Pitt (Pittsburgh), and embarked upon a moderately successful career of thinly disguised piracy along the lower Mississippi and other rivers emptying into the Gulf of Mexico. Capturing Natchez in early 1778, Willing raided British Florida with some success until the Crown beefed up its local garrisons. Faced with more serious opposition, Willing's force soon dispersed through desertion.

Private Marines

Many of the ships which served as privateers—free enterprise raiders commissioned by Congress or the various states to attack British shipping—included contingents of men armed and trained to fight as Marines. Their service in the Revolutionary War, and, indeed, later in the War of 1812 and in Confederate Service during the Civil War, is largely unremembered.

Marine Participation in the Revolutionary War

Strength of the Corps
Total Marines in Service During the War   c.3,500
Wartime Peak Strength of the Marine Corps   c.1,500 (mid-1778)

Casualties

Killed/Mortally Wounded in Action	47
Non-Combat Deaths	??
Wounded in Action	117
Prisoners-of-War	c.300
Total	at least 464

The Ten Most Notable Continental Marine Operations of the Revolutionary War

1. New Providence, Nassau, the Bahamas, 3 March 1776
2. USS *Cabot* vs HMS *Glasgow*, 6 April 1776*
3. Second Battle of Trenton (Assanpink Creek), 2 January 1777
4. Defense of the Delaware Forts, October-November 1777
5. Second Nassau Expedition, 27 January 1778
6. HMS *Yarmouth* vs USS *Randolph*, 7 March 1778
7. John Paul Jones' Whitehaven Raid, 27-28 April 1778
8. Penobscot Expedition, 26 July-13 August 1779
9. USS *Bon Homme Richard* vs HMS *Serapis*, 23 September 1779
10. Defense of Charleston, 12 February-12 May 1780

* In ship-vs-ships actions, the victor has been given first.

The Four Most Notable Operations by State Marines in the Revolutionary War

1. Capture of Fort Ticonderoga, 10 May 1775, Connecticut Marines
2. Battle of Valcour Island, Lake Champlain, NY, 11-13 October 1776, Massachusetts Marines
3. Penobscot Expedition, 26 July-13 August 1779, Massachusetts Marines
4. George Rodgers Clark's Illinois Expedition, 1779-1783, Virginia Marines

The Six Most Notable Marines of the War for Independence

1. 1LT Robert George, commanded a company of Marines that served with George Rogers Clark in the Ohio Territory.
2. MAJ Samuel Nicholas, the first U.S. Marine, and senior officer of the Corps, led the Nassau Expedition, commanded a battalion of Marines in Washington's Army during the Trenton-Princeton Campaign and later took part in the defense of the Delaware River approaches to Philadelphia.
3. 1LT Edward Stack, a Franco-Irish Marine commissioned in the Continental Marines, he commanded the Marines aboard John Paul Jones' *Bon Homme Richard* in her famous fight with HMS *Serapis.*
4. CPT John Trevett, who took part in both expeditions to the Bahamas, and was wounded in the action between the USS *Trumbull* and the British Privateer *Watt.*
5. 1LT Samuel Wallingford, commanded the Marines aboard John Paul Jones' *Ranger* during the raids on Whitehaven and St. Mary's Isle, Britain, and was later killed in action in Jones' fight with HMS *Drake.*

6. CPT John Welsh commanded the combined Continental and state marine battalion in the Penobscot Expedition, during which he was killed in action.

Three Black Continental Marines

1. John Martin, recruited in April 1776, served as a Marine aboard the brig *Reprisal*. Martin—who was also known as Keto—served in the ship for more than a year, during which she took seven British prizes and tangled with a ship-of-the line. On 1 October 1777 *Reprisal* foundered in a gale off Newfoundland with the loss of all hands save the ship's cook.
2-3. Isaac Walker and "Orange" enlisted in late 1776 at the famed Tun Tavern by its proprietor, CPT Robert Mullan. Assigned to Mullan's company, they accompanied it when it joined MAJ Samuel Nicholas' Marine Battalion in reinforcing Washington's Army for the Trenton-Princeton Campaign of December 1776-January 1777.

Daily Ration Allowance, the Continental Marines, 1775

> 1 pd bread
> 1 pd meat (including pork, beef, or fish, usually salted)
> 1 pd potatoes or turnips, or .5 pd pease
> .5 pt rum

There were also periodic issuances of butter, pudding, and other delicacies and condiments.

The Quasi-War with France, 1798-1801

Marine Participation in the Quasi-War

Strength of the Corps

Total Marines in Service During the War	c.1,200
Wartime Peak Strength of the Marine Corps	c.600 (mid-1800)

Casualties

Killed/Mortally Wounded in Action	6
Non-Combat Deaths	??
Wounded in Action	11
Prisoners-of-War	??

Total at least 17

The Four Most Notable Actions by the Marine Corps during the Quasi-War

1. USS *Constellation* vs FNS *L'Insurgent*, 1 February 1799 *.
2. USS *Constellation* vs FNS *La Vengance*, 1 February 1800.
3. Raid on Puerto Plata, Hispaniola, 11 May 1800.
4. Defense of Curacao, Netherlands Antilles, 10-24 September 1800.

There were literally scores of actions involving Marines during the Quasi-War, which merged somewhat into the ongoing anti-piracy campaign in the Caribbean at the time.

* In ship to ship actions, the victor is listed first.

The Three Most Notable Marines of the Quasi-War

1. MAJ William W. Burrows, the CMC, who virtually created the Corps.
2. CPT Daniel Carmick, commanded the Marines at Puerto Plata.
3. 1LT Bartholomew Clinch, Commander of Marines, USS *Constitution,* twice cited by Congress for conspicuous service.

One Marine Officer Twice Cited by Congress for Services in the Quasi-War with France

1LT Bartholomew Clinch, Commander of Marines, USS *Constitution*
>   1. For the capture of FNS *Insurgente,* 1 February 1799.
>   2. For the capture of FNS *La Vengance,* 1 February 1800.

The Barbary Wars, 1801-1805 & 1815

Marine Participation in the Barbary Wars

Strength of theCorps

Total Marines in Service During the War	c.1,500
Wartime Peak Strength of the Marine Corps	c.550 (mid-1805)
Marines Committed to Action	c.400
Casualties	
Killed/Mortally Wounded in Action	4
Non-Combat Deaths	??
Wounded in Action	10
Prisoners-of-War	c.43
Total	at least 55

Figures are for the First Barbary War. Those of the Second War, which lasted only about seven months, seem to have gone unrecorded.

The Ten Most Notable Actions of the Barbary Wars in Which the Marines Took Part

1. USS *Enterprise* vs the Tripolitanian *Tripoli,* 1 August 1801 *
2. Commodore John Rodgers Raid on Tripoli Harbor, 20 May 1803
3. USS *John Adams* vs the Tripolitanian *Mashuda,* 22 May 1803
4. Burning of USS *Philadelphia* in Tripoli Harbor, 16 February 1804
5. Naval Battle off Tripoli, 3 August 1804
6. Bombardment of Tripoli, 3 August-12 September 1804 **
7. Capture of Derna, 27 April 1805
8. Defense of Derna, 13 May-10 June 1805 ***
9. Capture of the Algerian *Mashuda* off Spain, 17 June 1815
10. Capture of the Algerian *Estedio* off Spain, 19 June 1815

* In ship to ship actions, the victor is listed first.

** During this period Tripoli was bombarded on 3, 7, 25, and 28 August, and 3, 10, and 12 September

*** Lieutenant O'Bannon and his tiny garrison beat off three assaults during this period, 13 and 28 May and 10 June.

The Two Most Notable Marines of the Barbary Wars

1. 1LT Presley N. O'Bannon, who commanded the Marines on the Derna Expedition.
2. SGT Solomon Wise, who led the Marines in the burning of the USS *Philadelphia*.

Two Notable Comments Made During the Barbary Wars

1. "The most bold and daring act of the age," said by Vice Admiral Sir Horatio Nelson upon hearing of the burning of the USS *Philadelphia* in Tripoli Harbor.
2. "My head or yours," said by the governor of Derna when summoned to surrender by William Eaton.

Marines Who Received the Gratitude of Congress During the Barbary Wars

1. For the capture of frigate *Tripoli* by USS *Enterprise*, 1 August 1801, 2LT E.S. Lane.
2. For the burning of the former USS *Philadelphia* in Tripoli Harbor, 16 February 1804, SGT Solomon Wise, CPL Duncan Mansfield, PVT James Noble, PCT John Quinn, PCT Isaac Canbell, PVT Reuben O'Brien, PVT William Pepper, and PVT John Wolsfronduff.
3. For gallantry during operations against Tripoli, July-September 1804, CPT John Hall, 1LT John Johnson, and 2LT Robert Greenleaf.
4. For gallantry at Tripoli, 7 August 1804, SGT John Meredith and PVT Nathaniel Hudson, during which they were both killed in action.

Prior to the institution of the Medal of Honor in 1862, Congress often proclaimed its thanks or granted special awards, such as swords of honor, to men it wished to single out for special praise.

The American Members of the Derna Expedition *

1. "General" William Eaton, U.S. Consul at Tunis, overall commander
2. 1LT Presley N. O'Bannon, commanding the Marines
3. Midshipman Pascal Paoli Peck, USN
4. Marine SGT Derek
5. Marine Crawford
6. Marine Evans
7. Marine Elroy
8. Marine Langley
9. Marine Wafe
10. Marine Busch

* In addition to the ten Americans there were some 500 other men on the expedition, of whom about 100 were Greek mercenaries and the rest adherents of Hamet, the apirant Pasha of Tripoli.

The West African Anti-Slavery Patrol, 1808-1861

Eleven Notable Anti-Slavery Operations in Which Marines Took Part

1. USS *Cyane* captures seven slaver ships, off West Africa, 7-12 April 1820
2. USS *Grampus* captures the slaver *Fenix*, off Cap Hatien, Haiti, 5 June 1830
3. Raid on slaver villages, Berribee, Ivory Coast, 13-16 December 1843
4. USS *Yorktown* captures the slaver *Pons* off Kahaula, 30 November 1845
5. USS *Perry* captures the slaver *Martha* off Luanda, Angola, 6 June 1850
6. USS *Constitution* captures the slaver *Gambril* off West Africa, 3 December 1853
7. USS *Perry* captures the slaver *Glamorgan* off West Africa, 10 March 1854
8. USS *Marion* captures the slaver *Brothers* off the southwest African coast, 8 September 1858
9. USS *Marion* captures the slaver *Orion* off the Congo, 21 April 1859
10. USS *Marion* captures the slaver *Ardennes* off the Congo, 27 April 1859
11. Raid on slaver villages, Kisembo, Portuguese Angola, 1-4 March 1860*

*In cooperation with the Royal Marines

The War of 1812, 1812-1815

Marine Participation in the War of 1812

Strength of the Corps	
Total Marines in Service During the War	c.3,000
Wartime Peak Strength of the Marine Corps	c.750 (mid-1814)
Casualties	
Killed/Mortally Wounded in Action	46
Non-Combat Deaths	??
Wounded in Action	33
Prisoners-of-War	c.100
Total	at least 200

The Ten Most Notable Actions Involving Marines During the War of 1812

1. USS *Constitution* vs HMS *Guerriere*, 9 August 1812 *
2. USS *United States* vs HMS *Macedonian*, 26 October 1812
3. USS *Constitution* vs HMS *Java*, 29 December 1812
4. HMS *Shannon* vs USS *Chesapeake*, 1 June 1813
5. Battle of Lake Erie, 10 September 1813
6. USS *Wasp* vs HMS *Reindeer, 28* June 1814
7. Battle of Bladensburg, Maryland, 24 August 1814
8. Defense of Fort McHenry, 12-14 September 1814
9. HMS *Endymion* vs USS *President*, 15 January 1815 **
10. USS *Consitution* vs HMS *Cyane* and HMS *Levant*, 20 February 1815 **

* In ship to ship actions, the victor is listed first.
** Both these actions occurred after the formal end of the war.

The Ten Most Distinguished Marines During the War of 1812

1. SGT William D. Barnes, of USS *Wasp*, who rallied the ship's Marines and crew to take HMS *Reindeer, 28* June 1814.
2. 1LT John Brooks, the only Marine officer with the Lake Erie Squadron, who trained backwoodsmen to serve as Marines, and led them in action during the battle of 10 September 1813, in which he was mortally wounded.
3. 2LT William S. Bush, of USS *Constitution,* killed in action 19 August 1812 as he led the boarding of HMS *Guerriere.*
4. CPT Daniel Carmick, who commanded the Marines at New Orleans.
5. 1LT James Marshall Gamble, of USS *Essex,* who commanded the British prize *Greenwich* in 1813, thus becoming the only Marine ever to command a US warship, in which capacity he took the British merchantman *Seringaptam* as a prize.
6. CPT Archibald Henderson, commanding the Marines aboard USS *Constitution,* who so distinguished himself in the taking of HMS *Cyane* and *HMS Levant,* 20 February 1815, that he received a special mention in the official report of the action.
7. CPT James Lambert, of USS *Constitution,* mortally wounded as he led the boarding of *HMS Java.*
8. CPT Samuel Miller, who commanded the Marine Battalion in Commodore Joshua Barney's Naval Brigade during the Battle of Bladensburg, 24 August 1814.
9. CPT Alexander Sevier, second in command of the Marines at Bladensburg, for which he was breveted a major.
10. 1LT Levi Twiggs, of USS *President,* who distinguished himself in action against HMS *Endymion,* 15 January 1815.

Occasions for Which Specific Marines Received the Gratitude of Congress during the War of 1812 *

1. For the battle between USS *Constitution* and HMS *Guerriere*, 9 August 1812, to 1LT William Bush (KIA) and 2LT John Contee.
2. For the capture of HMS*s Detroit* and *Caledonian*, on Lake Erie, 8 October 1812, to 1LT William H. Freeman and 2LT John Contee.
3. For the action between USS *United States* and HMS *Macedonian*, 26 October 1812, 1LT William Anderson and 2LT James L. Edwards.
4. For the Battle of Lake Erie, 10 September 1813, CPT George Stockton, CPT William Webster, 1LT John Brooks (KIA), 1LT John Heddlestone, SGT James Artis, SGT Joseph Beckly, SGT Johnathan Curtis, SGT William S. Johnson, SGT Sandord A. Mason, SGT James Tull, CPL Joseph Berry, CPL John Brown, and CPL David Little.
5. For the action between USS *Wasp* and HMS *Reindeer*, 28 June 1814, to SGT William O. Barnes.
6. For the Battle of New Orleans, 8 January 1815, to MAJ Daniel Carmick and the Marines of the New Orleans Battalion.

* This could consist of anything from a citation to a sword of honor.

The Florida War, 1835-1842

Marine Participation in The Florida War

Strength of the Corps

Total Marines in Service During the War	c.3,000
Wartime Peak Strength of the Marine Corps	c.1,600 (early -1838)
Forces Committed to Action	c.1,000

Casualties

Killed in Action/Mortally Wounded	25
Non-Combat Deaths	36
Wounded in Action	??
Prisoners-of-War	0
Total	at least 61

The Principal Marine Actions in the Florida War

1. Relief of Fort Brooke, 22 January 1836
2. Battle of Wahoo Swamp, 21 November 1836
3. Lake Ahopoka, 23 January 1837
4. Hatchee-Lustee, 27 January 1837
5. "Mosquito Fleet" Operations, July 1838-July 1842

The Three Most Distinguished Marines of the Florida War

1. CPT John Harris (CMC #6), who won the battle of Lake Ahopoka at the head of a company of "Horse Marines."
2. CMC COL Archibald Henderson, who commanded a mixed Marine-Army-volunteer-Indian brigade at the Battle of Hatchee-Lustee.
3. MAJ Samuel Miller, who commanded the Marines with the Army of the South after the departure of Henderson.

The War with Mexico, 1846-1848

Marine Participation in the War with Mexico

Strength of the Corps

Total Marines in Service During the War	c.3,000
Wartime Peak Strength of the Marine Corps	c.2,000 (mid-1847)
Casualties	
Killed/Mortally Wounded in Action	11
Non-Combat Deaths	??
Wounded in Action	47
Prisoners-of-War	0
Total	at least 58

The Dozen Most Notable Marine Actions of the War with Mexico, 1846-1846

1. Capture of Monterey, California, 7 July 1846
2. Capture of Tampico, 14 November 1846
3. Battle of San Pascual, California, 6 December 1836
4. Battle of Santa Clara, California, 2 Janaury 1847
5. Battle of San Gabriel, California, 8 January 1847
6. Battle of La Mesa, California, 9 January 1847
7. Capture of Vera Cruz, 9 March 1847
8. Second Tabasco Expedition, 14 June-21 July, 1847
9. Storming of Chapultepec Castle, 13 September 1847
10. Capture of Mazatlan, 11 November 1847
11. Capture of Guaymas, 17 November 1847
12. Battle of San Jose, California, 19 November 1847

Chapultepec is by far the more famous action in this war ("...the Halls of Montezuma ..."). However, the Marines were useful but not essential to the American victory there. The most notable feats of arms involving Marines during the war were the battles of San Gabriel and La Mesa, fought on successive days, during which a battalion of Marines supplemented some Army troops in defeating superior Mexican forces, and Guaymas, on Mexico's west coast, in which some 65 Marines and bluejackets landed from the USS *Dale* drove about 350 Mexican troops from the town.

The Ten Most Distinguished Marines in the War with Mexico

1. CPT Alvin Edson, who commanded a battalion of Marines in the landing at Vera Cruz and during the subsequent investment and capture of the city, 9-29 March 1847.
2. 1LT Archibald H.Gillespie, confidential agent of President Polk, who distinguished himself in numerous actions in California, being wounded at La Mesa on 9 January 1847.
3. 2LT Charles A. Henderson (son of CMC Archibald Henderson), who took part in the seizure of the San Cosme Gate, at Mexico City, being wounded in the process.
4. CPT John G. Reynolds, who assumed command of the Marines during the storming of Chapultepec, after Levi Twiggs was killed.
5. 2LT Jabez C. Rich, took part in the pursuit of Mexicans after the fall of Chapultepec Castle, and was one of the Marines who seized the San Cosme Gate.
6. 1LT John D. Simms, took part in the pursuit of the Mexicans after the capture of Chapultepec, and helped seize the San Cosme Gate.
7. CPT George H. Terrett, who pressed the pursuit of the Mexican forces retreating from Chapultepec.
8. MAJ Levi Twiggs, commanded the Marines who took part in the storming of Chapultepec Castle, until killed in action.
9. LTC Samuel E. Watson, who commanded the Marine battalion that reinforced MG Winfield Scott's army for its final assault on Mexico City, dying of natural causes shortly afterwards.
10. 1LT Jacob Zeilin, Jr., later CMC, commanded the Marines during the occupation of Santa Barbara, San Pedro, and Los Angeles, relieved the Mexican siege of Warren's Ranch, retook Los Angles after it was lost to Mexican forces, distinguished himself in the battles of San Gabriel and La Mesa, and, having been promoted to captain and brevet major, led the Marines and Bluejackets who captured Mazatlan.

The Civil War, 1861-1865

Marine Participation in the Civil War

Strength of the Corps

Total Marines in Service During the War	c.5,000
Wartime Peak Strength of the Marine Corps	c.3,800 (early 1865)

Casualties

Killed/Mortally Wounded in Action	148
Non-Combat Deaths	312
Wounded in Action	131
Prisoners-of-War	c.200
Total	c.791

Officers Present with the Marines at the Capture of John Brown at Harper's Ferry in 1859

1. LTC. Robert E. Lee, USA, later Gen., C.S., senior officer, in command.

2. 1LT. James B. Fry, USA, later Brig. Gen., C.S.
3. 1LT. Albion P. Howe, USA, later Brig. Gen., U.S.
4. 1LT. James E.B. Stuart, USA, volunteer *aide-de-camp* to Lee, and later became Lt. Gen., C.S.
5. Maj. W.W. Russell, USMC Paymaster, who went along for the excitement
6. 1LT. Israel Green, USMC, who actually commanded the Marines who stormed the engine house to capture John Brown, and later became a Confederate Marine.

Marine Casualties during the Storming of the Engine House at Harper's Ferry

1. PVT Luke Quinn, mortally wounded.
2. PVT Matthew Rupert, seriously wounded in the face.

The 12 Most Notable Civil War Actions Involving the USMC

1. Battle of Bull Run, 12 July 1861
2. Hatteras Inlet Landings, 28-30 August 1861
3. Capture of Wassaw Island, 5 December 1861
4. Battle of Hampton Roads (Sorties of CSS *Virginia* against the US squadron and the USS *Monitor*), 8- 9 March 1862
5. Capture of New Orleans, 24-29 April 1862
6. Farragut's Mississippi River Campaign against Vicksburg, 18 May-26 July 1862
7. Scuttling of the USS *Mississippi,* Port Hudson, Louisiana, 14 March 1863
8 Attempted storming of Fort Sumter, 6 September 1863
9. Red River Expedition, 10 March-2 May 1864
10. USS *Kearsarge* vs *Alabama*, off Cherbourg, France, 19 June 1864
11. Battle of Mobile Bay, 5 August 1864
12. Storming of Fort Fisher, 15 January 1865

Four Notable Civil War Marines

1. CPT Charles Heywood, later CMC, took part in the Hatteras Inlet expedition, fired the last shot from the USS *Cumberland* as she was sinking during the attack by the Confederate *Virginia (Merrimac)*, commanded the Marines aboard Farragut's flagship *Hartford* from late 1863 until the end of the war, leading the boarding party that seized the Confederate ram *Tennessee* during the Battle of Mobile Bay, and in the capture of several forts during the closing months of the war, earning a promotion to major and brevet lieutenant colonel by age 24.
2. CPT Charles G. McCawley, later CMC, took part in the capture of Fort Wagner and Morris Island, and in the attempt to storm Fort Sumter on 9 September 1863, ending the war as a brevet major.
3. CPL John F. Mackie, the first Marine to earn a Medal of Honor, for rallying the demoralized gunners of USS *Galena* at Drewry's Bluff.
4. MAJ John G. Reynolds, a seasoned veteran who commanded the Marines at Bull Run with some distinction and later on blockade duty and in raids on the Atlantic Coast.

Marine Corps Officer Loss at the Onset of the Civil War

Officers Available, 31 December 1860	48
Officers Deserting to the Confederacy	21 (43.8%)
Officers Resigning to Join the Volunteer Army	3 (6.2%)
Officers Resigning to Return to Civil Life	3 (6.2%)
Officers Remaining from the Prewar Corps	21 (43.8%)

Officers Who Left the Marine Corps to Join the Confederacy

Officer	D/R?	Wartime Activity
1. MAJ Henry B. Tyler *	D	LTC, CSMC
2. MAJ George Terrett	D	MAJ, CSMC
3. CPT Jabez C. Rich	D	CPT, CSMC; dismissed, October 1862.
4. CPT Algernon S. Taylor	D	MAJ & Quartermaster, CSMC
5. CPT Robert Tansill	D	CPT, CSMC; resigned, February 1862
6. CPT John D. Simms	D	CPT, CSMC
7. 1LT Israel Greene	D	MAJ & Adjutant, CSMC
8. 1LT John R.F. Tattnall	D	CPT, CSMC; later COL 29th Alabama
9. 1LT Andrew J. Hays	R	CPT, CSMC; later LTC, staff, PACS **
10. 1LT William W. Kirkland	R	BG, PACS **
11. 1LT George Holmes	R	CPT, CSMC
12. 1LT Adam N. Baker	D	1LT, CSMC; deserted, November 1861.
13. 1LT Henry B. Tyler, Jr.	D	1LT, CSMC; dismissed, December 1861
14. 1LT Julius E. Meiere	D	CPT, CSMC
15. 1LT George P. Turner	D	CPT, CSMC; dismissed, December 1862
16. 1LT Thomas S. Wilson	D	CPT, CSMC
17. 1LT Alexander W. Stark	D	Officer, Confederate Army
18. 1LT Jacob Read	R	CPT, CSMC; dismissed, February 1863
19. 2LT Calvin L. Sayre	R	CPT, CSMC
20. 2LT Henry L. Ingraham	R	1LT, CSMC; resigned, November 1861
21. 2LT Beckett K. Howell	R	CPT, CSMC

As a consequence of the secession of various slave states, 21 officers "abandoned the service in its hour of need," as CMC John Harris put it, amounting to 43.8% of the active officers in the Marine Corps. This was a higher proportional loss than that of either the Army or the Navy, both of which lost about a third of their officers through desertion to the Confederacy.

Key: Sen = Seniority among those leaving the Corps; *D/R?* = Dismissed or Resigned?—Before 1 May 1861 any officer who tendered his resignation had it accepted. After that date, unless the officer was resigning to accept a commission in the U.S. Volunteer Army, all offers of resignation were rejected and the officers in question were summarily dismissed from the service. Several officers who "went South" did so without offering a formal resignation, and were dismissed as deserters.

* The second ranking man in the Corps, as Adjutant and Inspector General.

** Provisional Army of the Confederate States.

Marine Officers Who Left the Corps to Join the Army During the Civil War

1. 2LT George W. Cummings became an officer in the 15th Ohio Volunteers.
2. 2LT Joel H. Rathbone became a captain in Regular Army's 12th Infantry.
3. 2LT David M. Sell became an officer in the 107th U.S. Colored Infantry, rising to colonel.

Officers Who Left the Marine Corps for Civil Life During the Civil War

1. 1LT S.H. Matthews
2. 1LT Charles A. Henderson *
3. 1LT Robert Kidd

* Son of the late CMC Archibald Henderson; retired for reasons of health in December 1861, died July 1865.

Brothers Who Served in Opposing Marine Corps During the Civil War

1. MAJ Philip R. Fendall, Jr, USMC, and his brother, 2LT James R.Y. Fendall, CSMC. Cousins of the Lees of Virginia, a third of the seven Fendall brothers served through the war as an officer in the U.S. Coast Survey.
2. 1LT Charles A. Henderson, USMC, and his brother, 1LT Richard H. Henderson, CSMC, sons of the late CMC Archibald Henderson; a third brother, Octavius C. Henderson, was a captain in the Confederate 1st Virginia Battalion.

Six Enlisted U.S. Marines Known to Have Joined the Confederacy

1. SGT ?? Myers, USMC, deserted from the Norfolk Navy Yard, April 1861, and was appointed a captain in the 6th Virginia.
2. PVT Julius F. Heilman, USMC, deserted from the Norfolk Navy Yard, April 1861, and was appointed a lieutenant in Virginia's Henrico Artillery.
3. PVT Joshua Charlesworth, USMC, deserted to become a SGT in the CSMC, from which he also deserted.
4. SGT Thomas Grogan, USMC, deserted to become 1SGT CSMC.
5. 1SGT Jacob S. Scholls, USMC, discharged from the USMC in 1856, joined the CSMC in 1861 and rose to 1SGT.
6. CPL William Toombs, USMC, deserted to join the Confederate Marines as Private in 1861.

In the great crisis of 1860-1861 enlisted men proved far more loyal to their oaths "to support and defend the Consitution of the United States" than did their officers. Only five of approximately 1,700 enlisted Marines deserted to the Confederacy, a record matched by the approximately 14,500 Army enlisted men, of whom only some dozens betrayed their oath.

The Confederate States Marine Corps

Year End Strength of the Confederate States Marine Corps, 1861-1865

Year	Officers	Enlisted	Total	EP/Officer
1861	29	325	354	11.2*
1862	27	535	562	10.8
1863	31	550	581	17.7
1864	40	575	615	14.4
1865	38	400	438	10.5**

* Includes two Army officers on temporary duty with the CSMC.

** As of April. The last detachment of Confederate Marines to surrender were three officers and 24 enlisted men, on 10 May 1865. However, a detail of about two dozen Marines were still serving in the cruiser *Shenandoah,* who were discharged along with the rest of the ship's company in England in November. A total of 58 men were commissioned in the CSMC during the Civil War, and approximately 1200 enlisted. Only one officer died on active service, of disease.

Seniority of Virginia Marine Corps Officers

1. CPT Aden N. Baker, former 1LT, USMC
2. CPT John C. Rich, former CPT, USMC
3. 1LT C. Miles Collier, formerly Lieut., USN
4. 1LT Ander Weir, late Lieut. , USN
5. 1LT J. Oty Bradford, late Passed Midshipman, USN

Virginia appears to have been the only Confederate state to have much success in forming a marine corps, doing so on 18 April 1861. On 8 June 1861 the corps was disbanded, most of the five officers and approximately 100 enlisted men being transferred to the CSMC, with the balance entering the Confederate Army or Navy.

One U.S. Marine Who Became a Confederate General

1. William Whedbee Kirkland, Lt., U.S.M.C., 1855-1860, resigned from the Corps in late 1860, was appointed a captain in the Confederate Army in 1861 and by August of 1863 had been promoted to brigadier general.

Three Confederate Marines Who Had Very Strange Military Careers

1. Henry B. Tyler, Jr.
   a. Dismissed as 1LT, USMC, 21 June 1861
   b. Dismissed as 1LT, CSMC, 10 December 1861

2. Edward C. Stockton
   a. Cadet, USNA, Annapolis, 1846-1850
   b. Passed Midshipman (i.e., junior ensign), USN, 1850-1852, dismissed, for "conduct unbecoming an officer"
   c. Lieutenant in the South Carolina State Navy, April-May 1861
   d. Second Lieutenant, CSMC, May-September 1861, dismissed
   e. Captain, 21st South Carolina, January-April, 1862
   f. Lieutenant, Confederate States Navy, April 1862 onwards
3. Jabez C. Rich
   a. Second Lieutenant, USMC, June 1834
   b. First Lieutenant, USMC, February 1839:
      i. Sentenced to be dismissed from the Corps for "conduct unbecoming an officer," July 1848, but was reprieved by the CMC
      ii. Scheduled to be "riffed," March 1849, but was reprieved by Act of Congress.
   c. Captain, USMC, November 1853
      i. Sentenced to dismissal by court martial, 1856, but was reprieved by the President
      ii. Deserted to the Confederacy, April 1861, and was dismissed from the USMC, May 1861
   d. Captain, Virginia Marine Corps, May 1861, but was shortly afterwards dismissed
   e. Captain, CSMC, October 1861, until he deserted to the Union, in October 1862.

Notable Actions in Which Confederate Marines Took Part

1. Defense of Ship Island, 9 July 1861
2. Battle of Hampton Roads (sorties of the CSS *Virginia* against the U.S. squadron and the USS *Monitor*), 8-9 March 1862
3. Defense of Drewry's Bluff, Virginia, 15 May 1862
4. Cutting out of the USS *Underwriter*, New Bern, North Carolina, 2 February 1864.
5. Defense of Drewry's Bluff, Virginia, 12-16 May 1864
6. Battle of Mobile Bay, 5 August 1864
7. Defense of Fort Fisher, North Carolina, 24-27 December 1864 and 6-15 Janaury 1865,
8. Battle of Sayler's Creek, Virginia, 6 April 1865

The Only Occasions on Which the USMC and the CSMC Fought Each Other

1. Battle of Drewry's Bluff, Virginia, 15 May 1862
2. USS *Kearsarge* vs CSS *Alabama*, off Cherbourg, France, 19 June 1864
3. Battle of Mobile Bay, 5 August 1864

The U.S. Army's Marines

In order to provide a landing force to support the Union river flotilla on the Mississippi, the U.S. Army formed the Mississippi Marine Brigade in mid-1862. The brigade (which should properly have been called the "Mississippi Riverine Brigade"), comprised:

1st Battalion Mississippi Marine Brigade Infantry

1st Mississippi Marine Brigade Light Artillery Battery
1st Battalion Mississippi Marine Brigade Cavalry *

* Appropriately enough, the "horse marines" were raised in Missouri.

The War with Spain, 1898

Marine Participation in the War with Spain, 1898

Strength of the Corps

Total Marines in Service During the War	c.4,200
Wartime Peak Strength of the Marine Corps	c.4,200 (August 1898)
Forces Committed to Action	c.1,000

Casualties

Killed/Mortally Wounded in Action	7
Non-Combat Deaths	??
Wounded in Action	20
Prisoners-of-War	0
Total	at least 27 *

* Figures omit the 28 Marines killed when the USS *Maine* blew up on 14 February 1898.

The Dozen Most Important Operations Involving Marines During the War with Spain

1. Battle of Manila Bay, 1 May 1898
2. Capture of Cavite, 3 May 1898
3. Cable Cutting Expedition, Cienfuegos, Cuba, 11 May 1898 (12 Medals of Honor awarded)
4. Occupation and Defense of Guantanamo Bay, 10-14 June 1898
5. Battle of Cuzco Well, 14 June 1898
6. Fisher's Point Raid, Cuba, 11 June 1898
7. Caimanera Raid, 15 June 1898
8. Manzanillo Raid, 30 June-1 July 1898
9. Naval Battle of Santiago, 3 July 1898
10. Capture of Guanica, Puerto Rico, 25 July 1898
11. Capture of Ponce, Puerto Rico, 27 July 1898
12. Raid on Cape San Juan, Puerto Rico, 9 August 1898

The Two Most Distinguished Marines of the War with Spain

1. LTC Robert W. Huntington, who commanded the Marine Battalion at Guantanamo Bay.
2. SGT John H. Quick, who earned a Medal of Honor by repeatedly exposing himself to hostile fire to prevent the USS *Dolphin* from shelling Marine positions during the Battle of Cuzco Well.

## CHAPTER 6

"Send in the Marines!"

1898-1940
Expeditionary Service in the Early Twentieth Century

From the end of the war with Spain to the eve of the Second World War the primary duty of the Marine Corps was as a colonial fire brigade, securing American interests in the Caribbean and in Asia, while undertaking what were the biggest operations in its history to that time, in France during World War I. During this same period, forward thinkers in the Marine Corps developed new technologies which would serve the Corps well in a greater war to come, notably close air support and amphibious operations.

The Philippine Insurrection
1899-1902

Marine Participation in the Philippine War

Strength of the Corps

Total Marines in Service During the War	c.10,500
Wartime Peak Strength of the Marine Corps	c.6,000 (early 1902)
Forces Committed to Action	c.2,600

Casualties*

Killed/Mortally Wounded in Action	c.50
Non-Combat Deaths	300
Wounded in Action	?
Prisoners-of-War	0
Total	350

* Estimated

The Four Most Important Marine Actions of the Philippine War

1. Battle of Novaleta, 8 October 1899
2. Battle of the Sohoton River, 5 November 1901
3. Storming of the Sohoton Cliffs, 15 November 1902
4. The March Across Samar, 8 December 1901-17 January 1902

The Five Most Distinguished Marines of the Philippine War

1. LTC George F. Elliot, who commanded the 1st Marine Brigade in the Philippines.
2. MAJ Littleton W.L. Waller, who commanded the march across Samar.
3. GySGT John Henry Quick, who took part in the march across Samar.
4. CPT David Dixon Porter, who fought at Novaleta (Brevet Medal #2), Sohoton Cliffs (Medal of Honor #84), and marched across Samar.
5. CPT Hiram I. Bearss, who fought at the Sohoton Cliffs (Medal of Honor #83) and was on the march across Samar.

The Boxer Rebellion
("The China Relief Expedition")

Marine Participation in the China Relief Expedition, 1900-1901

Strength of the Corps	
Total Marines in Service During the War	c.5,500
Wartime Peak Strength of the Marine Corps	c.5,500
Forces Committed to Action	c.2,000
Casualties	
Killed/Mortally Wounded in Action	9
Non-Combat Deaths	??
Wounded in Action	17
Prisoners-of-War	0
Total	at least 26

The Nine Principal Marine Actions of the Boxer Rebellion

1. Capture of the Taku Forts, 17 June 1900
2. Battle of Tang T'su (First Relief Expedition), 20-21 June 1900
3. Defense of the Peking Legations, 20 June-14 August 1900
4. Battle of the Eastern Arsenal, Tientsin, 19 June 1900
5. First Battle of Tientsin, 24 June 1900

6. Battle of the Imperial Arsenal, Tientsin, 9 July 1900
7. Second Battle of Tientsin, 13-14 July 1900
8. Battle of Yang T'sun, 5-6 August 1900
9. Battle of Peking, 13-19 August 1900

The Five Most Distinguished Marines of the Boxer Rebellion

1. MAJ William P. Biddle, who commanded the 1st Marines in the Second Relief Expedition.
2. 2LT Smedley D. Butler, who earned a brevet promotion, plus nominations for the Medal of Honor and Victoria Cross, at Tientsin, 13 July 1900.
3. PVT Daniel Daly, who earned his first Medal of Honor helping to defend the Peking Legations.
4. CPT John Twiggs Myers, who commanded the Marines guarding the Peking Legations, during which he was wounded.
5. MAJ Littleton W.T. Waller, who commanded the Marines in the First Relief Expedition, 10-26 June 1900, and a battalion in the Second Relief Expedition.

Six Marine Corps that Took Part in the China Relief Expedition

1. French *Fusiliers marins*
2. Imperial German Marines
3. Imperial-and-Royal Austro-Hungarian Marines
4. Royal Marines
5. Russian Naval Infantry
6. U.S. Marines

Marines in World War I, 1917-1919

Marine Participation in The Great War

Strength of the Corps

Total Marines in Service During the War	c.78,800	
Wartime Peak Strength of the Marine Corps	c.60,000	(mid-1918)
Forces Committed in Europe	c.30,000	

Casualties

Killed/Mortally Wounded in Action	2,461
Non-Combat Deaths	9,520
Wounded in Action	390
Prisoners-of-War	25
Total	c.12,386*

* Includes Marine aviation casualties, 47, of whom 3 were combat deaths.

Service of Marine Units in Europe, 1917-1919

Organization	Activities
4th Marine Brigade (2nd Division)	
5th Marines	Front line duties
6th Marines	Front line duties
6th Machinegun Battalion	Front line duties
5th Marine Brigade (Independent)	
11th Marines	Security and training assignments
13th Marines	Security and training assignments
5th Machinegun Battalion	Disembarking at the Armistice
10th Marines (Artillery)	Security assignments
1st Marine Aero Company	ASW patrol from the Azores
1st Marine Aviation Force	Bomber missions in Belgium

The 5th Marines had the longest service in Europe, arriving as part of the Army's 1st Division on 26 June 1917. The 4th Marine Brigade was not completed until late 1917, with the arrival of the 6th Marine Machine Gun Battalion, and served thereafter in the 2nd Division. The other Marine units arrived in France from 25 September through 9 November 1918. The 5th Marine Brigade never saw action, and in fact never served together. A proposal to organize a Marine Division from the 4th and 5th Marine Brigades and the 10th Marines was scotched by GEN John J. Pershing, as it would have meant breaking up the 2nd Division, which was probably his best. In any case, the Army would have had to supply most of the artillery and other supporting arms and services for the proposed division. The 1st Marine Aviation Force comprised four squadrons, and operated under Allied control from mid-1918. The 1st Marine Aviation Company arrived in the Azores in January of 1918.

Senior Marine Commanders in France, 1917-1919

That MG John A. Lejeune commanded the AEF's 2nd Division during World War I is rather common knowledge. It is less well known that several other Marine officers commanded major units of the Army as well, either in a permanent or an acting capacity. Some of the more notable were:

Division Commanders

2nd Division

BG Charles A. Doyen, USMC acting	c.30 October-11 November 1917 *
BG John A. Lejeune, USMC, acting	26-27 July 1918
permanent	28 July-3 August 1919 **
BG W.C. Neville, USMC, acting	17-22 June 1919

41st Division ***

BG Elik Cole, USMC	29 October-27 December 1918

* Thus Doyen, not Lejeune, was the first Marine to command a division, albeit not in combat.

** Lejeune was promoted to MG 1 August 1918

*** This unit had become the 1st Depot Division, a replacement training command, and saw no combat.

Brigade Commanders

2nd Infantry Brigade, 1st Division

COL Charles A. Dyer, USMC, acting		22 July- 9 August 1917
	acting	14-19 August 1917
	acting	26-29 August 1917

4th Marine Brigade, 2nd Division

1. BG Charles A. Dyer, USMC   23 October 1917-7 May 1918
   LTC Hiram Bearss, USMC, acting   9 November 1918-8 December 1917
   1COL W.C. Neville, USMC, acting   9-11 April 1918
2. BG Charles A. Doyen, USMC   23 October 1917-7 May 1918
   BG James G. Harbord, USA   7 May-15 July 1918
   LTC Harry Lee, USMC, acting   15-17 July 1918
   COL W.C. Neville, USMC, acting   17-26 July 1918
3. BG John A. Lejeune, USMC   26-28 July 1918
4. COL/BG W.C. Neville, USMC   28 July 1918-3 August 1919
   COL Logan Freland, USMC, acting   2-14 March 1919
   COL Harry Lee, USMC, acting   11 May 1919-16 June 1919
   COL Harold C. Snyder, USMC, acting   17-22 June 1919
   COL Harry Lee, USMC, acting   12-23 July 1919

8th Infantry Brigade, 4th Division

   COL Frederick M. Wise, USMC, acting 15-25 January 1919

51st Infantry Brigade, 26th Infantry Division *

   COL Hiram I. Bearss, USMC, acting   15-25 October 1918
                 acting   9-24 November 1918

* During the Meuse-Argonne Offensive

The Ten Principal Actions of the 4th Marine Brigade During World War I

1. Defensive Operations, Toulon Sector, Verdun Front, 15 March-13 May 1918
2. Aisne Defensive, 31 May-5 June 1918
3. Battle of Belleau Wood, 6 June-9 July 1918
4. Soissons Offensive, 18-20 July 1918
5. Morheche Sector, 9-16 August 1918
6. St. Mihiel Offensive, 12-16 September 1918
7. Battle for Blanc Mont, 2-6 October 1918
8. Capture of St. Etienne, 6-8 October 1918
9. Breaching of the Kriemhulde-Freya Lines, 1-2 November 1918
10. Crossing of the Meuse, 2-11 November 1918

The Soissons Offensive was part of the French Aisne-Marne Counteroffensive. Mont Blanc, St. Etienne, the breaching of the Kriemhulde and Freya Lines (which involved the combats of Landreville, Bayonville, the Barricourt Heights), and the approach to and crossing of the Meuse were integral parts of the American Meuse-Argonne Offensive.

The Nine Most Distinguished Marines of the First World War

1. COL Hiram I. Bearss, who at various times commanded the 3rd Battalion, 9th Infantry, the 9th Infantry, and the 102nd Infantry, U.S. Army, as well as serving as serving as acting commander of the 51st Infantry Brigade and the 4th Marine Brigade, all in combat, earning a Distinguished Service Cross before being permanently disabled.
2. 1LT Clifton B. Cates, who led the capture of Bouresches, on the first day at Belleau Wood, and held it against enemy counterattacks, and later at Soissons held a forward position against heavy German counterattacks with fewer than two dozen men.
3. SGM Daniel Daly, who said "Come on, you sons of bitches—do you want to live forever?"
4. COL Robert H. Dunlap, who served on GEN Pershing's staff in the early months of the war, helping to plan the AEF, and Marine participation in it, and later went on to command the Army's 17th Field Artillery in the Meuse-Argonne, earning a Navy Cross in the process.
5. MAJ Thomas Holcomb, who commanded the 2nd Battalion, 6th Marines.
6. MG John A. Lejeume, who rose to command the 2nd Division.
7. COL Wendell C. Neville, who commanded the 5th Marines at Belleau Wood, and the 4th Marine Brigade, from Soissons to the end of the war.
8. SGM John H Quick, who fought in every action of the 6th Marines, and added a Navy Cross and Distinguished Service Cross to his Medal of Honor.
9. LTC Frederick M. Wise, commanded the 2nd Battalion, 5th Marines at Belleau Wood, and later the Army's 59th Infantry at St. Mihiel and in the Meuse-Argonne.

The Five German Divisions Against Which the 4th Marine Brigade Fought in Belleau Wood

1. 5th Guards Division
2. 28th Division
3. 87th Division
4. 197th Division
5. 237th Reserve Division

These divisions formed part of the German IV Reserve Corps, also known as *Group Conta*, from its commanding officer, General der Infanterie von Conta. The 237th Reserve Division and the 197th Division were in the front lines at the beginning of the battle for Belleau Wood. The 87th and 28th Divisions relieved these two divisions in the course of the fighting. The 5th Guards Division was brought in as a counterattack force.

Marine Units Winning the French *Fourragere* During World War I

1. 5th Marine Regiment
2. 6th Marine Regiment
3. 6th Marine Machinegun Battalion

The *Fourragere* is a braided rope in the colors of the *Croix de guerre,* green and scarlet, granted to units that have been thrice collectively awarded the *Croix de guerre*. Worn looped over the right shoulder, they are derisively nicknamed "pogey ropes" by those Marines belonging to regiments who do not have this honor.

One U.S. Marine World War I Combat Action Against the Germans Not on the Western Front

1. SMS *Kormoran*, Agaña Harbor, Guam, 7 April 1917

Closely pursued by elements of the Imperial Japanese Navy, SMS *Kormoran*, a German armed merchant raider operating in the Pacific, had interned herself at Agaña in late 1914. Her presence lent some excitement to the social life of the sleepy town. On 7 April 1917, when the U.S. declared war on Germany, the governor ordered the ship seized. By chance a cutter from the vessel was at dockside when word of the impending seizure spread. The cutter cast off from the dock, to bring word to the ship. A detail of Marines at dockside was ordered to fire on the cutter, and one German seaman was struck. The survivors made it to *Kormoran*, whose skipper shortly blew the vessel up, even as several boatloads of bluejackets and Marines were closing in on her. A number of the crew were killed and the rest sent to a P/W camp in the U.S.

The "Banana" Wars

Marine Casualties in the Principal Twentieth Century Expeditions in the Caribbean

Country	Years	KIA/MW	WIA	Died	Total
Dominican Republic	1916-1922	17	50	66	133
	1965	9	25	0	34
Grenada	1983	3	15	0	18
Haiti	1915-1934	10	26	136	172
Mexico	1914	5	13	??	18?
Nicaragua	1912-13	5	16	16	21
	1927-1933	47	66	89	202
Panama	1989	2	3	0	5

Twenty-one operations that resulted in no reported casualties have been omitted.

Key: *KIA/MW*, killed in action or mortally wounded; *WIA*, wounded in action; *Died*, deaths from all other causes; *Total*, summary of all casualties.

The Thirteen Most Notable Actions of the "Banana Wars"

1. Battle of El Cuero, Cuba, 9 June 1912
2. Storming of Coyotepe, Nicaragua, 3-4 October 1912
3. Capture of Vera Cruz, 20-21 April 1914
4. Battle of Fort Dipitie, Haiti, 24-25 October 1915
5. Battle of Fort Riviere, Haiti, 17 November 1915
6. Battle of Guayacanas, Dominican Republic, 2-3 July 1916
7. Battle of San Francisco de Macoris, Dominican Republic, 29 November 1916

8. Battle of Port-au-Prince, Haiti, 7 October 1919
9. Battle of Port-au-Prince, Haiti, 14 January 1920
10. Battle of La Paz Centro, 16 May 1927
11. Battle of Ocotal, Nicaragua, 16 July 1927
12. Defense of Quilali, Nicaragua, 30 December 1927-8 Jane 1928
13. Railway Battle, El Sauce, Nicaragua, 26 December 1932

The Dozen Most Distinguished Marines of the "Banana Wars"

1. MAJ Smedley D. Butler, who won his second Medal of Honor in Haiti, and also served in Panama, the Dominican Republic, and Nicaragua
2. 1LT Louis Cukela, who served in the Dominican Republic and Haiti
3. GySGT Daniel Daly, who won his second Medal of Honor in Haiti
4. COL Robert H. Dunlap, who commanded the 11th Marines in Nicaragua
5. CPT Merritt A. Edson, who played an important role in the Sandino War in Nicaragua
6. SGT Herman H. Hanneken, who killed *Caco* leader Charlemagne Peralte, at Grand Riviere, Haiti, 31 Oct 1919
7. BG Harry Lee, Commander, 2nd Marine Brigade, the Dominican Republic, 1922-1924
8. SGT William A. Lee, who won the Navy Cross three times in Nicaragua
9. COL Douglas C. McDougal, who commanded, at various times, both the *Gendarmerie d'Haiti* and the *Guardia Nacional de Nicaragua*
10. 1LT Lewis "Chesty" Puller, who served in Haiti, and went on to win two Navy Crosses in Nicaragua
11. 1LT Alexander A. Vandegrift, who served with distinction in Haiti and Nicaragua
12. SGT Faustin E. Wirkus, the "White King" of Gonave, Haiti, 1925-1929

The Seven Most Capable Enemy Commanders of the "Banana Wars"

1. GEN. Benjamin Zeledon, Nicaragua, 1912
2. GEN. Victoriano Huerta, Mexico, 1914
3. Charlemagne Peralte, Haiti, 1915-1919
4. GEN. Ramon Natera, Dominican Republic, 1917-1922
5. Benoit Batraville, Haiti, 1919-1920
6. GEN. Augusto Cesar Sandino, Nicaragua, 1926-1933
7. GEN. Manuel Jiron, Nicaragua, 1926-1928

Three Constabulary Forces Trained by the USMC in the Caribbean and Central America

1. *Gendarmerie d'Haiti,* began forming in late 1915, and was formally activated in 1916; renamed the *Garde d' Haiti* in 1928.
2. *Guardia Nacional Dominicana,* formed in 1917, renamed the *Policia Nacional Dominicana* in 1922.
3. *Guardia Nacional de Nicaragua,* formed 1927.

Thirteen Occasions on Which the Marines Have Intervened in Nicaragua

1. San Juan del Sur (Greytown), 1852, assistance in fire fighting
2. San Juan del Sur (Greytown), 11-13 March 1853, arrest of filibustering expedition
3. San Juan del Sur (Greytown), 12-15 July 1854, protection of American life and property
4. Punta Arenas, 8 December 1857, arrest of the filibuster William Walker
5. Bluefields, 6 July-7 August 1894, restoration of order
6. Corinto, 2-4 May 1896, protection of American life and property
7. Bluefields, 7-8 February 1898, protection of American life and property
8. San Juan del Sur (Greytown), 24-28 February 1898, protection of American life and property
9. Corinto, 22 February 1910, protection of American life and property
10. Bluefields, 19 May-4 September, restoration of order
11. Various points, 17 August 1912-9 June 1913, restoration of order
12. Various points, 25 January-11 February 1922, restoration of order
13. Nationwide, 7 May 1922-8 January 1933, restoration of order

Thirteen Occasions on Which the Marines Have Intervened in Panama

1. 20 September 1856, to protect the isthmian railroad
2. 27 July-8 October 1860, to prevent secession from Colombia
3. 7-12 May 1873, to protect the isthmian railroad
4. 23 September-9 October 1873, to protect the isthmian railroad
5. 18-19 January 1885, to protect the isthmian railroad
6. 16-25 May 1885, to protect the isthmian railroad
7. 8-9 March 1895, to prevent secession from Colombia
8. 24 November-4 December 1901, to prevent secession from Colombia
9. 16-22 April 1902, to prevent secession from Colombia
10. 17 September-18 November 1902, to prevent secession from Colombia
11. 3 November 1903-1 June 1914, to support secession from Colombia
12. 30 August-15 September 1921, to prevent a border war between Panama and Costa Rica
13. 20-28 December 1989, to arrest Manuel Noriega

Three Notable Firsts of the "Banana Wars"

1. First employment of a Marine artillery battalion, Vera Cruz, 1914.
2. First use of dive bombing in support of ground forces, Ocotal, Nicaragua, 16 July 1927.
3. First successful "medevac" flights from a besieged garrison. Quilali, Nicaragua, 1-8 January 1928.

The "China Marines," 1911-1941

Seven "China Marines" Who Became Commandants of the Marine Corps

1. Alexander A. Vandegrift, the 18th Commandant
2. Clifton B. Cates, the 19th Commandant
3. Lemuel C. Shepherd, Jr., the 20th Commandant
4. Randolph McC. Pate, the 21st Commandant
5. David M. Shoup, the 22nd Commandant
6. Wallace M. Greene, Jr., the 23rd Commandant
7. Robert E. Cushman, Jr., the 25th Commandant

Some Other Notable Marines Who Served in China, 1911-1941 *

1. Smedley D. Butler, who commanded the 3rd Marine Brigade, 1927-1929.
2. Evans Carlson, the Marine Raider, who eventually became a brigadier general, served three tours in China, his last during the late 1930s, when he spent some four months as an observer with the Communist Chinese Eighth Route Army during the Sino-Japanese War.
3. Merritt A. Edson, the Marine Raider, who eventual rose to brigadier general, served in China on several occasions, most notably in the mid-1930s.
4. Samuel I. Howard, who was forced to surrender the 4th Marines at Corregidor, had commanded them in Shanghai for some time prior to the outbreak of the Pacific War.
5. William A. Lee, holder of three Navy Crosses, served in China in the late 1930s, and was captured there with the other legation guards at the outbreak of World War II.
6. Michael J. Mansfield, who later was a U.S. Senator from Montana, served as a private in China in the early 1920s.
7. Lewis "Chesty" Puller, served several tours in China, and actually commanded the "Horse Marines" of the Peking Legation Guard in 1933.
8. William H. Rupertius, who commanded the 1st Marine Division at Peleliu, did several tours in China.

* Actually, just about anyone who served more than one enlistment in the Marine Corps between the World Wars was likely to have served in China at some time, particularly in the late 1920s, when about a quarter of the Corps was at Shanghai.

Marine Units Serving in China, 1911-1941

Peking Legation Guard Battalion, 1911-1941
4th Marines, 1927-1941
6th Marines, 1927-1929
10th Marines, 1927-1928

114

12th Marines, 1927-1928
5th Engineer Company, 1927- 1929
Provisional Military Police Company, 1927-1928
Light Tank Platoon, 1927-1929
VF-3M, 1927-1928
VF-6M, 1928
VO-1M, 1928

The Legation Guard aside, these forces formed the 3rd Marine Brigade, 1927-1929, under BG Smedley D. Butler. The 10th Marines, an artillery regiment, comprised only one battalion. This listing, of course, omits the services in northern China of the 1st Marine Division, 1945-1949, and the 6th Marine Division, 1945-1947.

The Marines and the Development of Amphibious Doctrine 1900-1941

Ten Marines Who Played Essential Roles in the Development of Amphibious Doctrine

1. COL Charles D. Barrett, who headed the board that prepared *Tentative Manual for Landing Operations*, in 1934, which became *Fleet Training Publication 167*, the first official handbook on amphibious warfare.
2. BG Randolph C. Berkeley, who used the Marine Corps Schools, at Quantico, to prepare the first experimental manuals for landing operations, 1931-1933.
3. MG William P. Biddle, the 11th Commandant, who created the "Advanced Base Force" in 1911.
4. LTC Earl "Pete" Ellis, who promulgated the idea that the primary mission of the Marine Corps in a Pacific War would be the seizure of advanced bases, and wrote *Advanced Base Operations in Micronesia*, in 1921, outlining the basic requirements for an offensive in the Central Pacific.
5. BG Roy S. Geiger, who worked on developing close air support for the Fleet Marine Force.
6. CPT Victor H. Krulak, who played an important role in the adoption of the LCVP and the LTV landing vehicles.
7. CMC John A. Lejeune, who saw to it that Ellis' views were adopted as *OpPlan 712*, and began a series of amphibious exercises to develop and refine doctrine.
8. MG Holland M. Smith, the "Father of Amphibious Warfare," who began putting theory into practice, and by June of 1941 was conducting multi-divisional exercises, while training several divisions in amphibious techniques.
9. MG John H. Russell, who pressed for the establishment of the "Fleet Marine Force" in 1933, a permanent standing expeditionary force prepared to effect landings in support of naval operations.
10. MAJ Dion Williams, who began advocating that amphibious operations ("Advanced Base" operations in the terminology of the times) was an essential Marine Corps mission as early as 1902, and who by the mid-1920s was orchestrating landing exercises in the Caribbean.

Two Important Amphibious Landings that the USMC Failed to Study before World War II

1. The German landings on Oesel and Dago Islands, the Baltic Sea, Russia, October 1917.
2. The Spanish landings at Alhucemas Bay, Morocco, 8-9 September 1925.

One of the principal activities of the Marine Corps between the two world wars was the development of the technique of amphibious landings against opposition. Although the officers who developed the technique paid careful attention to a number of amphibious operations, notably the American landings at Vera Cruz in 1847 and 1914, Japanese landings in Korea in 1904, and particularly the disastrous Anglo-French Gallipoli Operation of 1915, as well as the various Japanese operations against the Chinese in the 1930s, not to mention experience gained from maneuvers and exercises, they seem to have totally ignored two of the most notable landings of the first quarter of the twentieth century.

Although hastily organized and admittedly conducted against light resistance, the German landings on Oesel and several adjacent islands proved enormously successful, helping to hasten the final collapse of Russia. The Spanish landings at Alhucemas Bay were meticulously planned by the Spanish Army in cooperation with the *Infanteria de Marina*, and the Spanish Navy. The operation included attention to such details as combat loading and the provision of specialized equipment. There was a carefully orchestrated naval bombardment, and surprisingly effective close air support. The operation broke the back of the Rif Rebellion, which had been dragging on for more than a decade at enormous cost in blood and treasure. Interestingly, perhaps because the Alhucemas Landings had been witnessed by a number of British officers, it was studied by the planners for the Normandy invasion.

Two Civilians Critical to the Development of Amphibious Warfare

1. Andrew J. Higgins, noted boat designer, who designed some of the first landing craft, including the prototype LCVP.
2. Donald Roebling, Jr., of the Brooklyn Bridge family, who designed the amphibious tractor, or LVT.

Civil War Battles "Reenacted" by BG Smedley D. Butler and the Marine Corps in the 1920s

1. Battle of the Wilderness, 1921
2. Battle of Gettysburg, 1922
3. Battle of New Market, 1923
4. Battle of Antietam, 1924

These "reenactments" were large scale affairs (that at Gettysburg included the 4th Marine Brigade, composed of the 5th and 6th Marines, plus a battalion of the 10th Marines for artillery support) attended by literally tens of thousands of onlookers. Historical verisimilitude was not particularly good. At "Gettysburg" Marine aircraft gave a demonstration of air combat, accompanied by an attack that included tanks and mortars, while at the "Wilderness" the Marines conducted an "amphibious assault" across the Rappahannock River. These ahistorical elements were critical to the primary purpose of the "reenactments," to gain a favorable press for the Marine Corps.

## CHAPTER 7

World War II, 1941-1945 The Golden Age of Amphibious Warfare

The Second World War was the most heroic era in the history of the Marine Corps, from the spirited defense of Wake Island to the "uncommon valor" of Iwo Jima and Okinawa. It was an era that made the Marines the definitive masters of amphibious warfare, an art at which they remain so skilled that the mere threat of its employment can tie down numbers of hostile forces.

Marine Participation in World War II

Strength of the Corps

Total Marines in Service During the War	669,100
Wartime Peak Strength of the Marine Corps	485,113 (Aug 1945)

Casualties

Killed/Mortally Wounded in Action	19,733
Non-Combat Deaths	4,778
Wounded in Action	67,207
Prisoners-of-War	2,278
Total	93,996

The August 1945 figure of 485,113 was the greatest number of Marines serving in uniform at the same time. With the exception of the approximately 18,000 women in the Corps, virtually every Marine saw overseas service during the war. Indeed, about 98% of the officers and 89% of enlisted persons served in the Pacific Theater. Apparently only 348 Marines became prisoners of war in the normal course of operations, including four taken by the Germans in France in 1944 and four by the French at Oran in November 1942. The balance of the men who fell prisoner did so as a result of formal surrenders to the Japanese at Chingwangtao and Tientsin, in China, and at Guam and Wake Island, in December 1941, and in the Philippines in April and May 1942. Only 1,756 of the 2,270 Marines captured by the Japanese were still alive at the end of the war. Of the 514 Marines who died while P/Ws, at least 184 were killed by the actions of American forces. Despite a number of attempts, apparently only nine Marines succeeded in escaping from Japanese P/W camps. A number of others escaped, but were shortly recaptured or killed in the attempt.

Marine Divisional Casualties in World War II

Division	Combat Deaths	All Other Casualties	Total	Ratio
1st	5,435	13,849	19,284	2.5
2nd	2,729	8,753	11,482	3.2
3rd	1,932	6,744	8,676	3.5
4th	3,317	13,006	16,323	3.9
5th	2,113	6,450	8,563	3.1
6th	1,637	6,590	8,227	4.0

Key: Combat Deaths, number killed in action or died of wounds; *All Other Casualties* includes wounded, as well as deaths from disease and accidents; *Total,* Combat Deaths and Other Losses combined. *Ratio,* the number of Other Casualties for each Combat Death. In general, the lower this figure the more intense the combat was likely to have been.

Six Divisions Trained in Amphibious Warfare by Holland M. Smith

1. 1stMarine Division, which not only made several amphibious landings of its own but with the
2. 2ndMarine Division, which had a distinguished record as well, went on to parent four more Marine Divisions.
3. 1stInfantry Division, which landed in North Africa, Sicily, and Normandy.
4. 3rd Infantry Division, which landed in North Africa, Sicily, and at Anzio.
5. 7thInfantry Division, which landed on Attu, Kiska, Kwajelein, Leyte, and Okinawa.
6. 9thInfantry Division, which landed in North Africa, Sicily, and Normandy.

Commissioning Background of USMC Generals in World War II

Commissioned from	Number	Notes
Annapolis	11	
Army Enlisted Service	4	A
Citadel	6	B
Civil Life	49	
Coast Guard Academy	1	C
Marine Corps Enlisted Service	12	
National Guard Enlisted Service	5	D
Naval Militia Service	1	
Norwich University	2	E
Pennsylvania Military College	1	
Texas A&M	2	
VMI	5	

Most Marine generals in World War II secured their commissions through direct appointment from civilian life. These were usually college men commissioned during World War I, often after a stint at one of the "Plattsburgh Plan" camps. The second most common source was men who had attended a military academy or college. Total exceeds the actual number on active duty during the war (96) due to double counting of three officers, as indicated in the Notes.

A. Includes one who later graduated from the Citadel.

B. Includes one who had served as an enlisted man in the Army.

C. Includes one with prior enlisted service in the National Guard.

D. Includes one who later graduated from the Revenue Service School (now the Coast Guard Academy), and one who later graduated from Norwich University.

E. Includes one with prior enlisted service in the National Guard.

Birthplaces of Marine Generals in World War II

States and Territories of the United States

Alabama	1	Missouri	3
California	5	Nebraska	2
Connecticut	1	New Jersey	3
Delaware	2	New York	5
D.C	4	Ohio	4
Florida	1	Oklahoma	1
Georgia	1	Pennsylvania	3
Idaho	1	Puerto Rico	1
Illinois	2	South Carolina	8
Indiana	3	Tennessee	1
Iowa	4	Texas	4
Kansas	2	Utah	1
Kentucky	2	Vermont	2
Louisiana	3	Virginia	7
Maryland	4	Washington	3
Massachusetts	5		
Michigan	1	**Foreign Countries**	
Minnesota	2	Germany	1
		Japan	1

Nine World War II Marine Generals with Prior Service in the Army

1. Thomas E. Bourke (1896-1978) enlisted in the Army in 1916, was commissioned in the Marine Corps in 1917. He was promoted to BG in 1943, MG in 1994, commanded the 5th Marine Division 1945-1946, and retired with the rank of LTG in 1946.

2. William O. Brice (1898-1972) served in the Army 1918-1919, graduated from The Citadel in 1921, and was commissioned in the Marine Corps. A BG in January 1945, by which time he was XO in the Division of Plans and Policies, HQ, USMC, Brice retired from the Marines in 1956 as a full general.

3. Graves B. Erkine (1897-1973) enlisted in the Louisiana National Guard shortly before World War I. Commissioned in the Marine Corps in 1917, he was promoted to brigadier general in 1943, major general in 1944, commanded the 4th Marine Division on Iwo Jima, and retired as a full general in 1953.

4. Walter G. Farrell (1897-1990) enlisted in the Illinois National Guard in 1916, entered the Marine Corps Reserve in 1917, and was commissioned that same year. A brigadier general in 1943, he ended the war as commander of the 3rd Marine Air Wing, and retired as a major general in 1946.

5. Franklin A. Hart (1894-1967) served in the Georgia National Guard 1915-1917. Commissioned in the Marine Corps in 1917, he reached brigadier general in 1944, and served as assistant division commander, 4th Marine Division, 1944-1945. He retired as a full general in 1954.

6. Ralph S. Keyser (1883-1955) served as an enlisted man in the Army 1902-1905, and was then commissioned in the Marines. He retired in 1937 as a brigadier general, but was recalled to duty in 1941. Serving as assistant to the CMC, he retired for the second time in 1942 as a major general.

7. Edward A. Osterman (1882-1969) served as an enlisted man in the army 1899-1902 and again 1904-1905. Commissioned in the Marines in 1907. A brigadier general in 1939, he served as Adjutant and Inspector General, USMC, until he retired as a major general in 1943. He was Marine Medal of Honor Winner # 94.

8. William H. Rupertius (1889-1945) served as an enlisted man in the District of Columbia National Guard 1907-1910. He then attended the Revenue Cutter Service School (now the USCG Academy), and was commissioned in the Marine Corps upon graduation in 1913. A brigadier general in 1942, he was promoted to major general in mid-1943, commanded the 1st Marine Division on Peleliu, and died of natural causes while on active duty in 1945.

9. Seth Williams (1880-1963) served in the Vermont National Guard 1901-1903, while attending Norwich University. Upon graduation in 1903 he was commissioned in the Marine Corps. A brigadier general in 1937, he was Quartermaster of the Marine Corps, from then until his retirement as a major general in 1944.

Average Ages of Marine Generals at the Start of World War II

Rank	Number	Average
General	1	54
Lieutenant General	3	59
Major General	42	52
Brigadier General	50	49
All	96	51

Overall Marine generals were slightly older than the average for the approximately 2,400 generals and admirals on active duty during the war, if only because there were a surprising number of "boy" generals in the Army, particularly in the Army Air Forces, which had 105 men who attained flag rank during the war but had not passed age 40 as of 1 January 1942.

Key: *Number* is restricted only to those who held the indicated rank as their highest rank (so officers who went from BG to MG, etc., during the war are not counted in their lower rank); *Average* is age as of 1 January 1942. *Note that only one full general is shown, Alexander A. Vandegrift, as Thomas Holcomb's promotion to full general took place upon his retirement.

The Five Oldest Marine Generals on Active Duty During World War II

1. BG Russell B. Putnam, born 7 January 1878, retired February 1942.
2. MG Louis McCarty Little, born 16 January 1878, retired February 1942.
3. LG CMC Thomas Holcomb, born 5 August 1879, retired December 1943, promoted to general.
4. MG Seth Williams, born 19 January 1880, retired February 1944.
5. MG Emile Phillips Moses, born 27 May 1880, retired May 1944.

The Five Youngest Marine Generals on Active Duty During World War II

1. BG William O. Brice, born 10 December 1898
2. BG Ivan W. Miller, born 16 July 1898
3. BG William L. McKittrick, born 30 June 1897
4. MG Graves B. Erskine, born 28 June 1897
5. BG Lewis Griffth Merrit, born 26 June 1897

Marine Generals Who Died During World War II

1. MG William P. Upshur, CG Department of the Pacific, died in an aircraft accident, 18 August 1943 (Medal of Honor #95)
2. MG Charles D. Barrett, CG I Marine Amphibious Corps, killed in an accidental fall, 8 October 1943
3. MG William H. Rupertius, Commandant, Marine Corps Schools, Quantico, died of natural causes, 25 March 1945
4. BG David J. Brewster, died of natural causes, 10 July 1945

Marine Generals Who Retired During World War II

1. LG Thomas Holcomb, CMC, 31 December 1943
2. MG Ralph S. Keyser, October 1942
3. MG Seth Williams, March 1942
4. MG Edward A. Ostermann, January 1943
5. MG Bennet Puryear, Jr. , May 1944
6. MG Emile P. Moses, May 1944
7. BG Louis McC. Little, February 1942
8. BG Russell B. Putnam, February 1942
9. BG Matthew H. Kingman, October 1944
10. BG Lyle H. Miller, June 1945

An Alphabetical Listing of the Ten Most Notable Marines of the Second World War

1. GySGT John Basilone (Medal of Honor #127)
2. MAJ Gregory "Pappy" Boyington (Medal of Honor #133)

3. LTC Evans F. Carlson
4. Master Gunner Leland "Lou" Diamond
5. LTC, later BG Merrit J. Edson (Medal of Honor #124)
6. CPT Henry T. Elrod (Medal of Honor #117)
7. BG, later LTG, Roy S. Geiger
8. LTC Lewis "Chesty" Puller
9. MG, later GEN Holland McT. Smith
10. MG, later GEN CMC Alexander A. Vandergrift (Medal of Honor #121)

Five Marines Who Distinguished Themselves Serving with the OSS

1. COL Peter Ortiz
2. CPT Peter DeVries
3. CPT John Hamilton
4. CPT Walter R. Mansfield
5. 1LT Robert H. Barrow

The OSS (Office of Strategic Services, the precursor of the CIA) undertook secret missions behind enemy lines during World War II, including such diverse activities as conducting sabotage, bringing out personnel, and training guerrillas. Marines in the OSS served in Europe, China, and Southeast Asia. The actual number of Marines who served with the OSS during the war is unclear, but the men listed were certainly among the most notable. COL Ortiz, served in the Foreign Legion, 1932-1940. Captured by the Germans on the fall of France, he escaped, made his way to the U.S. and joined the Marines, shortly being assigned to the OSS. In 1943 he parachuted into Occupied France, where he trained resistance fighters. Captured in 1944, he spent the rest of the war in a P/W camp. After the war he was awarded the Navy Cross twice and the *Croix de Guerre* five times, as well as the Order of the British Empire and the French *Legion d'Honneur*. CPT Hamilton (who in civilian life used the screen name Sterling Hayden) actually was in training with the Commandos in Britain shortly before the U.S. entered the War. Operating out of Italy from 1943 he ran guns to the Yugoslav partisans and himself took part in several missions behind German lines. CPT DeVries was a noted novelist and playwright, author of *But Who Wakes the Bugler?* (Boston: 1940), *The Fruits of Wickedness* (Boston: 1954), and *Reuben, Reuben* (Boston: 1964), among other works. CPT Mansfield had the unique distinction of serving in both theaters of war, parachuting into Yugoslavia to help train partisans in 1943, and then in late 1944 going into China with the same mission. 1LT Barrow also served in China, and nearly 25 years later became the 27th Commandant of the Marine Corps.

Casualties in the Principal Marine Campaigns of World War II

Dates	Campaign	Marine Corps Casualties		USN Casualties	
		KIA/MW	WIA	KIA/MW	WIA
7 Dec 41	Pearl Harbor	108	75	0	0
8-10 Dec 41	Guam	5	13	0	0
8-23 Dec 41	Wake	56	44	0	0
8 Dec 41-6 May 42	Philippines	331	357	2	26
8 Dec 41-6 Jun 42	Midway	48	39	0	0
7 Aug 42-8 Feb 43	Guadalcanal	1,440	2,966	36	101
17-18 Aug 42	Makin Raid	30	16	0	0
20 Jun-16 Oct 43	New Georgia	221	415	3	11
28 Oct 43-15 Jun 44	Bougainville	536	1,243	12	30
20 Nov-8 Dec 43	Tarawa-Apamama	1,085	2,233	30	59
26 Dec 43-1 Mar 44	Cape Gloucester	438	815	12	30
20 Jan-8 Feb 44	Kwajelein-Majuro	387	631	6	36
17 Feb-7 Mar 44	Eniwetok	258	568	*	*
6-8 Mar 44	Talasea	37	133	0	4
11 Jun-10 Jul 44	Saipan	3,147	8,575	77	337
21 Jul-15 Aug 44	Guam	1,568	5,365	51	206
24 Jul-1 Aug 44	Tinian	368	1,921	26	40
6 Sep-14 Oct 44	Peleliu	1,236	5,450	61	249
19 Feb-26 Mar 45	Iwo Jima	5,928	17,272	209	641
1 Apr-22 Jun 45	Okinawa	3,332	18,899	117	442
7 Dec 42-2 Sep 45	Air Operations	1,041	448	10	18
7 Dec 42-2 Sep 45	Miscellaneous	2	6	0	0
7 Dec 42-2 Sep 45	Naval Operations	301	402	0	0
Total		**21,903**	**67,886**	**652**	**2,230**

Most of the operations shown here were composed of numerous individual actions. The Kwajelein-Majuro operation, for example, included two major amphibious landings (one each by the Army and the Marines on Kwajelein Atoll), as well as more than 30 smaller ones, to clear Majuro and numerous small islets near both island groups, while the Eniwetok operation required two regimental sized landings (again one each by the Army and the Marines), plus nearly 30 more to clear smaller islands in the vicinity. *Key*: *Dates* are from the onset of the campaign to its official conclusion, or the withdrawal of Marine forces. *Operation*, the name shown encompasses related operations in adjacent areas. Thus, for example, casualties on Tulagi, Gavutu, and Florida Island during the Guadalcanal Campaign are included under Guadalcanal. "Air Operations" includes all Marine air activity, anywhere. "Miscellaneous" includes casualties in other theaters, notably the liberation of the Philippines, operations in China, and the European-Middle Eastern-North African Theater. "Naval Operations" includes men lost aboard ship in naval actions. Marine Aviation casualties during the liberation of the Philippines in 1944-1945 are included under "Air Operations," and ground casualties under "Miscellaneous." *KIA/MW*, includes men killed in action, mortally wounded, or missing and later declared dead. *WIA*, includes men wounded in action. Navy casualties are shown only if they were incurred as part of a Marine operation: most of the men included here were Navy Medical Corpsmen serving with the Marines.* indicates that Navy casualties have been included with those for Kwajelein-Majuro. Figures for Makin include nine men captured by the Japanese and later murdered.

Note the discrepancy between the casualty figures given here and those at the beginning of this chapter, yet both are drawn from official sources. The difference seems to be the result of calculating casualties at different times, using different criteria, such as including some non-combat related casualties among the figures for those killed or wounded, or overestimating the number of men missing in action and presumed killed.

The Ten Toughest Marine Battles of World War II

1. Wake Island, 8-23 December 1941
2. Tarawa, 20-24 November 1943
3. Iwo Jima, 19 February-26 March 1945
4. Saipan, 11 June-10 July 1944
5. Peleliu, 6 September-15 October 1944
6. Okinawa, 1 April-22 June 1945
7. Gavutu-Tonambogo, 7-9 August 1942
8. Guadalcanal, 7 August 1942-8 February 1943
9. Bougainville, 1 November 1943-31 January 1944
10. Cape Gloucester, New Britain, 26 December 1942-1 March 1943

The ranking of some of the actions perhaps needs some explanation. Wake is first because of the remarkable intensity of the defense against extraordinary odds. Tarawa second because there was a very real fear that the assault might fail. The assault on the twin islands of Gavutua-Tanambogo, just north of Guadalcanal is included because the fighting was so intense that the Marines who took the islands (the 1st Parachute Battalion and 3/2nd Marines, plus a tank platoon) suffered more than 10% casualties, in what was actually part of the first opposed Marine landing of the war (the other part was the landing on Tulagi, as there was virtually no resistance to the landing on Guadalcanal).

The Easiest Marine Amphibious Assault of the War

1. Emirau Island, 20 March 1944.

Not until after the 4th Marines were ashore did it become apparent that the Japanese were not in occupation of Emirau. There were no casualties.

Four Marine Combat Landings in the European-Middle Eastern-North Africa Theater

1. Arzeu, near Oran, Algeria, 8 November 1942: Shortly after midnight, CPT W.C. Ansell, USN, of the USS *Philadelphia* led a landing party composed of USN, USMC, and Royal Navy personnel in the capture of Grand Quay and Fort de la Pointe, at Mirs-el-Kebir, to prevent the French defenders from damaging vital harbor installations, a mission which was accomplished against negligible resistance. The force included a dozen Marines under the command of LTC I.C. Plain.

2. Oran, Algeria, 8 November 1942: LtCdr G.D. Dickey, USN, led a detail of 35 men, including six Marines, in a landing from HMS *Hartland*, one of two destroyers carrying over 400 U.S. personnel—mostly Army troops—on a predawn mission to seize port facilities and ships in Oran harbor. The attack failed in the face of fierce resistance, with both vessels sunk, and about half of the troops being killed, and the balance becoming prisoners of war for several days until the French concluded an armistice. Two Marines were killed and 4 taken prisoner in the disaster.

3. Safi, Morocco, 10-11 November 1942: Led by CPT W.C. Ansell, USN, Marines and blue-ackets of the USS *Philadelphia* landed to assist the 47th Infantry in capturing the airport at La Senia.

4. Marseilles, France, 28 August 1944: CPT W.C. Ansell, USN, skipper of the USS *Philadelphia*, led a party of Marines from his ship and the USS *Augusta*, to accept the surrender of some 730 Germans holding the forts of Ratonneau, Pomeques, and the notorious Chateau d'If, wherein Edmund Dantes was fictionally imprisoned in *The Count of Monte Cristo*.

In addition to these landing operations, Marines engaged in combat in the ETO and adjacent areas on numerous occasions, as part of the crews of warships operating against Axis forces. Some 300 Marines were involved in the Normandy Invasion, including several officers on Eisenhower's staff. On D-Day itself, Marines were assigned as sharpshooters to detonate mines in the way of warships closing on the French coast to take up bombardment positions.

One Naval Officer Who Thrice Led Marines in Landing Parties in the ETO

CPT W.C. Ansell, USN, skipper of the cruiser USS *Philadelphia*, at Arzeu, Algeria, 8 November 1942, at Safi, Morocco, on 10 November 1942, and at Marseilles, France, 28 August 1944.

Marine Units With Service in the ETO

1st Provisional Marine Brigade, organized in June 1941 and shipped to Iceland, where it arrived on 7 July, remaining there until relieved in February and March 1942. The principal components of this brigade were:

> 6th Marines
> 10th Marines (one battalion)
> 5th Marine Defense Battalion

Four World War II Army Generals Who Were Former Marines

1. BG Clarence L. Burpee (b. 1894) served as an enlisted Marine 1918-1919. After World War I he became a railroadman, and was commissioned in the Army Corps of Engineers shortly before World War II. During World War II he rose to brigadier general and Assistant Chief of Transport of the Military Railroads Division of the ETO.

2. BG Harold A. Bartron (1894-1975) served in the Marines 1912-1916. Commissioned in the Army Air Service in 1918, he rose to brigadier general, USAAF in 1943, serving for a time as Commanding General Air Transport Services, North Africa.

3. MG William E. Kepner (1893-1982) served in the Marines 1909-1913. Commissioned in the Indiana National Guard in 1916, he rose to commanding general of the 2nd Bombardment Division, Eighth Air Force.

4. BG Harold C. Vanderveer (1889-1969) served in the Marines 1907-1911. Commissioned in the Coast Artillery in 1912, he became a brigadier general in 1942, and commanded the artillery of the 5th Infantry Division, 1942-1946.

One Army General Who Was Relieved by a Marine

1. MG Ralph Smith, GC 27th Infantry Division, by MG Holland McT. Smith, Saipan, 24 June 1944.

Citing what he said were instances of disobedience of orders on the part of Ralph Smith, and deficiencies in the performance of the 27th Infantry Division, "Howling Mad" Smith requested that his superiors relieve Ralph Smith. The relief was effected by Admiral Raymond Spruance, though this has generally been overlooked in the ensuing controversy. The justice of the case is rather difficult to determine, colored as it is by interservice rivalry (the matter is still one of "fighting words" in the New York National Guard). However, Ralph Smith does not seem to have served his division well, either in the field or in his relations with higher headquarters. In fact, during the Saipan operation, although the 27th Infantry Division incurred fewer casualties overall than did either Marine division present, it had the worst ratio of killed-to-wounded of all three divisions:

Division	KIA/MW	Wounded	Ratio
2nd Marine	1,256	6,170	1: 4.9
4th Marine	1,107	6,612	1: 5.9
27th Infantry	1,034	3,566	1: 3.4

The incident greatly exacerbated inter-service tensions. It is, however, worth noting that four other Army division commanders were relieved during the war in the Pacific, several with less justification than in Ralph Smith's case, but no comparable controversy resulted. Three reliefs were by Army commanders and one was by an admiral, which also sparked some controversy.

One Occasion in World War II When Marines and Soldiers Fought "Shoulder-to-Shoulder"

Battle of the Matanikau, Guadalcanal, 24-26 October 1942: On the first night of the battle "Chesty" Puller's 1st Battalion, 7th Marines, heavily beset by the Japanese Kawaguchi Force, was reinforced by the 2nd Battalion, 164th Infantry, which was fed right into the Marine lines, so that during the night's fighting battalions intermingled under Puller's command through the night of 24-25 October.

The Two Biggest "Tank Battles" of the Pacific War

1. Saipan, 16 June 1944. At dawn on 16 June 1944, the 4th Company of the Japanese 9th Tank Regiment, with about a dozen Type 97 Medium Tanks, and an SNLF "Imperial Marines" tank company, with about a dozen Type 95 Light Tanks, took part in a major attack against the beachhead. Engaged by the Shermans of the Marines' 2nd and 4th Tank Battalions, they were beaten off.

2. Saipan, 17 June 1944. At 0200, the entire 9th Tank Regiment (c.40 tanks, mostly Type 97s, with some Type 95s) essayed another attack, this time attempting to carry infantry into the Marine lines. The assault was met by heavy infantry anti-tank fire, and was then struck by a counter attack from elements of the Marine 2nd and 4th Tank Battalions, which broke up the attack with very heavy losses. This was the largest Japanese tank attack in the Pacific outside of China.

The Principal Actions of the Marine Raiders and Parachutists

1. Capture of Tulagi, 7-8 August 1942, 1st Raider Battalion
2. Capture of Gavutu, 7 August 1942, 1st Parachute Battalion
3. Makin Raid, 17-18 August 1942, 2nd Raider Battalion
4. Raid on Tasimboko, Guadalcanal, 8 September 1942, 1st Raiders and 1st Parachute Battalion
5. Battle of Edson's Ridge, Guadalcanal, 12-14 September 1942, 1st Raiders and 1st Parachute Battalion
6. Carlson's Guadalcanal Raid, 4 November-4 December 1942, 2nd Raider Battalion
7. Capture of Sequi Point, Viru, and Vanguni, New Georgia, 21 June-1 July 1943, 4th Raider Battalion
8. Battle for Enogai and Bairoko, New Georgia, 5-24 July 1943, 1st Raider Battalion
9. Choiseul Raid, 28 October 1943, 2nd Parachute Battalion
10. Capture of Cape Torokina, 1 November 1943, 2nd and 3rd Raider Battalions
11. Koiari Raid, Bougainville, 29 November 1943, 1st Parachute Battalion

Five Notable Marine Raiders and Parachutists

1. LTC Evans Carlson, who commanded the 2nd Raiders at Makin and on Guadalcanal
2. LTC Merritt A. Edson, who commanded the 1st Raiders during the Guadalcanal Campaign
3. LTC Samuel B. Girffith II, who commanded the 1st Raiders on New Georgia
4. LTC Victor H. Krulak, who commanded the 2nd Parachute Battalion on Choiseul
5. MAJ James Roosevelt, who served with the 2nd Raiders at Makin and on Guadalcanal, and later commanded the 4th Raiders for a time

Japanese Destroyers Sunk by the Marine Defenders of Wake Island

1. *Hayate*, sunk 11 December 1941, by coast defense artillery fire
2. *Kisarigi*, sunk 11 December 1941, by air attack

Two Marines Who Rescued the Enemy

1. PVT Guy Gabaldan, on Saipan
2. 1LT Spencer V. Silverthorne, on Okinawa

Gabaldan, a Japanese language expert with the 2nd Marine Division, repeatedly exposed himself to enemy fire while talking nearly a thousand Japanese soldiers and civilians into surrendering. Silverthorne, also a Japanese language specialist, managed to talk 58 Japanese soldiers into surrendering on 12 June 1945.

The Flag Raisings on Mt. Suribachi

The ultimate image of American dedication and courage in World War II is the famous Joe Rosenthal photograph of five Marines and a Navy corpsman raising the Stars and Stripes atop Mt. Suribachi, on Iwo Jima on 23 February 1945. There were actually two flag raisings that morning, of which the more famous was the second. Both flags were raised by the 3rd Platoon, E Company, 28th Marines. Of the 40 men in the platoon on that day, only four escaped death or injury on Iwo Jima.

The Men Who Raised the First Flag

1LT Harold G. Schrier, USMC

Pl. Sgt Ernest I. Thomas, USMC, later killed in action

SGT Henry O. Hansen, USMC, later killed in action

CPL Charles W. Lindberg, USMC, later wounded in action

PFC James R. Michelis, later wounded in action

PVT Louis Charlo, later killed in action

The Men Who Raised the Second Flag

CPL Harlan H. Block, USMC, later killed in action

PM2 John H. Bradley, USN

CPL Rene A. Cagnon, USMC

PFC Franklin R. Sousley, USMC, later killed in action

SGT Michael Strank, USMC, later killed in action

CPL Ira Hayes, USMC

The Men Who Took the Pictures

Louis Lowery, USMC, took a still of the first flag raising for *Leatherneck* magazine.

William Campbell, USMC, photographed the lowering of the first flag as the second was being raised

William Genaust, USMC, shot the motion picture of the second flag raising, and was later killed in action

Joe Rosenthal, Associated Press, took the world famous photograph

The Iwo Jima/Marine Corps Memorial

A statue, over 100 feet tall, based on the Joe Rosenthal photograph of the raising of the Stars and Stripes on Mt. Suribachi, is located at the Arlington National Cemetery, Arlington, VA.

Dedicated November 10, 1954

Sculpted by Felix de Weldon

Funded entirely by individual Marine Corps and U.S. Navy personnel, veterans and friends

The original full-sized sculpture from which the bronze Arlington monument was cast can be seen today at the Visitors Center in Harlingen, Texas. Further information about the Texas Iwo Jima Memorial may be had from 210-423-6006 or 800-365-6006.

Three Unnecessary Marine Amphibious Assaults

1. Tarawa, 20-24 November 1943.
2. Cape Gloucester, New Britain, 26 December 1943-16 January 1944
3. Peleliu, 15 September-25 November 1944.

Although Tarawa, one of the toughest Marine fights of the war, was important for the refinement of amphibious assault techniques, in retrospect MG Holland M. Smith decided that it could have been avoided, to be by-passed and neutralized by air and sea power, a conclusion which naval historian—and rear admiral—Samuel Eliot Morison later extended to the Cape Gloucester operation. The wisdom of taking Peleliu, which proved another extremely difficult fight, was actually questioned before the assault began, but Admiral Chester W. Nimitz decided to go ahead anyway, one of his few major errors of judgment in the Pacific War.

Four Marines Who Became Prisoners of War in the ETO

1. MAJ Peter Ortiz, 16 August 1944
2. SGT John P. Badnor, 16 August 1944
3. SGT Jack R. Risler, 16 August 1944
4. 2LT Walter W. Taylor, 21 August 1944

During World War II 2,278 Marines became prisoners of war. Of these 2,270 were captured by the Japanese. These four men were working with the OSS in France when captured by the Germans. MAJ Ortiz and Sergeants Badnor and Risler were operating in support of French Resistance forces in Haute Savoie. On 16 August 1944 they were trapped by German forces in a populated area. Rather than risk civilian casualties they surrendered. Lieutenant Taylor was acting as a liaison officer with elements of the 36th Infantry Division as it advanced northwards from the beaches of Southern France when he was captured in a frontline skirmish. All four men proved uncooperative prisoners. Four other Marines were taken prisoner by French forces at Oran on 8 November 1942, but were released when the French concluded an armistice with the Allies on 11 November.

Sources of Marine Weapons, Equipment, and Supplies During World War II

Rank	Source	Percent
1	Army Procurement System	65
2	Commercial Sources	25
3-tie	Navy Procurement System	5
4-tie	Marine Specialized Procurement	5

Data is based on types of equipment, rather than amount of materiel procured.

Principal Amphibious Warfare Vessels of World War II

Type	Name	Displ	Speed	Crew
AGC	Amphibious Command Ship	2.2-7.4	16	600
AKA	Attack Cargo Ship	4.0—8.0	12-20	100-400

Type	Name	Displ	Speed	Crew
APA	Attack Transport	6.8-21.0	15-20	150
LCI	Landing Craft, Infantry	0.39 (0.25)	14	25-30
LCM	Landing Craft, Medium	0.05	10	4
LCT	Landing Craft, Tank	0.29	8	12
LCVP	Landing Craft, Vehicle and Personnel	0.01	10	3
LSM	Landing Ship, Medium	1.0 (.74)	12	50-60
LSD	Landing Ship, Dock	4.5	15	240
LST	Landing Ship, Tank	4.0 (2.4)	12	100

Notes: *Type* indicates whether the vessel is capable of beach landings or not (L= beach capable). Vessels shown as *LS* were seagoing, those shown *LC* were not. *Displacement*, is given in thousands of tons. Where a range is shown it indicates that there were several models of the type in service. Figures in parentheses indicate maximum displacement for beaching operations. *Speed* is maximum, in knots. *Crew* indicates the number of men needed to operate the vessel.

An LST could lift up to 20 tanks, in the right circumstances, an LCT only 3 or 4. An LCI had the capacity to land about a company, 200-250 troops, and LCVP, a little more than a platoon, up to 60 men in certain circumstances.

Beaching operations were extremely wearing on the vessels. The survivability rate of LSTs was only about 85%, that is, an LST had a 15% chance of being rendered unsuitable for service each time it hit a beach.

Planned Marine Participation in the Invasion of Japan

Operation Olympic, the Invasion of Kyushu, scheduled for 1 November 1945
> V Marine Amphibious Corps
>> 2nd Marine Division
>> 3rd Marine Division
>> 5th Marine Division

Operation Coronet, the Invasion of Honshu, scheduled for 1 March 1946
> III Marine Amphibious Corps
>> 1st Marine Division
>> 4th Marine Division
>> 6th Marine Division
>> Netherlands *Korps Mariniers* Brigade

The U.S. Marines were to spearhead both invasions. In addition to men in British warships, a Royal Marine Brigade was to form part of the British Empire Corps, in reserve for Coronet. French Marines were to serve in French warships supporting the invasion. Estimates of casualties were quite high, and at least one Marine division was not included in planning for operations beyond the first few days, on the assumption that it would be burned out.

The Last Marine Combat Action of World War II

Peleliu, 17 March-21 April 1947. After a series of guerrilla attacks, nearly 100 Marines were assigned to ferret out Japanese holdouts on the island, which had been secured in October 1944. With surprisingly light casualties, some 34 Japanese soldiers were induced to surrender.

## CHAPTER 8

The Cold War and After, 1945-1996

The end of the Second World War brought a long and bitter "Cold War" with Communist expansionism. Marked by "small" wars, the era saw the Marine Corps evolve into the nation's primary "Rapid Deployment Force," for swift response in times of crisis. The abrupt end of the Cold War in the late 1980s brought new and different challenges.

The Korean War, 1950-1953

Marine Participation in the Korean War

Strength of the Corps

Total Marines in Service During the War	424,000
Wartime Peak Strength of the Marine Corps	261,343 (Sept 1953)
Forces Committed to Action	c.150,000
Wartime Peak Strength in Korea	35,206 (April 1953)

Casualties *

Killed/Mortally Wounded in Action	4,267
Non-Combat Deaths	339
Wounded in Action	23,744
Prisoners-of-War	221
Total	28,571

*Note that alternative figures have been given at various times, for a total of 30,544 casualties, of whom 4,262 were battle deaths, 244 non-battle deaths, and 26,038 wounds not mortal. Of the 221 prisoners of war, only 194 were repatriated, most at the end of the war, but 20 succeeded in escaping, and two others were voluntarily released by the enemy during the war. The fate of the other 27 men is undetermined.

Principal Marine Units in the Korean War

1st Marine Division
    1st Marines
    5th Marines *
    7th Marines

      11th Marines (Artillery)
1st Marine Aircraft Wing
      Marine Air Group 12
      Marine Air Group 33 *

*With the 1st Battalion, 11th Marines, Marine Aircraft Group 33 and some additional elements, the 5th Marines formed the 1st Provisional Marine Brigade, which fought in the Pusan Perimeter until shortly before the Inchon landings.

The Dozen Most Important Marine Actions of the Korean War

1. Chinju Counterattacks, 7-12 August 1950
2. Battles for the Naktong Bulge, 17 August-5 September 1950
3. Amphibious Landing at Inchon, 15-16 September 1950
4. Liberation of Seoul, 20-30 September 1950
5. Battle of Sudong, 7-8 November 1950
6. Chosin Defensive and Breakout, 27 November-11 December 1950
7. Operations Killer-Ripper, 21 February-10 April 1951
8. Fifth Chinese Offensive, 22 April-15 May 1951
9. Hwanchon Offensive, 23 May-17 June 1951
10. The "Punchbowl" Offensive, 27 August-20 September 1951
11. Defense of the "Jamestown" Line, August-October 1952
12. Battles for Outposts "Vegas," "Reno," and "Carson," 26 March -1 April 1953.

The Ten Most Notable Marines of the Korean War

1. CPT William E. Barber, who held the Taktong Pass with F Company, 7th Marines (Medal of Honor #213)
2. CPT Robert H. Barrow, who, while commanding A Company, 1st Marines, played important roles in the battle for Seoul and in the battles around the Chosin Reservoir.
3. LTC Olin L. Beall, after conducting a personal reconnaissance under enemy fire, organized and led the rescue of hundreds of wounded and frostbitten troops—the survivors of the Army's disastrous Task Force Faith—on the ice of Chosin Reservoir, 2 December 1950.
4. CPT John S. Bolt, Jr., who became the Marine Corps' only jet ace.
5. BG Edward A. Craig, who commanded the 1st Marine Brigade in the Pusan Defensive.
6. 1LT Baldomero Lopez, the first man ashore at Inchon, and the first Marine to earn a Medal of Honor in Korea, when he was killed shortly thereafter, smothering a grenade (Medal of Honor #197).
7. MG Field Harris, who commanded the 1st Marine Air Wing with commendable effectiveness, particularly during the Chosin Campaign in 1950.
8. COL Lewis "Chesty" Puller, who led the 1st Marines at Inchon and the Chosin Reservoir, earning his fifth Navy Cross for "superb courage" commanding the rear guard at Koto-ri.
9. MG Oliver P Smith, who led the "attack in another direction" from the Chosin Reservoir.
10. MG Gerlad C. Thomas, who commanded the 1st Marine Division in 1951.

The Marine Corps That Participated in the Korean War

1. Colombia's *Infanteria de Marina* *
2. Netherlands, *Korps marniers* **
3. Republic of Korea Marine Corps
4. Royal Marines
5. U.S. Marine Corps

* Officers and men of the *Infanteria de Marina* served with the Colombian infantry battalion in Korea.

** Netherlands Marines served aboard Dutch warships operating in support of United Nations activities in Korea.

The Vietnam War, 1962-1975

Marine Participation in the Vietnam War

Strength of the Corps

Total Marines in Service During the War	c.788,000
Wartime Peak Strength of the Marine Corps	317,107 (Mar 1969)
Forces Committed to Action	c.450,000 *

Casualties

Killed/Mortally Wounded in Action	13,067
Non-Combat Deaths	1,624
Wounded in Action	88,633
Prisoners-of-War/Missing in Action	c.152
Total	c.103,449

* Peak strength in Vietnam was c.86,000 in late 1968. Of these, 35 were women Marines (seven officers and 28 enlisted personnel), the first women Marines ever to serve in a combat zone.

The Principal Marine Units in the Vietnam War

III Marine Amphibious Force
    1st Marine Division
        1st Marines
        5th Marines
        7th Marines
        11th Marines
    3rd Marine Division
        3rd Marines
        4th Marines
        9th Marines
        12th Marines
    5th Marine Division
        26th Marines

27th Marines
1st Marine Aircraft Wing
    MAG 11, attack aircraft
    MAG 12, attack aircraft
    MAG 13, fighter
    MAG 15, fighter
    MAG 16, helicopter
    MAG 36, helicopter

Ten Notable Marine Operations in Vietnam

1. Battle for An Hoa, 20 -24 March 1966
2. Defense of Hill 488, Chu Lai, 15-16 June 1966
3. First Battle of Khe Sanh, 24 April-10 May 1967
4. Operation Kingfisher, Hai Lang Forest, 1-30 October 1967
5. Action at Quang Nam, Phouc Ninh, 20-21 Dec 1967 *
6. Defense of Khe Sanh, 20 January-14 April 1968
7. Liberation of Hue City, 30 January-25 February 1968
8. Battle for Dai Do, 30 April-2 May 1968
9. Operation Dewey Canyon, Quang Tri, 22 January-28 February 1969
10. Operation Imperial Lake, Que Son, 31 August 1970

* This action resulted in the award of the Meritorious Unit Citation to the 1st Platoon, D Company, 7th Marines, one of the smallest units ever to win such an honor, and the smallest to do so in Vietnam.

One Marine General Killed in Vietnam

1. MG Bruno A. Hochmuth, CG 3rd Marine Division, killed in an aviation accident, 14 November 1967.

Ten Notable Marines in Vietnam

1. COL Robert H. Barrow, who served several tours, and commanded the 9th Marines, 1968-1969.
2. COL Victor J. Croizal, who arrived 2 August 1954 and helped organize the Vietnamese Marine Corps.
3. LG Robert E. Cushman, who assumed command of III Marine Amphibious Force, 1967-1969, after having served for a time as deputy commander.
4. COL Stanley S. Hughes, who commanded the Marines in the retaking of Hue.
5. LCPL Miguel Keith, who earned a posthumous Medal of Honor (#295) single handedly beating off about 30 of the enemy, killing at least seven in the process.
6. COL David E. Lownds, who commanded the 26th Marines at Khe Sanh.
7. CPL Larry L. Maxam, who at Cam Lo on 2 February 1968, single handedly defended half the base's defensive perimeter for some two hours, before dying of his wounds (MoH #265), in the process accounting for nearly a dozen of the enemy.
8. LG Herman Nickerson, Jr., who was successively commander of the 1st Marine Division, Deputy Commander of the III MAF, and commander of the III MAF, 1967-1970.

9. LTC Frank E. Petersen, Jr., the highest ranking black Marine in Vietnam, commander of VMF-214, flying 280 combat missions, during one of which he was shot down.
10. LG Lewis W. Walt, who commanded III Marine Amphibious Force, 1965-1967.

Two Marine Corps That Fought Alongside the USMC in Vietnam

1. Republic of Vietnam Marine Corps
2. Republic of Korea Marine Corps

The Beirut "Peacekeeping" Mission, 1982-1983

Marine Participation in the Beirut Mission

<u>Strength of the Corps</u>

Total Marines in Service During the Operation	c.195,000
Forces Committed to Action	c.10,000
<u>Casualties</u>	
Killed/Mortally Wounded in Action	238
Non-Combat Deaths	??
Wounded in Action	151
Prisoners-of-War/Missing in Action	0
Total	at least 389

Maximum strength on the ground at any one time was c.5,000-6,000 in mid- to late-1983. In addition to Marines attached to the embassy security detail, several Marines remained behind in Lebanon on United Nations missions. A number of Marine casualties occurred in Lebanon after the withdrawal of the "peacekeeping" forces in February 1984, including one man kidnapped and murdered and a number of others wounded, as late as 1989.

Chronological Listing of Marine Units That Took Part in the Beirut Operation

MAU 32 (2/8th Marines and HMM 261) 17-24 June 1982
                                      15 August-10 September 1982
                                      25 September-1 November 1982
MAU 24 (3/8th Marines and HMM 263) 1 November 1982-15 February 1983
MAU 22 (2/6th Marines and HMM 264) 15 February-29 May 1983
MAU 24 (1/8th Marines and HMM 162) 30 May-19 November 1983
MAU 22 (2/8th Marines and HMM 261) 19 November 1983-27 February 1984

This listing omits Marines of the Embassy Security Detachment or those assigned to UN agencies in Lebanon. MAU 32 was redesignated MAU 22 between its rotation from Beirut on 1 November 1982 and its return there on 15 February 1983.

Two Marines Who Particularly Distinguished Themselves in Lebanon

1. CPT Robert K. Dobson, Company G, 8th Marines, who was awarded the Leftwich Trophy as the best ground combat commander in the Marine Corps for his performance in Grenada in 1983 and Lebanon in 1984.
2. CPT Charles B. Johnson, Company L, 9th Marines, who, on 2 February 1983 personally stopped an Israeli tank column with a .45 and the words "You'll have to come through me."

Marine Corps Taking Part in the Beirut Operation

1. Italy's *Reggimento San Marco*
2. USMC

Elements of the French *Troupes de Marine* were also present, but they are not Marines or naval infantry.

The Grenada Operation, 25 October-1 November 1983

Marine Participation in the Grenada Operation

Strength of the Corps

Total Marines in Service During the War	c.195,000
Marines Committed to the Operation	c.1,200
Casualties	
Killed/Mortally Wounded in Action	3
Non-Combat Deaths	0
Wounded in Action	15
Prisoners-of-War	0
Total	18

Marine Units Taking Part in the Grenada Operation

MAU 22 (2/8th Marines and HMM 261)

The Panama Operation, 1989

Marine Participation in the Panama Operation

Strength of the Corps

Total Marines in Service During the Operation	c.197,000
Marines Committed to the Operation	c.1,200

Casualties

Killed/Mortally Wounded in Action	2
Non-Combat Deaths	0
Wounded in Action	3
Prisoners-of-War	0
Total	5

Principal Marine Units in the Panama Operation

Marine Forces Panama
     I, 6th Marines *
     K, 6th Marines
     D, 1st Light Armored Infantry Battalion
     Marine Corps Security Company Panama
     1st Fleet Antiterrorism Security Team Platoon
     G, Brigade Security Support Group 6

* Arrived 28 December, all other units were already pre-positioned in Panama. Marine Forces Panama also had under command 2/27th Infantry, USA, from 22 December.

The Gulf War
(Operation Desert Shield/Desert Storm), 1990-1991

Marine Participation in the Gulf War

Strength of the Corps

Total Marines in Service During the War	c.215,000 *
Wartime Peak Strength of the Marine Corps	c.215,000 *
Marines Committed to the Gulf	c.94,000 **

Casualties

Killed/Mortally Wounded in Action	22 (14 by "friendly fire")
Non-Combat Deaths	9
Wounded in Action	82 (6 by "friendly fire")

Prisoners-of-War	5
Total	118

* Includes 13,066 Marine reservists.

** This was the greatest number of Marines ever concentrated for a single operation. It included c.2,275 women, the largest overseas deployment of women in the history of the Marine Corps.

Principal Active Marine Corps Organizations in the Gulf War

Superior Headquarters

    I Marine Expeditionary Force

Forces Serving in Saudi Arabia

    1st Marine Division

        1st Marines

        3rd Marines

        7th Marines

        11th Marines (Artillery)

    2nd Marine Division

        4th Marines

        6th Marines

        8th Marines

        10th Marines (Artillery)

    1st Marine Aircraft Wing *

        Marine Aircraft Group 11

        Marine Aircraft Group 13

        Marine Aircraft Group 16

        Marine Aircraft Group 26

        Marine Air Control Group 38

        Marine Wing Support Group 37

    5th Marine Expeditionary Brigade

        5th Marines

        Marine Aircraft Group 50

        Battalion Service Support Group 5

Forces Serving Afloat

    4th Marine Expeditionary Brigade

        2nd Marines

        Marine Aircraft Group 40

        Battalion Service Support Group 4

        13th Marine Expeditionary Unit (SOC – Special Operations Capable)

Logistical Forces

    1stForce Service Support Group

    2nd Force Service Support Group

* The 2nd Marine Air Wing was incorporated in the 1st MAW.

Principal Marine Corps Reserve Units Activated for the Gulf War

4th Marine Division
    14th Marines (Artillery)
    23rd Marines (2nd & 3rd Battalions)
    24th Marines
    25th Marines
4th Marine Aircraft Wing
    Marine Aircraft Group 41
    Marine Aircraft Group 42
    Marine Aircraft Group 46
    Marine Aircraft Group 49
    Marine Air Control Group 48
    Marine Wing Support Group 47
4th Force Service Support Group

The Principal Marine Operations of the Gulf War

1. The Air Campaign, 17 January-2 March 1991
2. Battle of Khafji, 30-31 Janaury 1991
3. Breaching of the Iraqi Front Lines, 23-24 February 1991
4. Advance on Kuwait City, 24-26 February 1991
5. Battle of Kuwait International Airport, 26 February 1991

The Senior Marine Commanders of the Gulf War

1. LTG Walter E. Boomer, CG I MEF
2. MG Harry W. Jenkins, Cdr, 4th Marine Expeditionary Brigade
3. MG William M. Keys, Cdr 1st Marine Division
4. MG Royal N. Moore, Cdr, 3rd Marine Air Wing
5. MG James A. Myatt, Cdr 2nd Marine Division
6. BG James A. Brabham, Cdr 1st Force Service Support Group
7. BG Charles C. Krulak, Cdr 2nd Force Service Support Group
8. BG Peter J. Rowe, Cdr 5th Marine Expeditionary Brigade

Ranking of Marine Fixed Wing Sorties in the Gulf War Air Campaign

Rank	Service	Sorties	%
1	US Air Force	65,156	59.3
2	US Navy	17,580	16.0
3	Allied Air Forces	17,250	15.7
4	Marine Corps	9,890	9.0
	Total	109,876	

Of course, if the "Allied Air Forces" figure was broken down by country, the Marine ranking would be 3rd.

Distribution of Marine Fixed Wing Sorties in the Gulf War by Mission

Type	Sorties	%
Combat	8,308	84
Other	1,582	16
Total	9,890	

Combat sorties include close-air-support, strike missions, and the like. *Other* includes all other types of missions.

Three Marine Corps Participating in "Operation Provide Comfort," 1991-

1. Royal Marines
2. Netherlands *Korps Mariniers*
3. USMC

"Operation Provide Comfort" provides security and relief for Kurdish refugees in Northern Iraq in the aftermath of the Gulf War.

## CHAPTER 9

The Commandants

Because the Marines are a corps—in effect a single body—they have always been under the direct command of a single officer, the Commandant. Some of the thirty-two commandants were notable leaders, who helped make the Marine Corps what it is today. Others were little more than time servers. Taken together, however, they have proven a surprisingly interesting group of men.

Commandants of the Marine Corps, 1775-1997

# Name	Served	Notes
1. CPT (MAJ) Samuel Nicholas (1744-1790)	28 Nov 1775- Aug 1781	
None	Aug 1781-12 Jul 1798	
2. MAJ (LTC) William W. Burrows (1758-1805)	12 Jul 1798-6 Mar 1804	A
3. LTC Franklin Wharton (1767-1818)	7 Mar 1804- 1 Sep 1818	
MAJ Samuel Miller (acting)	2 Sep 1818-15 Sep 1818	
MAJ Archibald Henderson (1783-1859) (acting)	16 Sep 1818-3 Mar 1819	
4. LTC (COL) Anthony Gale (1782-1843)	3 Mar 1819-16 Oct 1820	B
5. LTC (COL) Archibald Henderson (1783-1859)	17 Oct 1820-6 Jan 1859	
6. COL John Harris (1795-1864)	7 Jan 1859-12 May 1864	
MAJ Augustus S. Nicholson (acting)	13 May 1864- 9 Jun 1864	
7. COL (BG) Jacob Zeilin (1806-1880)	10 Jun 1864- 31 Oct 1876	
8. COL Charles G. McCawley (1827-1891)	1 Nov 1876-29 Jan 1891	
9. COL (MG) Charles Heywood (1839-1915)	30 Jan 1891- 2 Oct 1903	
COL Clement D. Hebb (acting)	30 Jan 1899-10 Feb 1899	C
10. BG(MG) George F. Elliot (1846-1931)	3 Oct 1903-30 Nov 1910	
COL William P. Biddle (1853-1923) (acting)	1 Dec 1910- 2 Feb 1911	
11. MG William P. Biddle (1853-1923)	3 Feb 1911-24 Feb 1914	
12. MG George Barnett (1859-1930)	25 Feb 1914-30 Jun 1920	D
13. MG John A. Lejeune (1867-1942)	1 Jul 1920- 4 Mar 1929	
14. MG Wendell C. Neville (1870-1930)	5 Mar 1929- 8 Jul 1930	
15. MG Ben H. Fuller (1870-1937)	9 Jul 1930-28 Feb 1934	
16. MG John H. Russell (1872-1947)	1 Mar 1934-30 Nov 1936	
17. MG (LTG) Thomas Holcomb (1879-1965)	1 Dec 1936-31 Dec 1943	
18. LTG (GEN) Alexander A. Vandegrift (1887-1973)	1 Jan 1944-31 Dec 1947	
19. GEN Clifton B. Cates (1893-1970)	1 Jan 1948-31 Dec 1951	
20. GEN Lemuel C. Sheperd, Jr. (1896-1990)	1 Jan 1952-31 Dec 1955	
21. GEN Randolph McCall Pate (1898-1961)	1 Jan 1956-31 Dec 1959	
22. GEN David M. Shoup (1904-1983)	1 Jan 1960-31 Dec 1963	
23. GEN Wallace M. Greene, Jr. (1907-)	1 Jan 1964-31 Dec 1967	

24. GEN Leonard F. Chapman, Jr. (1913-)	1 Jan 1968-31 Jan 1971
25. GEN Robert E. Cushman, Jr. (1914-1985)	1 Jan 1972-30 Jun 1975
26. GEN Louis H. Wilson (1920-)	1 Jul 1975-30 Jun 1979
27. GEN Robert H. Barrow (1922-)	1 Jul 1979-30 Jun 1983
28. GEN Paul X. Kelley (1928-)	1 Jul 1983-30 June 1987
29. GEN Alfred M. Gray, Jr. (1928-)	1 Jul 1987-30 Jun 1991
30. GEN Carl E. Mundy, Jr. (1935-)	1 Jul 1991-30 Jun 1995
31. GEN Charles C. Krulak (1942-)	1 Jul 1995-

NB: Rank is that at time of appointment, final rank on active duty, if different, is given in parentheses.

A. Strictly, Burrows was the first Marine to bear the title "Commandant, " Nicholas being merely the senior officer in the Continental Marines.

B. Dismissed by court martial.

C. BG Heywood was seriously ill during this period.

D. Barnett's rank as a major general was a temporary one; his substantive rank was colonel 1914-1916, then brigadier general, 1916-1921. In 1921 he was promoted major general on the retired list. He was the first commandant to serve a statutory four year term, which was extended.

Commandants Who Held the Medal of Honor

1. Wendell C. Neville, the 14th Commandant, earned his as a LTC with the 2nd Regt of Marines & Sailors at Vera Cruz, on 21-22 Apr 1914.
2. David M. Shoup, the 22nd Commandant, received his as colonel of the 2nd Marines on Tarawa, in 1943.
3. Alexander A. Vandegrift, the 18th Commandant, won the Medal of Honor as a major general commanding the 1st Marine Division on Guadalcanal in 1942.
4. Louis H. Wilson, Jr., the 26th Commandant, earned it as a captain commanding a company of the 9th Marines on Guam in 1944.

Commandants Who Held Both the Brevet Medal and the Medal of Honor

1. Wendell C. Neville, the 14th Commandant
     Brevet Medal #14, at Guantanamo, Cuba, 13 June 1898
     Medal of Honor #89, at Vera Cruz, on 21-22 Apr 1914.

The Nine Most Important Commandants of the Marine Corps

1. LTC William W. Burrows, the 2nd Commandant, 12 Jul 1798- 6 Mar 1804
2. COL Archibald Henderson, the 5th Commandant, 17 Oct 1820- 6 Jan 1859
3. MG Charles Heywood, the 9th Commandant, 30 Jan 1891- 2 Oct 1903
4. MG John A. Lejeune, the 13th Commandant, 1 Jul 1920- 4 Mar 1929
5. MG John H. Russell, the 16th Commandant, 1 Mar 1934-30 Nov 1936
6. MG Thomas Holcomb, the 17th Commandant, 1 Dec 1936-31 Dec 1943
7. GEN Alexander A. Vandegrift, the 18th Commandant, 1 Jan 1944-31 Dec 1947
8. GEN Robert H. Barrow, the 27th Commandant, 1 Jul 1979-30 Jun 1983
9. GEN Alfred M. Gray, Jr., the 29th Commandant, 1 Jul 1987-30 Jun 1991

Some Commandant Firsts

First Commandant, Samuel Nicholas (actually the seniormost officer in the Continental Marines)
First Commandant to be a Lieutenant Colonel, William W. Burrows
First Commandant to be a Colonel, Archibald Henderson
First Commandant to be a Brigadier General, Jacob Zeilin
First Commandant to be a Major General, Charles Heywood
First Commandant to be a Lieutenant General, Thomas Holcomb
First Commandant to be a General, Alexander A. Vandegrift
First Commandant to be tried by court martial, Franklin Wharton
First Commandant to have attended the Army War College, John A. Lejeune
First Commandant to hold a Medal of Honor, Wendell C. Neville
First Commandant to live in the Commandant's House, Franklin Wharton
First Commandant to sit on the Navy's General Board, George Barnett
First Commandant who was a "Marine Brat, " Charles G. McCawley, his father having served in
    the Corps 1820-1836, rising to captain
First Commandant who was a Career Marine, Anthony Gale, rising from 2LT in 1798
First Commandant who was an Annapolis graduate, George Barnett
First Commandant to die in office, Franklin Wharton

Some Commandant "Onlys"

Only Commandant for whom there is no known picture, Anthony Gale
Only Commandant to be a Brevet Brigadier General, Archibald Henderson
Only Commandant to have commanded an army division in combat, John A. Lejeune
Only Commandant to have ever been dismissed by court martial, Anthony Gale
Only Commandant to have held the Brevet Medal, Wendell C. Neville
Only Commandant to have killed a man in a duel, Anthony Gale
Only Commandant who remained on duty after his term as CMC, Clifton B. Cates, who reverted
    to LG
Only Commandant who was a lawyer, William W. Burrows

Commandants Who Started out as Junior Officers in the Navy

1. George Barnett, USN, 1881-1883
2. John A. Lejeune, USN, 1888-1890
3. Wendell Neville, USN, 1890-1892
4. Ben H Fuller, USN, 1889-1891
5. John H Russell, USN, 1892-1894

Until early in the twentieth century, Annapolis graduates were not necessarily immediately commissioned in the Navy, but served, often for several years, as "Passed Midshipmen" until an ensign's billet opened up for them. These officers accepted second lieutenacies in the Marine Corps rather than wait for openings in the Navy. During the same period West Point graduates for whom there were no second lieutenacies served as "brevet second lieutenants."

The Commandants Who Were Annapolis Graduates

1. MG George Barnett, the 12th Commandant
2. MG John A. Lejeune, the 13th Commandant
3. MG Wendell C. Neville, the 14th Commandant
4. MG Ben H. Fuller, the 15th Commandant
5. MG John H. Russell, the 16th Commandant
6. GEN Wallace M. Greene, Jr., the 23rd Commandant
7. GEN Robert E. Cushman, Jr., the 25th Commandant
8. GEN Charles C. Krulak, the 31st Commandant

Two Commandants Who Were West Point Dropouts

1. Jacob Zeilin (CMC #7), entered West Point in 1822, and was dropped for deficiencies in philosophy and chemistry in 1825.*
2. George F. Elliot (CMC #10), entered the Military Academy in 1868, and was dropped for deficiencies in mathematics and French in 1870.**

* Among Zeilin's classmates who made it to graduation was Albert Sidney Johnston, who was later killed in action commanding a Confederate Army at Shiloh, in 1862.

** Another non-graduating member of the Class of 1872 was CMC Jacob Zeilin's son, William F. Zeilin, who had also entered the Military Academy in 1868, to be dropped in 1871, like his father also for deficiencies in philosophy. The younger Zeilin was commissioned a 2LT in the Corps in 1871, and rose to 1LT before he died of natural causes in 1880.

Two Commandants Who Had –*Gasp!*—Served in the Army

1. LTC William W. Burrows, CMC No. 2, served in the Army during the Revolutionary War, before joining the Marines in 1798.
2. GEN Leonard F. Chapman, CMC No. 24, was a reserve second lieutenant in the Army, 1935-1937, when he enlisted in the Marines, to be commissioned the following year.

The Commandants Who Died in Office

1. LTC Franklin Wharton, the 3rd Commandant
2. COL Archibald Henderson, the 5th Commandant
3. COL John Harris, the 6th Commandant
4. MG Wendell C. Neville, the 14th Commandant

The Commandants Who Never Lived in the Commandant's House

1. MAJ Samuel Nicholas, the 1st CMC
2. LTC William W. Burrows, the 2nd CMC, who arranged to have it built.

The Assistant Commandants of the Marine Corps

#	Name	Dates Served	Notes
1	LTC Eli K. Cole	9 Apr 1911- 1 Jan 1915	
2	COL (BG) John A. Lejeune	1 Jan 1915-10 Sep 1916	Later CMC
3	COL (BG) Charles G. Long	11 Sep 1916-13 Aug 1930	
4	MG Wendell C. Neville	14 Aug 1920-11 Jul 1923	Later CMC
5	Vacancy	12 Jul 1923	
6	BG Logan Feland	13 Jul 1923-31 Jul 1925	
7	BG Dion Williams	1 Aug 1925- 1 Jul 1928	
8	BG Ben H. Fuller	2 Jul 1928- 8 Jul 1930	
9	Vacancy	9 Jul 1930-31 Jul 1930	
10	BG John T. Myers	1 Aug 1930- 1 Feb 1933	
11	BG John H. Russell	2 Feb 1933-28 Feb 1934	
12	Vacancy	1 Mar 1934- 7 Apr 1934	
13	BG Douglas C. McDougal	8 Apr 1934-22 Apr 1935	
14	BG Louis McC. Little	22 Apr 1935- 6 May 1937	
15	Vacancy	7 May 1937-30 Mar 1939	
16	COL Holland M. Smith	1 Apr 1939-25 Sep 1939	
17	Vacancy	26 Sep 1939-29 Feb 1940	
18	COL (BG) Alexander A. Vandegrift	1 Mar 1940-18 Nov 1941	Later CMC
19	BG Charles D. Barrett	19 Nov 1941-12 Mar 1942	
20	Vacancy	13 Mar 1942-27 Mar 1942	
21	BG Ralph S. Keyser	28 Mar 1942-24 May 1942	
22	BG (MG) Harry Schmidt	25 May 1942- 1 Aug 1943	
23	MG Keller E. Rockey	2 Aug 1943-17 Jan 1944	
24	Vacancy	18 Jan 1944-19 Jan 1944	
25	MG DeWitt Peck	20 Jan 1944-30 Jul 1945	
26	Vacancy	31 Jul 1945-31 Aug 1945	
27	MG Allen H. Turnage	1 Sep 1945-16 Oct 1946	
28	MG Lemuel C. Sheperd	17 Oct 1946-14 Apr 1948	Later CMC
29	MG Oliver P. Smith	15 Apr 1948-19 Jul 1950	
30	MG (LG) Merwin H. Shiverthorn	19 Jul 1950- 1 Feb 1952	
31	Vacancy	2 Feb 1952- 7 Mar 1952	
32	LG Gerald C. Thomas	8 Mar 1952- 1 Jul 1954	
33	LG Randolph McC. Pate	1 Jul 1954-31 Dec 1955	Later CMC
34	LG Vernon E. Megee	1 Jan 1956-30 Nov 1957	
35	LG Verne J. McCaul	1 Dec 1957-31 Dec 1959	
36	LG John C. Munn	1 Jan 1960-31 Mar 1963	
37	LG Charles H. Hayes	1 Apr 1963-30 Jun 1965	
38	LG Richard C. Mangrum	1 Jul 1965-30 Jun 1967	
39	LG Leonard F. Chapman, Jr.	1 Jul 1967-31 Dec 1967	Later CMC

#	Name	Dates Served	Notes
40	LG (GEN) Lewis H. Walt	1 Jan 1968-29 Jan 1971	
41	GEN Keith B. McCutcheon	30 Jan 1971-11 Mar 1971	*
42	GEN Raymond G. Davis	12 Mar 1971-30 Mar 1972	
43	GEN Earl E. Anderson	31 Mar 1972-30 Jun 1975	
44	LG (GEN) Samuel Jaskilka	1 Jul 1975-30 Jun 1978	
45	GEN Robert H. Barrow	1 Jul 1978-30 Jun 1979	
46	GEN Kenneth McLennan	1 Jul 1979-30 Jun 1981	
47	GEN Paul X. Kelley	1 Jun 1981-30 Jun 1983	Later CMC
48	GEN John K. Davis	1 Jul 1983-31 May 1986	
49	GEN Thomas R. Morgan	1 Jun 1986-30 Jun 1988	
50	GEN Joseph J. Went	1 Jul 1988-31 Jul 1990	
51	GEN Joseph R. Dailey	1 Aug 1990-31 Aug 1992	
52	GEN Walter E. Boomer	1 Sep 1992-14 Jul 1994	
53	GEN Richard D. Hearney	15 Jul 1994-	

The title of this post tends to be somewhat uncertain. From 29 April 1911 to 31 March 1918 these officers were assigned to "Duty in the office of the Major General Commandant. " They were formally designated "Assistant to the Major General Commandant" on 1 April 1918. The title became "Assistant to the Commandant" 20 January 1942, "Assistant Commandant" 17 October 1946, "Assistant Commandant and Chief of Staff" 15 April 1948, back to "Assistant Commandant" on 1 December 1957, to "Assistant Commandant and Chief of Staff" once again on 1 July 1979, back to "Assistant Commandant" on 1 July 1983, to "Assistant Commandant and Chief of Staff" once more on 1 July 1988, and back again to "Assistant Commandant" on 1 September 1992. Note that rank is that at the commencement of service, final rank in the post is given in parentheses.

* Unable to perform his duties due to illness, he resigned.

Three Unusual Items Found in the Commandant's House

1. The Gamble Glassware: fourteen pieces which formerly belonged to LTC John Marshall Gamble.
2. Archibald Henderson's desk.
3. The Pate Butler's Table, made and donated by Randolf McC. Pate, the 21st Commandant, who was an accomplished carpenter.

## CHAPTER 10

Tell It to the Marines:
Miscellaneous Information About the Marine Corps

A lot of unusual information, lore, and paperwork tends to accumulate when an organization has been around for nearly 225 years. Some could be called "trivia," which is fine. "Trivia" is interesting,even important, information that is little known. There is certainly a lot of it about the Marine Corps.

Some Tales of Marines Being Marines

1. SGT Michael H. Garty, Master at Arms of the USS *Somers* and the only Marine aboard the ship in November of 1842. Rumors of mutiny were sweeping the ship. When the captain decided to move against the prospective mutineers on 29 November, Garty rose from his sick bed to assist in restoring order, then returned to his hammock. (It's worth noting that Garty had no part in the captain's illegal execution of three crewmen that followed a hasty court martial the next day.)
2. During the Battle of Mobile Bay (5 August 1864), the wooden sloop-of-war USS *Lakawanna* rammed the Confederate ironclad *Tennessee* with little effect save to herself. When several rebel crewmen stuck their heads out of her gun ports and addressed "opprobrious language" at the Yankee vessel, *Lakawanna's* Marines drove them back with a shower of holystones and spittoons, liberally seasoned with some musket balls.
3. In the wake of the "Custer Massacre" in 1876, CMC Jacob Zeilin volunteered the Marines for duty against the Sioux Indians, an offer which was rejected but garnered the Corps much publicity.
4. On 3 July 1916 a party of Marines under LTC Hiram I. Bearss was engaged against a band of rebels at Alta Mira, Dominican Republic. During the action, a private stuck his head up out of a trench, whereupon Bearss, who was standing atop the trench at the time, in full view of the enemy, shouted, "Get down, you damned fool! You'll get shot!"
5. In 1917 CPT Benjamin O. Davis, USA, was aboard a troop transport bound for the Philippines. When his Army colleagues refused to permit him to sit at mess with them, because he happened to be black (the only black Regular Army officer at the time), a contingent of

Marine officers led by 1LT Oliver P. Smith invited him to dine with them, placing him at the head of their table.

6. In mid-1942 recently reactivated MAJ Louis Cukela, who had a Medal of Honor from World War I, descended upon HQ USMC, and challenged his old World War I battalion commander, LTG Thomas Holcomb, CMC, to a one-on-one to determine whether he was fit enough to lead a battalion in combat.

7. On 18 January 1944, the Naval Group China established what was certainly the most oddly located naval base in history, in the Gobi desert of Mongolia, literally hundreds of miles from the sea. Commanded by MAJ Victor R. Bisceglia, USMC, the small group of sailors, Marines, and Coast Guardsmen operated a weather station there with Chinese assistance until the end of World War II. To provide protection from Japanese patrols, MAJ Bisceglia organized about 600 local Mongol tribesmen into a mounted security detail, to whom he arranged to have the Navy issue standard U.S. Army cavalry saddles. Using these troops, Bisceglia soon went on the offensive, occasionally attacking Japanese installations, and once defeating a Japanese motorized column of about 500 men.

8. While attached to Unit 8 of SACO ("Sino-American Cooperative Organization," a Chinese Army-USN/USMC/USCG special operations organization), 1LT Stuart L. Pittman, USMC, commanded a sailing junk on patrol off the coast of China on the morning of 20 August 1945, which, while in company with another SACO junk under LT Livingston Swentzel, USN, was attacked by a Japanese motorized junk. A 75-mm howitzer aboard the Japanese vessel severely damaged Swentzel's vessel. Pittman returned fire with his "main battery," a bazooka, and then laid his vessel alongside the Japanese one, and led his crew, armed with rifles, bayonets, and, in at least one instance, a meat cleaver, over the side to board and seize the enemy vessel.

The Seven Most Notable Courts Martial in the History of the Marine Corps

1. LTC Franklin Wharton, Commandant of the Corps, was acquitted in 1817 on charges of incompetence and cowardice stemming from his alleged failure to participate in the defense of Washington at Bladensburg, 24 August 1814.*

2. CPT John Heath, had an unseemly quarrel while on active duty, during which he traded blows with CPT Oliver Hazard Perry, skipper of the USS *Java*, in the Mediterranean. Both men were tried by courts martial in 1817 for "conduct unbecoming an officer." Both were convicted and sentenced to reprimands. The two later fought a duel, in which Heath missed, while Perry refused to fire.*

3. CMC Anthony Gale was convicted of "conduct unbecoming an officer" in 1820, for having been several times drunk in public and womanizing, and dismissed from his post.*

4. 1LT John S. Devlin, Quartermaster of the Marine Battalion that had helped storm Chapultepec Castle, in Mexico, 13 September 1847 (an action in which he had been slightly wounded), wrote a newspaper article in which he accused several of the officers taking part in the action of cowardice. Tried by court martial in 1852, he was convicted of slandering his fellow officers and dismissed from the Corps.

5. COL Littelton Waller Tazewell Waller, one of the most notable Marines of his day, commanded the Marines on Samar in October-December 1901. During the arduous campaign there was a mutiny among the native bearers accompanying the Marines and Waller had eleven of them shot summarily. Charges of war crimes were preferred by Army MG Adna R. Chafee, the

senior military officer in the Philippines, and an Army court martial was convened in early 1902. After 18 days of deliberations, the court concluded that it lacked jurisdiction, since Waller was a Marine officer, and the case was dropped. Although Waller eventually rose to major general, the incident clouded his career and probably was the principal reason he was twice passed over for the post of Commandant.

6. COL Alexander Williams, second-in-command of the Marine Barracks at San Diego, was arrested by his commanding officer, BG Smedley D. Butler, for public drunkenness. Tried by court martial, 12-21 April 1926, the colonel was convicted of "conduct unbecoming" in what was widely known as the "Cocktail Trial," suffering a loss of seniority and a transfer to a post of lesser importance.

7. SSG Matthew McKean, a Parris Island DI, was tried 16 July-4 August 1956 in the accidental death in training of six recruits (The Ribbon Creek Affair), in a case that rocked the Corps to its foundations. McKean was found guilty of negligent homicide and drinking on duty, but cleared of manslaughter charges, probably as a result of the testimony of retired LG Lewis B. Puller. He was sentenced to reduction to private, a fine, confinement for nine months, and a dishonorable discharge, which was reduced by the Secretary of the Navy to the reduction in grade and three month's confinement.

* Until 1834 the terms of existing legislation placed the Marine Corps under Army Regulations when ashore, and Naval Regulations when at sea. As a result, the courts in the trials of Wharton and Gale were composed of Army officers, while that in the trial of Heath consisted of Navy Officers.

Three Notable Duels Involving Marines

1. 1LT Anthony Gale (later CMC #4) killed LT Allan McKenzie, USN, as a result of a personal quarrel on 12 April 1799.

2. LT Richard Lawson, USN, of the USS *Constellation*, vs CPT James McKnight, USMC, commander of Marines aboard the same ship, as a result of quarrel over rank and privilege. They fought on 14 October 1802, and neither man was seriously injured.

3. CPT Oliver Hazard Perry, USN, skipper of the USS *Java*, vs CPT John Heath, USMC, commander of Marines of that ship, having had a unseemly public quarrel while on duty in the Mediterranean, during which Perry struck Heath, and for which both were convicted by courts martial and sentenced to reprimands. They fought on 19 October 1818. Heath fired first, missing his man, whereupon Perry refused to fire.

Six Occasions on Which Units of Marines and Army Troops Have Been Brigaded Together

1. Trenton-Princeton Campaign, December 1776-January 1777, Marine MAJ Samuel Nicholas' Battalion (130 Marines) served in BG John Cadwalader's Brigade, of Washington's Army, during which they fought in the Second Battle of Trenton (also known as Assunpink), 2 January 1777.

2. First Seminole War, December 1836-June 1837: A battalion of Marines served in the 2nd Brigade, Army of the South, along with regular army, volunteer, and militia troops, as well as allied Indians, all under the command of COL Archibald Henderson, USMC, fighting in the Battle of Hatchee-Lustee, 27 January 1837.

3. Winfield Scott's Expedition to Mexico, August 1847-January 1848: MAJ Levi Twiggs' Marine Battalion served in Brevet MG John A. Quitman's 4th Division, taking part in the storming of Chapultepec Castle on 13 September 1847.

4. Bull Run Campaign, 16-21 July 1861: MAJ Reynolds' Marine Battalion served in the 1st Brigade, 2nd Division, Union Army of Virginia, alongside the 8th, 14th (Brooklyn's Own), and 27th Regiments of New York Militia, two scratch battalions of Army recruits, and Battery D, 5th Artillery (Alexander Hamilton's Own), to which it was directly attached.

5. World War I, 1917-1918: The 4th Marine Brigade, consisting of the 5th and 6th Marines, plus the Marine 6th Machine Gun Battalion served with the division throughout the war.

6. Guadalcanal Campaign, January-February 1943: CAM (Combined Army-Marine) Division, a provisional division-sized task force formed from the Army's 147th Infantry Regiment (Separate) and 182nd Infantry (Americal Division), plus the 6th Marines (2nd Marine Division), with the artillery of the Americal Division, under the control of the headquarters of the 2nd Marine Division, spearheaded the final offensive against the Japanese on the island.

This listing excludes occasions on which Marine units may have been temporarily attached to Army units for special duties, or vice versa, or where the attachment was essentially administrative, as during the Philippine Insurrection.

A Sampler of Marine Recruiting Slogans Since 1775

First to Fight.
A Few Good Men.
Tell it to the Marines.
Let's go, U.S. Marines.
An opportunity to see the world.
The Few, The Proud, The Marines.
We didn't promise you a rose garden.
If you want to fight, join the Marines.
The Marines are looking for few good men.
No one likes to fight, but someone should know how.

The Five Dumbest Things Ever Issued by the Marine Corps

1. The Experimental 1942 Camouflage Uniform: A snap fastened blouse with trousers, on one side the uniform was patterned in blocks of various shades of green, for jungle cover, while on the other it was a light brown, for dry grass and sand. It was also too hot to wear for long, dehydrating and exhausting the men to whom it was experimentally issued, a bad thing, considering that they were storming Tarawa at the time.

2. The M501A1 Ontos (Greek for "Thing") was a tracked, self-propelled light anti-tank weapons system equipped with six 106mm self-propelled recoilless rifles. Originally developed by the Army, which subsequently refused to adopt it, which should have tipped off the Marine Corps. In combat in Vietnam, the gun mounts proved fragile. The system proved very effective in combat, if one only needed to fire six rounds. After that it proved almost impossible to reload under fire. Ontos was withdrawn by 1970.

3. The M278 "Mechanical Mule" was a 15 mph, four wheel drive vehicle weighing 925 pounds, which was capable of carrying over a thousand pounds, and could even operate with one wheel

broken ("hobbled"). For a time, Marine battalions were supplied with 30 of the beasts, eight of which were equipped with a 106mm recoilless rifle. But the Mule was noisy, and rather delicate, and wholly unsuited to combat. It was withdrawn early in the Vietnam War.

4. The V-neck tee shirt, issued for use with the Class C (tieless) uniform, which forced many Marines to shave their chests in order to meet grooming standards.

5. The Stock, a 3.5-inch high, stiff leather collar authorized for issue from 1798-1872, officially to protect men from having their throats cut in hand-to-hand combat, but was considered a torture device by the average Marine, albeit that from it was derived the name "Leathernecks."

Marine Customs, Traditions, and Lore

The Emblem of the Marine Corps

1. A silver or pewter "foul anchor," adopted in 1776, readopted in 1798, and slightly modified occasionally thereafter, until replaced.
2. A brass eagle, adopted in 1834.
3. A wreath partially encompassing the shield of the United States, charged with a bugle and an "M," adopted in 1859.
4. A gold foul anchor lying partially on its left side, charged with a globe showing the western hemisphere, surmounted by an eagle displayed, with a ribbon inscribed *Semper Fidelis*, adopted in 1868, and subject to slight modifications occasionally since. This appears to have been adopted in conscious imitation of the badge of the Royal Marines, adopted in 1827, which shows a globe with the eastern hemisphere.

Official Marine Music

1. *The Marine Hymn*, the official song
2. *Semper Fidelis*, the official march
3. The Marine Version of *The Navy Hymn*, the official hymn

Marine Corps Mottoes

1. *To the Shores of Tripoli* (1805)
2. *Fortitudine* (1812)
3. *From the Halls of Montezuma to the Shores of Tripoli* (1848)
4. *By Sea and by Land* (1850s) *
5. *Semper Fidelis* (1883)

* Adopted in translation from the motto the Royal Marines adopted in 1775, *Per mare per terram*.

Formal Colors of the USMC

Scarlet
Gold
Forest Green

Scarlet and gold are the official colors. Forest green is unofficial, its usage is established by long tradition, so that, for example, it appears on the "official" Marine Corps regimental tie and tartan.

Uniform Colors of America's Marines

British-American Colonial Marines

    1740   Canvas, with brown waistcoats.

The United States Marine Corps

    1775   Green with white or buff facings *

    1779   Green with red facings

    1798   Blue with scarlet facings.**

    1833   Green with white facings ***

    1840   Blue with scarlet trim, ordered 31 December 1839, with force from 4 July 1840.

* However, due to the impecuniousness of the infant United States, many Marines wore the Army's blue and white or other colors, as available, and even red with blue facings, in the case of the French Marines aboard John Paul Jones' *Bon Homme Richard*, who wore the uniform of the *Regiment de Walsh-Serrant*.

** One reason for the adoption of these colors for the newly recreated Marine Corps may have been because it enabled a penny pinching Congress to get rid of a large stock of uniforms left over from "Mad" Anthony Wayne's "Legion of the United States" (i.e., the Army).

*** Adopted because President Andrew Jackson decided the Corps should revert to its Revolutionary War colors. During the period the Marines also had a white canvas fatigue uniform.

The Confederate Marine Corps

    1861   Gray with black facings *

* Due to the poverty of the Confederacy, it was not unusual for Confederate Marines to wear other colors, including captured US Army blue.

Eight Hoary Old Marine Corps Legends that Are Not True

1. The first Marine recruiting station was established in Tun Tavern, in Philadelphia, the proprietor of which was so adept at securing recruits, by liberally plying them with drink, that he was made a captain in the Corps. Alas for "romance," the story is untrue. It probably got its start from the fact that Samuel Nichols, effectively the first Marine Commandant, actually did own a tavern in Philadelphia, the Conestoga Wagon, which apparently served as his headquarters for a time. However the owner of the Tun Tavern did become a Marine officer, about a year after the creation of the Corps, which probably gave rise to the legend

2. The first woman Marine was one Lucy Brewer, who served aboard the USS *Constitution* in the guise of a man, during the War of 1812. While the tradition is doubtful, it is probably accurate in spirit, if not in fact, as several women certainly served in male dress from time to time in the Army

3. When the government hastily evacuated Washington in 1814, a considerable sum of money and specie was buried on the grounds of the Commandant's House, at "Eighth and Eye." Although several attempts have been made to unearth this, there seems to be no truth to the matter.

4. When the British captured and burned Washington in 1814, they spared the Commandant's house in recognition of the courage that the Marine Battalion had shown at the Battle of

Bladensburg. Actually, it appears that someone merely forgot to order it—and several other structures—to be put to the torch, in other words the house was spared due to "a bureaucratic oversight."

5.   Having lived there so long, CMC Archibald Henderson forgot that the Commandant's Quarters belonged to the United States, and upon his death willed it to his heirs. There is no substance to this legend.

6.   When the USS *Maine* blew up on 15 February 1898, SGT William Anthony, the skipper's orderly, made his way through the burning and sinking vessel to the captain's cabin, where he told Captain Charles D. Sigsbee, "I have to report, sir, that the ship is blown up and sinking." Although Anthony did report to the captain in the midst of the disaster, and was one of the last three men to abandon ship, he appears to have said nothing of the sort.

7.   When the Japanese were overrunning Wake Island, on 23 December 1941, the last message sent by the garrison was "Send us more Japs!" Actually, the last message was "Enemy on island issue in doubt."

8.   One night during the Guadalcanal Campaign, as Japanese ships shelled the Marine beachhead, Master Gunner Lou Diamond took an attacking cruiser under fire with a mortar, placing a round directly down her smokestack, causing considerable damage and forcing the ship to withdraw. Diamond did engage some Japanese vessels with mortar fire, and this may have helped convince them to withdraw, but there is no evidence that he inflicted any damage on them.

Some Unusual Customs and Traditions of the Marine Corps

1. The fighting on Samar during the Philippine Insurrection was so fierce that ever afterwards, whenever a veteran of that campaign was present, other Marines would rise to toast him with the phrase, "Stand, gentlemen, he served on Samar."
2. Marines take the right of the line or head of the column when in formation with elements of the other sea services (i.e., the Navy and the Coast Guard, not to mention NOAA).
3. All Marine posts have a bell, usually from a decommissioned ship of the Navy.
4. In the U.S. Navy, when "Abandon Ship" is ordered, the last person to leave the vessel before the captain is his Marines orderly.
5. On a warship Marines do not man the rail.
6. Whatever the regulations say, Marines do not use umbrellas.
7. As in the Navy, when Marines enter or leave a boat or other vehicle, the junior person enters first.
8. Wherever they are, and under whatever the circumstances, Marines attempt to celebrate the birthday of the Corps on 10 November, with appropriate ceremonial, including the cutting of a birthday cake, the first two slices of which are given respectively to the oldest and the youngest Marines present.
9. The Marine Hymn is the oldest official anthem of any U.S. military service.
10. Marines always stand at attention during the playing of the Marine Hymn.
11. The Marine Corps March, "Semper Fidelis" by J.P. Sousa, is the only march authorized by Congress for a particular service.
12. The "Mameluke" Sword, first adopted in 1826, is the weapon with the longest continual service in the U.S. Armed Forces.

13. Since 1869, the Marine Band has serenaded the CMC at his quarters on the morning of 1 January, after which they are invited in for some hot buttered rum and breakfast.

14. In the Marines, the phrase "I wish ..." or "I desire ..." uttered by a senior is considered an order.

15. The crowns of Marine officer's service caps are decorated with an embroidered *quatre foil*, a heritage of the days when such designs helped Marines in the rigging identify their officers on deck below.

16. Since 1850 Marine sergeants have been the only NCOs in the U.S. Armed Forces to have the privilege of carrying swords on ceremonial occasions, a weapon of a pattern that makes it the second oldest weapon in any of the service, the oldest being the Mameluke Sword used by Marine officers.

17. Officers and NCOs of the Marine Corps wear scarlet piping on their trousers, said to honor the blood shed by the Marines who stormed Chapultepec Castle in Mexico City on 13 September 1847, and traditionally called the "Blood Stripe."

18. In combat Marines never leave behind wounded comrades, and attempt to recover their dead as well.

The Soldiers of the Sea

The Marines are both soldiers and sailors, a part of the sea services. Reflecting this, their role in the defense establishment is both important and complex.

Missions of the Marine Corps

By Act of Congress, the Marine Corps shall be organized, trained, and equipped to:

1. Provide Fleet Marine Forces of combined arms, together with supporting air components, for service with the United States Fleet in the seizure or defense of advanced naval bases and for the conduct of such land operations as may be essential to the prosecution of a naval campaign.

2. Provide detachments and organizations for service on armed vessels of the Navy, and security detachments for the protection of naval property at naval stations and bases.

3. Develop, in coordination with the Army, Navy, and Air Force, the doctrines, tactics, techniques, and equipment employed by landing forces in amphibious operations. The Marine Corps shall have primary interest in the development of those landing force doctrines, tactics, techniques, and equipment which are of common interest to the Army and the Marine Corps.

4. Provide, as required, Marine forces for airborne operations, in coordination with the Army, the Navy, and the Air Force and in accordance with doctrines established by the Joint Chief of Staff.

5. Develop, in coordination with the Army, the Navy, and the Air Force, doctrines, procedures, and equipment of interest to the Marine Corps for airborne operations which are not provided for by the Army.

6. Be prepared, in accordance with integrated joint mobilization plans, for the expansion of the peacetime components to meet the needs of war.

7. Perform such other duties as the President may direct.

The collateral functions of the Marine Corps are to:

1. Maintain a Marine Corps Reserve for the purpose of providing trained units and qualified individuals to be available for active duty in the Marine Corps in time of war or national emergency and at such other times as the national security may require.
2. Provide Marine officer and enlisted personnel in support of the Department of State security program overseas.

The implied functions of the Marine Corps are to:

1. Organize, train, and equip Marine Corps forces for assignment to unified and specified commands in support of national war plans.
2. Assign such forces to unified and specified commands, as directed.
3. Support Marine Corps and other forces assigned to unified and specified commands, as directed.
4. Be prepared, in accordance with integrated joint mobilization plans, to expand peacetime components to meet the needs of war.

Marine Corps aviation shall be organized to provide supporting air components for the Fleet Marine Forces in the seizure or defense of advanced naval bases and in the conduct of such land operations as may be essential to the prosecution of a naval campaign; and, as a collateral function, to participate as an integral component of naval aviation in the execution of such other Navy functions as the fleet commanders may direct.

Marine Corps General Orders

1. "To take charge of this post and all government property in view."
2. "To walk my post in a military manner keeping always on the alert and observing everything that takes place within sight or hearing."
3. "To report all violations of orders I am instructed to enforce."
4. "To repeat all calls from posts more distant from the guardhouse than my own."
5. "To quit my post only when properly relieved."
6. "To receive, obey, and pass on to the sentry who relieves me, all orders from the Commanding Officer, Officer of the Day, officers and non-commissioned officers of the guard only."
7. "To talk to no one except in the line of duty."
8. "To give the alarm in case of fire or disorder."
9. "To call the Corporal of the Guard in any case not covered by instructions."
10. "To salute all officers, colors, and standards not cased."
11. "To be especially watchful at night, and during the time for challenging, to challenge all persons on or near my post and to allow no one to pass without proper authority."

CMC Charles G. Krulak's Five Pillars of the Marine Corps

1. Warfighting
2. People
3. Core Values
4. Education and Training
5. Naval Character

COL Robert D. Heinl's "Meaning of the Marine Corps"

1. Quality
2. Competence
3. Discipline
4. Valor
5. *Esprit*
6. Loyalty
7. Individualism
8. Volunteerism
9. Tradition

The Marines' Hymn

From the Halls of Montezuma,
to the shores of Tripoli.
We fight our country's battles,
in the air, on land, and sea.
First to fight for right and freedom,
and to keep our honor clean.
We are proud to claim the title
of United States Marines.

Our flag's unfurled to every breeze,
from dawn to setting sun.
We have fought in every clime and place,
where we could take a gun.
In the snow of far off northern lands,
and in sunny tropic scenes,
You will find us always on the job,
the United States Marines.

Here's health to you and to our Corps,
which we are proud to serve.
In many a strife we've fought for life,
and never lost our nerve.
If the Army and the Navy,
ever look on Heaven's scenes,
They will find the streets are guarded by,
United States Marines.

In a move that Marine aviators had been proposing for several years, during World War II the first stanza, the wording of the second half of the second verse was changed from "on the land and on the sea" to "in the air, on land, and sea."

Some Unauthorized Stanzas to the Marines' Hymn

So here we are at St. Nazaire,
      our guns have rusty bores.
We are working side by side with Huns
      and nigger stevedores
But if the Army and the Navy
      ever gaze on Heaven's scenes,
They will find the roads are graded
      by United States Marines*
Again in nineteen-forty-one,
      wc sailed a northward course
And found beneath the midnight sun,
      the Viking and the Norse.
The Iceland girls were slim and fair,
      and fair the Iceland scenes,
And the Army found in landing there,
      the United States Marines.**

* 5th Marine Brigade, France 1918, with apologies.
** 1st Provisional Marine Brigade, Iceland 1941-1942

A Rifleman's Prayer

Dear God, my Father, through Thy Son
Hear the prayer of a warrior son.
Give my eyes a vision keen
To see the thing that must be seen.
A steady hand I ask of Thee
The feel of wind on land or sea.
Let me not ever careless be
Of life or limb or liberty.
For Justice sake a quiet heart
And grace and strength to do my part.
To God and Country, Home and Corps
Let me be faithful evermore.
Amen

The Infantryman's Creed

This is my rifle. There are many like it but this one is mine. My rifle is my best friend. It is my life. I must master it as I master my life. My rifle, without me is useless. Without my rifle, I am useless. I must fire my rifle true. I must shoot straighter than any enemy who is trying to kill me. I must shoot him before he shoots me. I will ....

My rifle and myself know that what counts in this war is not the rounds we fire, the noise of or burst, nor the smoke we make. We know that it is the hits that count. We will hit ....

My rifle is human, even as I, because it is my life. Thus, I will learn it as a brother. I will learn its weakness, its strength, its parts, its accessories, its sights and its barrel. I will keep my rifle clean and ready, even as I am clean and ready. We will become part of each other. We will ....

Before God I swear this creed. My rifle and myself are the defenders of my country. We are the masters of our enemy. We are the saviors of my life. So be it, until victory is America's and there is no enemy, but Peace.

—MG William H. Rupertius, USMC

The Code of Conduct

As members of the Armed Forces of the United States, Marines are subject to the Code of Conduct, governing their behavior in circumstances where they may face becoming prisoners of war.

Article I. I am an American, fighting in the forces which guard my country and our way of life. I am prepared to give my life in their defense.

Article II. I will never surrender of my own free will. If in command, I will never surrender the members of my command while they still have the means to resist.

Article III. If I am captured I will continue to resist by all means available. I will make every effort to escape and to aid others to escape. I will accept neither parole nor special favors from the enemy.

Article IV. If I become a prisoner of war, I will keep faith with my fellow prisoners. I will give no information nor take part in any action which might be harmful to my comrades. If I am senior, I will take command. If not, I will obey lawful orders of those appointed over me and will back them in every way.

Article V. When questioned, should I become a prisoner of war, I am required to give name, rank, service number, and date of birth. I will evade answering further questions to the utmost of my ability. I will make no oral or written statements disloyal to my country or its allies or harmful to their cause.

Article VI. I will never forget that I am an American, fighting for freedom, responsible for my actions, and dedicated to the principles which made my country free. I will trust in my God and in the *United States of America*.

Marine Version of the Navy Hymn

Eternal Father, strong to save,
Whose arm hath bound the restless waves,
Who bidd'st the mighty ocean deep,
Its own appointed limits keep:
O hear us when we cry to Thee,
For those in peril upon the sea.

O Christ! Whose voice the waters heard
And hushed their raging at Thy word,
Who walked'st on the foaming deep,
And calm amidst its rage didst sleep;
Oh, hear us when we cry to Thee,
For those in peril on the sea!

Most Holy Spirit! Who didst brood
Upon the chaos dark and rude,
And bid its angry tumult cease,
And give, for wild confusion, peace;
Oh, hear us when we cry to Thee,
For those in peril on the sea!

Eternal Father, grant, we pray,
To all Marines, both night and day,
The courage, honor, strength and skill
Their land to serve, Thy law fulfill;
Be Thou the Shield forevermore
From ev'ry peril to the Corps

O Trinity of love and power!
Our brethren shield in danger's hour;
From rock and tempest, fire and foe,
Protect them wheresoe'er they go;
Thus evermore shall rise to Thee
Glad hymns of praise from land and sea.

Some Marine Wisdom on Soldiering

1. "To be a sergeant, you have to know your stuff. I'd rather be an outstanding sergeant than just another officer," GySGT Dan Daly.
2. "Paper work will ruin any military force," LTG Louis B. Puller.
3. "You don't hurt 'em if you don't hit 'em," LTC Louis B. Puller.
4. "Being ready is not what matters. What matters is winning after you get there," LG Victor H. Krulak.
5. "Doctrine cannot be considered sound until it has been proven in combat," MG Holland M. Smith.
6. "There is no such thing as low intensity violence," CMC Alfred M. Gray.

Some Critically Important Official Works on Warfighting by Marines

OpPlan 712, Advanced Base Operations in Micronesia, by MAJ Earl "Pete" Ellis (1921), which outlined the essential features of the U.S. offensive in the Central Pacific that was actually carried out in 1943-1945.

Tentative Manual for Landing Operations (Fleet Training Publication 167), by the Faculty and Staff of the Marine Corps Field Officers' School (1934), which established the basic procedures for conducting amphibious operations.

Small Wars Manual, by MAJ Samuel M. Harrington and MAJ Harold H. Utley (1935), which distilled the Corps' Caribbean and Central American experiences in counter-insurgency warfare into a useful handbook on the subject, a work which was unfortunately forgotten by the 1960s.

Warfighting (FMF Manual 1) by CPT John F. Schmitt (1988), which with

Campaigning (FMF Manual 1-1) by CPT John F. Schmitt (1988), formed the basis of the revision of Marine training and doctrine for modern war.

Three Major Twentieth Century Military Techniques Developed by the USMC

1. Amphibious Assault
2. Close Air Support
3. Vertical Envelopment (Airmobile Operations)

Granting that amphibious warfare is as old as naval warfare itself, in its twentieth century form it certainly differs radically from previous experience. In the course of the twentieth century there have been nine major innovative military techniques, the three above, plus *"Blitzkrieg,"* pioneered by the Germans, airborne attack by the Germans and Russians, submarine warfare by the Germans, the carrier warfare by the U.S., the Japanese, and British, strategic bombardment by the British and U.S., and electronic warfare by the British and U.S. So the USMC has been the leader in developing a third of these, not a bad record in the innovation department.

Watches

Like sailors, Marines stand watches. The day is divided into seven watches, five of four hours each and two of two hours.

Time	Name
0000-0400	Mid-watch
0400-0800	Morning Watch
0800-1200	Forenoon Watch
1200-1600	Afternoon Watch
1600-1800	First Dog Watch
1800-2000	Second Dog Watch
2000-2400	First Watch

As watches were anciently only stood at night, that beginning at 2000 Hours (8:00 p.m.) is traditionally known as the "First Watch."

The "dog watches" are so named because they are shortened, or "dogged." They exist to permit rotation of shifts.

Telling Time

Marines use the traditional maritime system of Bells, a matter which is enormously confusing to landlubbers, but is actually quite simple.

			Time of Day			
Bells	Predawn	Morning	Forenoon	Afternoon	Evening	Night
1	0030	0400	0830	1230	1630	2030
2	0100	0430	0900	1300	1700	2100
3	0130	0500	0930	1330	1730	2130
4	0200	0600	1000	1400	1800	2200
5	0230	0630	1030	1430	1830	2230
6	0300	0700	1100	1500	1900	2300
7	0330	0730	1130	1530	1930	2330
8	0400	0800	1200	1600	2000	2400

Bells are rung in pairs, with a short pause between each pair. They are no longer normally rung at night.

If you hear ding-ding, ding-ding, ding, and it's the afternoon, the time is 1430 Hours, or 2:30 p.m. in civilianese. If it's really dark out there, then it must by 0230, or 2:30 a.m., unless it's January and you're in the Aleutians, when it may be 0230 or 0630 or even 1830 or 2230.

## CHAPTER 11

Marines and Other Folks

The Marine Corps consists of people, who deal with other people, as a part of the American people. Some of these people did interesting deeds, some have said notable things.

Some USMC Personnel Firsts

First Marine: LT John Watson, appointed to the Massachusetts state ship *Enterprise*, 3 May 1775
First Marine Commandant: CPT Samuel Nicholas, 28 November 1775
First Marine Brigadier General: Jacob Zeilin*
First Marine Reserve Brigadier General, Littleton Waller Tazewell Waller, Jr., September 1942
First Marine Major General: Charles Heywood
First Marine Lieutenant General: Thomas Holcomb
First Marine General: Alexander A. Vandegrift**
First Black Marine (Continental Corps): PVT John Martin
First Black Marine (Modern Corps): PVT Howard P. Perry, 1 June 1942
First Black Marine Officer: 2LT Frederick C. Branch, 10 November 1945
First Black Marine General: BG Frank Peterson ***
First Marine Killed in Action: 2LT John Fitzpatrick, 6 Apr 1776, in the fight between USS *Alfred* and HMS *Glasgow*, on which occasion three other Marines (one officer and two enlisted men) were also killed.
First Marine to command a brigade in combat: COL Archibald Henderson, the Seminole War.
First Marine to command a division in combat: MG John A. Lejeune, the 2nd Division in France in 1918.
First Marine to command a corps in combat: LG Alexander A. Vandegrift, the I Marine Amphibious Corps in the Southwest Pacific, July 1943.
First Marine to command a multi-corps operation: LG Holland M. Smith, who directed his own V Amphibious Corps and MG Roy S. Geiger's III Amphibious Corps, during the Marianas Operation, in June-July 1944.
First Marine to command an army in combat: MG Roy Geiger, Tenth Army, Okinawa, 18-23 June 1945.
First Marine to serve on the joint Army-Navy Planning Committee: Holland M. Smith, 1921.
First Marine to sit on the Navy's General Board: COL George C. Reed, Adjutant and Inspector General of the Corps, 29 March 1900.
First Woman Marine (Traditional): Lucy Brewer, War of 1812
First Woman Marine (Modern): Ophra Johnson, 13 April 1918
First Woman Marine Aviator: 1LT Sarah Deal, Marine Heavy Helicopter Squadron 466, 26 Sep 1995

First Woman Marine officer: MAJ Ruth C. Streeter, 13 Feb 1943 ****
First Woman Marine brigadier general: Margaret Brewer, 11 May 1978
First Woman Marine lieutenant general: Carol A. Mutter, 1996

* Substantive rank. However, Archibald Henderson held a brevet brigadier generalcy.

** However, Thomas Holcomb was promoted to full general on the retired list before Vandegrift received his promotion on active duty.

*** Also the first black major general.

****Also the first woman lieutenant colonel and colonel.

One Unfortunate Marine Only

1. The only Marine to surrender a regiment: COL Samuel I. Howard, 4th Marines, on Corregidor, 6 May 1942.

Sergeants Major of the Marine Corps

1. Wilbur Bestwick   23 May 1957-31 Aug 1959
2. Francis D. Rauber   1 Sep 1959-28 Jun 1962
3. Thomas J. McHugh   29 Jun 1962-16 Jul 1965
4. Herbert J. Sweet   17 Jul 1965-31 Jul 1969
5. Joseph W. Dailey   1 Aug 1969-31 Jan 1973
6. Clinton A. Puckett   1 Feb 1973-31 May 1975
7. Henry H. Black   1 Jun 1975-31 Mar 1977
8. John E. Massaro   1 Apr 1977-15 Aug 1979
9. Leland D. Crawford   16 Aug 1979-27 Jun 1983
10. Robert E. Cleary   28 Jun 1973-26 Jun 1987
11. David W. Sommers   27 Jun 1987-27 Jun 1991
12. Harold G. Overstreet   28 Jun 1991-29 Jun 1995
13. Lewis H. Lee   30 Jun 1995-

Directors of Women Marines

1. COL Ruth C. Streeter   13 Feb 1943-7 Dec 1945
2. COL Katherine Towle   7 Dec 1945-Jun 1946
3. MAJ (COL) Julia E. Hamblet   Sep 1946-4 Nov 1948
4. COL Katherine Towle   4 Nov 1948-30 Apr 1953
5. COL Julia E. Hamblet   30 Apr 1953- Mar 1959
6. COL Margaret M. Henderson   Mar 1959- Jan 1964
7. COL Barbara J. Bishop   Jan 1964-31 Jan 1969
8. COL Jeanette I. Sustad   31 Jan 1969-31 Jan 1973
9. COL (BG) Margaret A. Brewer   31 Jan 1973- Jun 1977

Note: From February 1943 to November 1948, women Marines belonged to the Women's Reserve, USMC, under the Director, Women's Reserve, as listed above for those dates. From November 1948 through June 1977, women Marines formed a branch within the Corps, the "Women Marines," under a Director of Women Marines, listed above under the appropriate dates. In June 1977 the separate branch for women was abolished.

Sergeants Major of Women Marines, 1961-1976

1. SGM Bertha L. Peters   Jan 1961- Nov 1963
2. SGM Evelyn E. Albert   Nov 1963- Dec 1966
3. SGM Ouida W. Craddock   Dec 1966- Aug 1969
4. SGM Mavel A.R. Otten   Aug 1969- Apr 1972
5. SGM June V. Andler   Apr 1972- Apr 1974
6. SGM Grace A. Carle   Apr 1972- Oct 1976

Eight Marines Who Were Critically Important to the Development of the Modern Corps *

1. LTC Earl "Pete" Ellis, wrote *OpPlan 712, Advanced Base Operations in Micronesia*, in 1921, which essentially outlined the plan of the American amphibious offensive in the Central Pacific that was executed in 1943-1945.
2. LTG Holland M. Smith, the "Father of Amphibious Warfare."
3. GEN Gerald C. Thomas, rose from private to full general, helped fight the "unification" battle of the late 1940s and early 1950s, commanded the 1st Marine Division in Korea for a time, and was instrumental in the modernization of the Marine Corps during the 1950s.
4. MG Merritt A. Edson, not only had a distinguished combat record during World War II, but also played a critical role in engineering the preservation of the Corps during the "unification" battles of 1947-1952.
5. LTG Victor H. Krulak, helped design the landing craft used in World War II, helped plan Marine strategy in the post-World War II "Unification Battles," played a role in the creation of "vertical envelopment," helped develop counterinsurgency doctrine, and accumulated a distinguished combat record in three wars.
6. LTG Merrill B. Twining, the "Father of Vertical Envelopment," General Twining (the brother of Air Force General Nathan B. Twining, Chairman of the Joint Chiefs), also helped refine amphibious doctrine during World War II and designed the 1stMarine Division's shoulder patch.
7. MG Robert E. Hogaboom chaired a board in 1956 that resulted in a major reorganization of the Marine Corps, leading to more streamlined combat units, increased airmobile capability, more flexible artillery operations, and more, to better prepare the Corps for limited war.
8. CPT John F. Schmitt, who wrote *Warfighting* (FMF Manual 1) and *Campaigning* (FMF Manual 1-1) in the late 1980s, providing the theoretical underpinnings for the revision of Marine training and doctrine for modern warfare.

* Other than Commandants

The Ten Most Notable Marine Heroes

1. GySGT John "Manila John" Basilone, who won the Medal of Honor on Guadalcanal, refused a commission, volunteered to return to combat, and later earned a posthumous Navy Cross on Iwo Jima.
2. COL Hiram I. Bearss, who earned a Medal of Honor and ten other decorations for valor in the Philippines, in China, at Vera Cruz, in various "Banana Wars," and in World War I.
3. BG Smedley D. Butler, who earned the Medal of Honor twice, as well as the Brevet Medal and two Distinguished Service Medals, among other honors.

4. SGM Daniel Daly, who earned the Medal of Honor twice, as well as the Navy Cross, the Distinguished Service Cross, and both the French *Medaille Militaire* and the *Croix de Guerre,* the latter twice.
5. BG Evans F. Carlson, "father" of the Marine Raiders, who led the 2nd Raiders at Makin and on Guadalcanal, holder of three Navy Crosses.
6. CPT Henry T. Elrod, the only man to ever be awarded the Medal of Honor for both ground and air combat.
7. SGM John Henry Quick, who won the Medal of Honor and the Navy Cross.
8. 1LT Presley O'Bannon, who led a column of Marines and mercenaries on a grueling march across the African desert to plant Old Glory on the fortress of Derna in 1805.
9. LTG Lewis "Chesty" Puller, who won the Navy Cross five times.
10. MG Littleton W.T. Waller: Commissioned a 2LT in 1880, he rose to MG, serving at Alexandria, at Santiago, during the China Relief Expedition (for which he was later awarded a Brevet Medal), in the Philippine Insurrection, during which he commanded on Samar, in Cuba, at Vera Cruz, and in Haiti.

The Ten Most Colorful Marines

1. COL Hiram I. Bearss, a tough, eccentric, and profane hero of the Philippine Insurrection and the First World War.
2. MAJ Gregory "Pappy" Boyington, colorful air ace of World War II.
3. MG Smedley D. Butler, heroic, eccentric veteran of numerous campaigns from the 1890s to the 1930s, with two Medals of Honor.
4. BG Evans F. Carlson, eccentric creator of the Marine Raiders.
5. SGM Daniel Daly, most outstanding, and eloquent, enlisted man in the history of the Corps.
6. MGySGT Leland "Lou" Diamond, wonderfully eccentric hero of Guadalcanal.
7. BG Merritt Edson, "Banana War" veteran, notable Marine Raider, and hero of the post-war "Unification Battle," who held the Medal of Honor and two Navy Crosses.
8. COL Robert D. Heinl, noted author, often found at the front perfectly uniformed, with his swagger stick, who ranked high on Haitian Dictator Francois "Papa Doc" Duvalier's enemies list.
9. LTG Lewis "Chesty" Puller, most decorated Marine in history.
10. MAJ John Phillip Sousa, master musician and notable pitchman for the Marine Corps.

Eight Marines Who Held Unique Commands in Combat

1. COL Hiram I. Bearss served as acting commander of the 51st Infantry Brigade, 26th Division, in France, 15-25 October 1918 and 9-24 November 1918, during the Meuse-Argonne Offensive, and also commanded the 102th Infantry Regiment, in that same brigade, after having commanded the 9th Infantry for a time, and before that a battalion of the same regiment, thus becoming the only Marine ever to have commanded an army battalion, regiment, and brigade in combat.
2. BG Thomas E. Bourke, commanded the Army's XXIV Corps Artillery, in combat in the Pacific during 1943-1944 .
3. COL Robert H. Dunlap, an artilleryman, commanded the Army's 17th Field Artillery Regiment from October 1918 until after the end of World War I, notably during both the St. Mihiel and Meuse-Argonne Offensives.

4. 1Lt James Marshall Gamble, of the Marine detachment aboard the 32-gun frigate USS *Essex*, was given command of the British prize *Greenwich* (10 guns) in 1813, when *Essex* ran out of spare naval officers, thus becoming the only Marine ever to command a U.S. warship, during which service he captured the British privateer *Seringapatam* (22) on 14 July 1813.

5. MG Roy Geiger assumed temporary command of the Tenth Army when Army LG Simon Bolivar Buckner was killed in action on Okinawa, 18 June 1945, thus becoming the only Marine ever to command a field army, until LTG Joseph Stilwell arrived to assume command on 23 June.

6. BG John A. Lejeune, served as commander of the 2nd Division from 26 July 1918 until after the armistice of 11 November 1918, while rising to major general on 1 Aug, becoming not only the first Marine to ever command a division, but the only Marine who ever commanded an Army division in combat.

7. COL James T. Moore, a member of the U.S. Aviation Mission to Peru, served as commander of the Peruvian Air Force from October 1940 to October 1942.

8. MG Julian C. Smith, of the 1st Marine Division, assumed command of the Army's IX Corps 24 February 1951, when the corps commander died as a result of an accident, remaining in command until relieved on 5 March 1951, thus becoming the only Marine ever to command an Army corps in combat.

Two Presidents Who Were "Sort of" Marines

1. John Adams. Appointed Minister to France, Adams was a passenger aboard the 24-gun frigate USS *Boston* en route to France 15 February-31 March 1778. During the voyage, the frigate came across a British merchantman. *Boston's* skipper decided to seize the British vessel. As the frigate cleared for action, her Marines were mustered on deck. Adams fell in beside them with a musket in hand, but was ordered below by the commanding officer. The British vessel shortly struck her colors, without a shot having been fired.

2. Franklin D. Roosevelt. While serving as Assistant Secretary of the Navy, 1913-1920, Roosevelt paid several visits to "his" Marines in Haiti, the Dominican Republic, and Cuba, not to mention at the front in France. In France, he toured the trenches, was with Marines who had just come out of the line, and those who were about to go into action, and walked through Belleau Wood shortly after the Marines had taken it, about which he later said, "I have seen blood running from the wounded. I have seen men coughing out their gassed lungs. I have seen the dead in the mud....I have seen two hundred limping, exhausted men come out of the line—the survivors of a regiment of one thousand that went forward forty-eight hours before." On one occasion the assistant secretary passed down a communications trench literally minutes before a German artillery barrage slammed into it.

Two Presidents Who Were Comrades-in-Arms of the Marines

1. 1LT Ulysses S. Grant, USA, 13 September 1847: During the storming of Chapultepec Castle, LT Grant led a platoon of 20 soldiers that accompanied a detachment of about 40 Marines under CPT George H. Terrett in the pursuit of the enemy.

2. LT John F. Kennedy, USNR, 28 October 1943: While commanding *PT-59,* Kennedy helped evacuate the wounded from the 1st Parachute Battalion's Choiseul Raid, one of whom died in his bunk.

One President's Brother Who Was a Marine

Laurence Washington

George's older half-brother Laurence was commissioned a captain in William Gooch's Colonial Marine Corps in 1740, serving in the Caribbean under Admiral Lord Edward Vernon.*

Laurence's share of the prize money ("Armies loot, navies take prize") for his service enabled him to purchase a large plantation, which he named Mount Vernon, in honor of his former commander. The estate passed to George when Laurence died.

* Nicknamed "Old Grog," because of a grogham coat he always wore, Vernon introduced the watered rum ration into the Royal Navy, which was ever after called "Grog."

Two Presidents Who Sent Sons into the Marine Corps

1. Grover Cleveland's son Richard Cleveland served as a junior officer in the Marine Corps during World War I, but did not see combat.
2. Franklin D. Roosevelt's eldest son, James Roosevelt, joined the Marine Reserves shortly before World War I, and rose from captain to colonel during the war. Instrumental in securing the creation of the Marine Raiders, Roosevelt served as XO of the 2nd Raider Battalion (Carlson's Raiders), taking part in the Makin Island Raid in August 1942, winning a Silver Star, and in the famous "Thirty Day Raid" on Guadalcanal (4 November - 4 December 1942). He subsequently organized and trained the 4th Raider Battalion, October 1942-May 1943, before being assigned to staff duties.

One Presidential Son-in-Law Who Was a Marine

Charles S. ("Chuck") Robb, Captain, USMC, a Vietnam veteran, married Lynda Bird Johnson, daughter of President Lyndon Baines Johnson, in December 1967.

Eight Notable Americans Who Sent Their Sons into the Marine Corps

1. Secretary of the Navy Josephus Daniels: Josephus Daniels, Jr., served as an officer in the Marine Corps during World War I.
2. Presidential *alter ego* Harry Hopkins: PFC Stephen P. Hopkins was killed in action in the Marshall Islands in early 1944.
3. Admiral David Dixon Porter: David Dixon Porter, Jr., was commissioned in the Marines in 1899, earned a Medal of Honor (#84) during the Philippine Insurrection, and rose to brigadier general.
4. MG George G. Meade, USA, victor at Gettysburg: Robert L. Meade was commissioned in the Marine Corps in June 1862, and served for some 30 years, rising to colonel.
5. Adlai Stevenson II, Governor of Illinois, UN Ambassador, and Presidential also-ran: Adlai Stevenson III served in the Marines 1952-1954, and was a reservist until 1961.
6. Flag Officer Josiah Tattanall, USN: John Rogers Fenwick Tattanall served as a 1LT in the Marines until he resigned in 1861 to join the Confederacy.
7. Secretary of the Navy Gideon Welles: George M. Welles became a Marine officer in July 1862, and served during the Civil War and after, until he resigned as a 1LT in 1874.
8. Columnist Walter Winchell: Walter Winchell, Jr., was seriously injured in training, turning the father into an inveterate foe of the Corps.

Five Famous Marines Who Sent Their Sons into the Marine Corps

1. COL Archibald Henderson sent two sons into the Marine Corps, one of whom, 1LT Charles A. Henderson, USMC, remained loyal to the Union during the Civil War, but later resigned for reasons of health; the other, 1LT Richard H. Henderson, became a captain in the Confederate Marine Corps.
2. LTG Victor H. Krulak's son, Charles C. Krulak, became the 31st Commandant in 1995.
3. LTG Lewis B. Puller's son, Lewis B. Puller, Jr., served as a company officer in Vietnam, where he was seriously wounded.
4. GEN Alexnader A. Vandegrift's son Alexander A. Vandegrift, Jr., served as a battalion commander during World War II.
5. MG Littleton T.W.T Waller's son, Littleton T.W.T Waller, Jr., served in the Marine Corps 1907-1935, after which he was a Marine Reservist, becoming a major general during World War II, the first Marine Reservist to attain that rank.

One Marine the Army Loves to Hate

1. GEN Holland McT. "Howlin' Mad" Smith, who relieved Army MG Ralph Smith for incompetence on Saipan, in June 1944, in an incident widely known as "The War of the Smiths."

Two Notable Marines Who Also Served in the Army and the Navy

1. John Philip Sousa, USMC 1868-1892, US Army, 1898, US Navy, 1917-1919.
2. Gilbert H. "Hashmark" Johnson, US Army, 1923-1929, in the 25th Infantry, US Navy, 1933-1942, as a messman and steward, and in the USMC, 1942-1955, becoming one of the first black NCOs in the Corps, and rising to SGM.

Some Notable Marines Who Also Served in the Army

1. John "Manila John" Basilone, who earned a Medal of Honor on Guadalcanal (#127), had served in the Army for several years before joining the Marine Corps in the mid-1930s.
2. William W. Burrows, CMC No. 2, who served in the Army during the Revolutionary War, became a Marine in 1798.
2. BG Evans F. Carlson, of "Carlson's Raiders," rose from private to captain in the Army, 1912-1919; enlisted in the Marine Corps as a private in 1922, and began to rise again.
3. GEN Leonard F. Chapman, CMC No. 24, a reserve second lieutenant in the Army, 1935-1937; joined the Marines in 1937, and was commissioned a first lieutenant the following year.
4. Michael J. Mansfield, a noted champion of the Marine Corps in the Senate, 1953-1971, served as an enlisted man in the Army 1919-1920, before joining the Marine Corps 1920-1922.

Three Famous Marines Who Had Problems about Things They Said

1. MG Smedley D. Butler, who said "I was a racketeer for Wall Street," and became a noted isolationist and anti-interventionist.
2. LTG Lewis "Chesty" Puller, who spoke up in favor of harder training, and defended SSG Matthew McKean at his court martial for the deaths of several recruits in training.
3. GEN David M. Shoup, former CMC, who spoke in opposition to the war in Vietnam.

One Marine Who Became Presidential National Security Advisor

1. Robert C. McFarlane, who served under Ronald Reagan, had commanded F, 12th Marines 1965-1966, the first Marine artillery battery to arrive in Vietnam.

Four Marines Who Became Secretary of the Navy

1. Edwin Denby served in the Naval Militia during the War with Spain, rising to Gunner's Mate. He afterwards went into politics and the automotive industry, doing well in both. In 1917 he joined the Marines, and rose from private to major by 1919, before returning to civilian life as a reservist. He served as Warren Harding's Secretary of the Navy, 1921-1924.
2. John Chafee, a Marine during World War II and in Korea, was made Secretary of the Navy under President Richard M. Nixon, 1969-1972.
3. John Warner, a Marine during and for several years after the Korean War, was Secretary of the Navy under Nixon, 1972-1974.
4. James Webb, who earned a Navy Cross, two Bronze Stars, and two Purple Hearts as a platoon leader in Vietnam, served as Secretary of the Navy under Ronald Reagan, 1987-1989.

The Thirteen Toughest Enemy Commanders the Marines Have Ever Fought *

1. Osceola, Seminole Indian Chief, Florida, 1832-1838.
2. *General der Infanterie* von Conta, Commanding Officer, German IV Reserve Corps, Belleau Wood, 1918.
3. Charlemagne Peralte, *Caco* guerrilla Leader, Haiti, 1915-1919: killed in action 30 October 1919, by SGT Herman H.Hanneken, a Marine serving as a captain in the *Garde d'Haiti*.
4. Gen. Augusto Cesar Sandino, insurrectionary leader, Nicaragua, 1920s and 30s.
5. MG Kiyotake Kawaguchi, Commanding Officer, Japanese 35th Brigade, Battle of Edson's Ridge, Guadalcanal, 1942.
6. RAdm Keiji Shibisaki, C/O, Garrison Forces, Tarawa Atoll, 1943.
7. LTG Yoshitsugo Saito, CG, Japanese Thirty-First Army, Saipan, 1944.
8. COL Kunio Nakagawa, C/O, 2nd Infantry Regiment, Imperial Japanese Army, Peleliu, 1944.
9. LTG Tadamichi Kuribayashi, Commanding General, Japanese 109th Infantry Division, Iwo Jima, 1945.
10. LTG Mitsuru Ushijima, CG, Japanese Thirty-Second Army, Okinawa, 1945.

11. GEN Sung Shin-lun, CG, Ninth Army Group, Chinese People's Liberation Army, Chosin Reservoir Campaign, 1950.
12. MG Tran Qui Hai, commanding the forces that invested Khe San, 1968.
13. LTC Nguyen Tran Don, C/O, 6th VC Regiment, Hue City, 1968.

* Whoever commanded the insurgents on Samar in 1901 should also be on this list, but his name is unknown.

Three Senior Enemy Commanders Killed in Action by Marines

1. Ben Crack-O, King of Berribee, West Africa, mortally wounded by Marine bayonets, 13 December 1843.
2. Charlemagne Peralte, Haitian guerrilla leader, killed in action 30 October 1919, by SGT Herman H. Hanneken, a Marine serving as a captain in the *Garde d'Haiti*.
3. LG Takeshi Takashina, C/G Japanese 29th Infantry Division, killed in action on Guam 28 July 1944, by Marine machine gun fire.

One Notable Foreign Admirer of the Marine Corps

1. Sir Winston Leonard Spencer Churchill, who was so fond of the Marine Corps he could recite the entire *Marine Hymn* from memory.

Ten Military Organizations of Other Services Which Have Special Ties to the USMC

1. The Royal Marines, having served together during the Chosin Campaign, not to mention numerous other occasions.
2. The British 7th Armoured Brigade, "The Desert Rats" of World War II, which served with the I MEF in the early months of the Gulf War.
3. The Royal Welch Fusiliers (23rd Foot), having served together during the Boxer Rebellion.
4. The 7th Infantry, which twice relieved the 6th Marines, once in Belleau Wood and once in Korea.
5. The 9th Infantry Regiment, having served together in the 2nd Division during World War I.
6. The 23rd Infantry Regiment, having served together in the 2nd Division during World War I.
7. The 31st Infantry, which served alongside the 4th Marines in Shanghai in 1923, and received a Presidential Unit Citation for its performance alongside the 1st Marine Division during the Chosin Campaign.
8. The 165th Infantry Regiment (New York's "Fighting 69th"), which was nicknamed the "165th Marines" for its performance on Saipan, alongside the 2nd and 4th Marine Divisions.
9. The 1st "Tiger" Brigade, 2nd Armored Division, having served together during Operation Desert Shield/Desert Storm.
10. The Republic of Korea Marine Corps, which fought alongside the USMC at Inchon and many another field.

Two Dozen Marines Who Ought to Be Better Known

1. CPT William E. Barber: A veteran of Iwo Jima, in 1950 he commanded Co. F, 7th Marines, and held the three mile long Taktong Pass, in Korea, against extraordinary odds from 28 November through 3 December 1950 (his company had only 82 able men left when relieved, and had accounted for at least a thousand of the enemy) while severely wounded, thereby greatly facilitating the attack "in another direction" of the 1st Marine Division, for which he was awarded a Medal of Honor (#213), later rising to colonel.

2. BG Hiram I. Bearss: Earned a Medal of Honor as a junior officer during the Philippine Insurrection, and went on to fight in several "Banana Wars, " later serving in World War I, during which he commanded variously the 3rd Battalion, 9th Infantry, the 9th Infantry, and the 104th Infantry, US Army, as well as serving as acting commander of the 4th Marine Brigade and the 51st Infantry Brigade at various times, rising to colonel, before being permanently disabled, retiring as a brigadier general, with eleven decorations for valor.

3. COL Anthony J.D. Biddle: Scion of a wealthy Philadelphia family (and kinsman of William P. Biddle, the 11th Commandant), he was an expert with the sword, knife, and bayonet, as well as in jujitsu and boxing. He served as a close combat instructor in the Marine Corps in World War I, during which he taught Gene Tunney how to box, and was recalled at age 67 to perform the same duties in World War II. Although he never saw combat, surely a notable Marine.

4. MAJ John S. Bolt, Jr.: An ace in World War II, during the Korean War he was lent to the Air Force, and shot down six enemy aircraft, thereby becoming the only Marine ace of that war and the only Marine jet ace ever.

5. 1LT James Broome: Commander of Marines aboard the USS *Chesapeake*, killed attempting to board HMS *Shannon*, 1 June 1813, in an action that saw 14 Marines killed and 20 wounded, out of 44 aboard.

6. MAJ Daniel Carmick: One of the first Marines of the restored corps (commissioned on 5 May 1798), and the first to go to sea, Carmick served in the frigate *Constitution* during the Quasi-War with France, led the landing party that seized a French battery at Puerto Plata, Hispaniola, to liberate the captured British corvette *Sandwich* in 1800; commanded the Marines at New Orleans from 1804-1815, during which he took part in numerous expeditions to suppress piracy in the Gulf of Mexico and in support of the civil authority against bandits and Indians, helped suppress a slave rebellion in 1811, and guarded the Louisiana frontier against a threatened invasion from Spanish Mexico, 1812. Wounded in action against the British on 28 December 1814, he nevertheless fought at the Battle of New Orleans (8 January 1815), and eventually died of his wound more than a year later.

7. MG Albertus W. Catlin, who was commander of Marines aboard the ill-fated USS *Maine*, earned a Medal of Honor at Vera Cruz, fought in various "Banana Wars," and commanded the 6th Marines in France until seriously wounded at Belleau Wood.

8. 1LT Bartholomew Clinch, commander of Marines, USS *Constitution*, in the Quasi-War with France, 1798-1800, during which he was twice cited by Congress, for, despite commanding raw recruits, "...by his manly deportment he made them equal to the bravest."

9. CPT Alvin Edson: Commanding the Marine detachment aboard the 44-gun frigate USS *Potomac*, on 7 February 1832 he led a landing party of Marines and sailors in the raid on the pirate base of Quallah Batoo, Sumatra, and later went on to command the Marine battalion that took part in the landing at Vera Cruz, Mexico.

10. CPT Henry P.S. Elrod, The only man ever to be awarded the Medal of Honor for both ground and air combat (four victories), during the defense of Wake Island, 8-23 December 1941, in which he was killed.

11. CPT Richard E. Fleming: Awarded a Medal of Honor for a glide bomb attack on the heavy cruiser HIJMS *Mikuma* during the Battle of Midway, an attack that he pressed with such determination that when his airplane was hit by anti-aircraft fire, it crashed into the ship, an incident that caused even the Japanese to observe that "He was very brave."

12. CPT Joseph J. Foss: A Marine aviator, and the second highest scoring ace in the Corps, he was the first American pilot to break Eddie Rickenbacker's score from World War I, shooting down a total of 26 Japanese aircraft during World War II (20 Zeroes, four bombers, and two others), while he was shot down three times, earning a Medal of Honor in the process, and later going on to be governor of South Dakota.

13. LTC by brevet John Marshall Gamble: the only Marine ever to command a U.S. warship, Gamble saw extensive service ashore and afloat. He died on active duty as a lieutenant colonel. Of him David Porter (1812 naval hero father of Civil War naval hero David Dixon Porter, and grandfather of Marine hero David Dixon Porter), said, "No Marine officer in the service ever had such strong claims as Captain Gamble, and none have been placed in such conspicuous and critical situations, and none could have extricated themselves from them more to their honor," while CMC Archibald Henderson said, "One of the most gallant and patriotic officers we have ever had in the Marine Corps."

14. 1LT Archibald H. Gillespie served as a confidential agent of President James K. Polk, carrying secret orders to the Pacific Fleet and the noted explorer 1LT John C. Fremont concerning U.S. plans for war with Mexico, helped train American volunteers in California, and took part in numerous actions there from 1846-1848, during which he was wounded.

15. CPT Samuel Miller: Commanded the Marine Battalion of Commodore Joshua Barney's Naval Brigade at the Battle of Bladensburg (24 August 1814), which was just about the only American unit on the field not to run away. Wounded and captured, both Barney and Miller were feted by the British, to honor their courage on the battlefield.

16. BG John Twiggs Myers: An 1891 Annapolis graduate, he served as a Passed Midshipman until commissioned a 2LT in the Corps in 1895. Myers served at Guantanamo, in the Spanish-American War, during the early stages of the Philippine Insurrection, commanded the Marines in the defense of the Legation Quarter at Peking in 1900, saw service in numerous "Banana Wars," and was for a time Assistant CMC.

17. Chief Gunner William A. Lee: A veteran of World War I and the "Banana Wars," Lee earned three Navy Crosses in Nicaragua serving alongside "Chesty" Puller (his second and third Navy Crosses coincided with Puller's first and second), but had the misfortune to be among the Marines captured by the Japanese at Chingwangtao, China, on 9 December 1941.

18. SGM John H. Quick: Took part in the Guantanamo landing during the Spanish-American War, earning a Medal of Honor at the Battle of Cuzco Well, and fought on Samar, in several "Banana Wars," and in France, where he took part in every action of the 6th Marines, earning a Navy Cross, Distinguished Service Cross, and French *Fourragere*.

19. MAJ John G. Reynolds in a long and varied career helped storm Chapultepec (assuming command after Levi Twiggs was killed), commanded the Marines at Bull Run, and served on blockade and landing duties off the Atlantic Coast during the Civil War, serving 40 years as a Marine.

20. CPT John Stack, commander of the Marines—mostly Franco-Irish—aboard John Paul Jones' USS *Bon Homme Richard*, during her raid on Whitehaven, Britain, 27-28 April 1778 and her battle with HMS *Serapis*, 23 September 1779, one of the bloodiest engagements of the age of sail, and later served with the French Marines that accompanied the Comte de Rochambeau's army in the Yorktown Campaign.

21. Quartermaster Sergeant Simeon Stearns, commanded the Marines who accompanied the "United States Exploring Expedition" in the Pacific, 1838-1842, under Navy LT Charles Wilkes, during which he led numerous landing parties, and engaged in many skirmishes with hostile natives.

22. CPT George H. Terrett took part in the Marine landing at Quallah Batoo, Sumatra, in 1832, served with the "Mosquito Fleet" in the Florida War, and later distinguished himself at Mexico City, before going on to resign from the Corps and become a Confederate Marine.

23. CPT John Trevett, probably the most distinguished Marine of the American Revolution, served afloat during most of the war. As Lieutenant of Marines aboard the USS *Columbus* he commanded a company in the capture of New Providence, Nassau, in 1776, led the second raid on New Providence in 1778, capturing Fort Nassau and the brig *Mary*, while liberating many Americans held as prisoners-of-war, and lost an eye in the duel between the USS *Trumbull* and the British privateer *Watt* in 1780, one of the hottest sea fights of the age.

24. MAJ Levi Twiggs: After service in the war of 1812, during which he was captured when the USS *President* was taken by HMS *Endymion*, 15 January 1815, he saw considerable service ashore and afloat, including command of the Marine battalion in the Mexican Expedition, being killed during the storming of Chapultepec Castle, Mexico City.

Some Notable Underage Marines

1. Jimmy Baker (1931-) enlisted using forged papers when he was 12, in early 1943. His deception was not discovered for eight months, whereupon he was promptly issued an honorable discharge with some fanfare.

3. Art Buchwald (1925-), the humorist, who enlisted shortly before his 17th birthday and served until the end of the war.

4. Smedley D. Butler (1881-1940) secured a commission as a 2LT at age 16, through family influence.

5. PFC Jacklyn H. Lucas (1928-) enlisted using forged papers when he was 16, and went on to earn a Medal of Honor (#170) on Iwo Jima at the age of 17 years and 6 days, the youngest Marine to win the Medal of Honor, and the youngest American to do so in this century.

6. Hugh O'Brien (1925-), the actor, apparently enlisted in the Marines just short of his 17th birthday. When he was 18 he was made a junior DI, one of the youngest in the history of the Corps.

One Former Marine Who Became a President

1. Hussein Mohammed Aidid, formerly USMCR, was sworn in as President of Somalia (one of several claimants to this high office), in succession to his father, the notorious Mohammed Farah Aidid, 4 August 1996.

The First Woman Marine

1. Opha M. Johnson, enlisted 13 August 1918, the first of 305 women enlisted in the Corps under authority of the Secretary of the Navy, 12 August 1918. Authorized strength of the "Marinettes" was 350, but apparently peak strength was 277.

Four Women Veterans of World War I Who Served in the Marines in World War II

1. LTC Martese Ferguson, formerly a "Marinette," 1918-1919
2. LTC Helen G. O'Neil, a former "Yeoman (F)" in the Navy, 1918-1919
3. MAJ Lillian Daby, a former "Marinette"
4. CPT Edna Loftus Smith, also a former "Yeomanette"

Some Notable Marine Nicknames

"Bigfoot Brown"	MG W.S. Brown, for obvious reasons
"Black Sheep"	VMF-214 during World War II
"Brute"	Victor H. Krulak, because he was small, but sturdy
"Chesty"	Lewis Puller, from his barrel chest
"Deacon"	William P. Upshur, who won a Medal of Honor in Haiti
"Dopey"	Frederic May Wise, Jr., who commanded the Army's 59th Infantry in World War I, as a take-off on his family name
"Haiti"	Herman H. Hanneken, who distinguished himself in Haiti, earning a Medal of Honor (#111) for slaying *Caco* leader Charlemagne Peralte
"Handsome Jack"	John T. Myers, commander of the Marines at the Peking Legation during the Boxer Rebellion and later Assistant CMC
"Hashmark Johnson"	Gilbert H. Johnson, Montfort Point D.I., for his many years of service
"Hiking Hiram"	BG Hiram Bearss, after one of his favorite activities
"The Honker"	Leland "Lou" Diamond, from his stentorian voice
"Old Gimlet Eye"	Smedley D. Butler, from the odd gleam that could sometimes be seen in his eyes
"Pappy"	Gregory Boyington, because at 31 he was the oldest man in VMF-214.
"Polish Warhorse"	Chief Gunner Michael Wodarcyzk, hero of Ocotal, Nicaragua
"Uncle Ben"	Ben H. Fuller, the 15th Commandant, a quiet, avuncular sort of guy
"Whispering Buck"	Wendell Neville, the 14th Commandant, for his softness of speech

Eleven Famous Mustachioed Marines

1. MAJ Gregory "Pappy" Boyington, fighter ace and Medal of Honor winner #133
2. LTC Loius Cukela, Medal of Honor winner #105
3. MAJ James Devereaux, the Defender of Wake Island

4. Master Gunner Leland "Lou" Diamond, notable character *
5. BG Herman H. Hanneman, Medal of Honor winner #111
6. MG Charles Heywood, the 9th Commandant
7. COL David E. Lownds, who commanded the 26th Marines at Khe Sahn **
8. BG John Twiggs Myers, who defended the Peking Legation
9. CPL John F. Mackie, Medal of Honor winner #1 *
10. John Philip Sousa, "The March King" *
11. MG Littleton W. T. Waller, hero of Samar

*With a beard to go with it.

** Lownds shaved off his handlebars when he visited President Lyndon Johnson in order to accept the Presidential Unit Citation on behalf of the regiment.

One Notable Marine Who Had a Beard, but not a Mustache

1. BG Jacob Zeilin, the 7th Commandant

Four Notable Honorary Marines

1. Bugs Bunny was made an honorary private for making a recruiting pitch for the Marine Corps during World War II (in which he appeared in full dress uniform). By the time he was discharged, at the end of the war, he had risen to honorary sergeant.
2. Stephen Crane, war correspondent and author of *The Red Badge of Courage* accompanied the Marines who landed at Guantanamo Bay, in Cuba, in 1898. At the Battle of Cuzco Well on 12 June he took part in the fighting, after which he was made an honorary 2LT by the Marines.
3. BG James G. Harbord, U. S. Army, who commanded the 4th Marine Brigade, and later the 2nd Division, in France in 1918, was forever welcome among "his" Marines.
4. SGM Sir Jacob Vouza, of the Solomons Islands Defence Force, had many heroic adventures scouting for the 1st Marine Division on his native Guadalcanal. On the eve of the Japanese attack across the Tenaru River, he was captured behind Japanese lines. Finding a small American flag on his person, the Japanese tied him to a tree, beat him, bayoneted him several times, and then went off, leaving him to die. Vouza got loose from his bonds and crawled three miles through the jungle to warn the Marines of the impending attack. He later guided the Marine Raiders on their month long (4 November-4 December 1942) foray behind Japanese lines. While the U.S. awarded him a Silver Star and King George VI gave him a knighthood, he most appreciated his appointment as an honorary Marine by the men of the 1st Marine Division.

Note that the Marine Corps discourages its people from designating someone an "honorary" Marine, but the practice persists.

A Dozen People the Average Person Might Have Trouble Believing Were Marines

1. Hugh Brannum, television's Mr. Green Jeans
2. Art Buchwald, newspaper humorist
3. David Dinkins, former Mayor of New York

4. Edward Dugmore, abstract expressionist artist
5-6. The Everly Brothers (Don and Phil), purveyors of "blue eyed soul."
7. Ray Heatherton, television's Merry Mailman
8. Bob Keeshan, television's Captain Kangaroo
9. Ed McMahon, Sweepstakes spokesman
10. Paul Moore, Jr, former Episcopal Bishop of New York
11. Mark Russell, political satirist
12. Vincent Sardi, noted New York restaurateur

Eight Noted Athletes Who Were Marines

1. Carmen Basilio, boxer
2. Gil Hodges, baseball player
3. Bob Mathias, decathlete
4. Ken H. Norton, boxer
5. Leon Spinks, Jr, boxer
6. Lee Trevino, golfer
7. Gene Tunney, boxer
8. Ted Williams, baseball player*

* When Williams was in flight school during World War II he had a young classmate named George Bush.

Twelve Actors Who Were Marines

1. Gene Hackman
2. Sterling Hayden
3. Charlton Heston
4. Brian Keith
5. Steve McQueen
6. Lee Marvin
7. George Peppard
8. Tyrone Power
9. George C. Scott
10. Burt Reynolds
11. Robert Wagner
12. James Whitmore

Some Former Marines Who Served Prominently in the Senate

1. Henry Bellmon of Oklahoma, 1969-1981: USMC, 1942-1946.
2. Daniel Brewster of Maryland, 1969-1981: USMC 1942-1946.
3. Dale Bumpers of Arkansas, 1975-1993: USMC 1943-1946.
4. Francis Case of South Dakota, 1951-1962: USMC 1918-1919, and later served in both the Army and Marine Corps Reserve.
5. John Chaffee of Rhode Island, 1977-1989: USMC 1942-1945 and 1951-1953.
6. James P.S. Devereaux of Maryland, 1951-1959: USMC, 1923-1948, rising to BG.

7. Paul Douglas of Illinois, 1949-1957: USMC, 1942-1945 (enlisting at age 50, he rose to LTC).
8. John East of North Carolina, 1981-1986: USMC, 1953-1955.
9. John H. Glenn, Jr., of Ohio, 1974-1997: USMC, 1942-1965.
10. Howell Heflin of Alabama, 1979-1991: USMC 1942-1946.
11. Joseph R. McCarthy of Wisconsin, 1946-1957: USMC, 1942-1945.
12. Michael J. Mansfield, of Montana, 1953-1971: USA, 1919-1920, USMC, 1920-1922.
13. Charles S. Robb of Virginia, 1989-present: USMC Vietnam.
14. James Sasser of Tennessee, 1977-1989: USMC 1957-1963.
15. George Smathers of Florida, 1951-1969.
16. Adlai Stevenson III of Illinois, 1970-1981: USMC 1952-1961.
17. Stephen Douglas Symms of Idaho, 1981-1993: USMC 1960-1963.
18. John Warner of Virginia, 1979-1991: USMC 1952-1956.
19. Pete Wilson of California, 1983-1989: USMC 1955-1958.

Note that several of these men served in the House of Representatives before moving on to the Senate. The number of former Marines who served in the House is too great to list here conveniently.

Nine Notable American Soldiers and Sailors Who Were Boosters of the Marine Corps

1. Commodore Thomas Truxton wrote one of the earliest "manuals" for Marine service aboard ship, and supported expansion of the Marine Corps as an important factor in enhancing the professionalism of the Navy.
2. Commodore William Bainbridge urged the enlargement of the Corps during the 1820s.
3. ADM David Dixon Porter supported the corps in bureaucratic battles after the Civil War ("If the Marines were abolished half the efficiency of the Navy would be destroyed."), and whose son was himself a Marine and Medal of Honor winner.
4. Admiral of the Navy George Dewey, who, after his victory at Manila Bay (1 May 1898), wired Washington deploring the fact that he didn't have enough Marines to capture Manila, and later fought hard to preserve and strengthen the Marine Corps.
5. MG James G. Harbord, sometime commander of the Marines in France during World War I, who so admired *his* Marines that upon hearing one of his tales about the Leathernecks, General of the Armies John J. Pershing replied, "No wonder the Marines like you, when you can tell whoppers like that."
6. RAdm Ellis M. Zacharias, submariner and prominent naval intelligence officer during World War II, who lent his support to the Marine Corps during the "Unification Battle" of 1947-1952.
7. MG Frank E. Lowe, USA, an aide to President Truman, who reported so glowingly on the performance of the Marines in Korea as to have a positive effect on the political survival of the Corps.
8. MG Johnson Hapgood, USA, who said "No one can ever say that the Marines have ever failed to do their work in handsome fashion. "
9. Fleet Admiral Chester W. Nimitz, who made the comment about "uncommon valor. "

Ten Journalists Who Were Special Friends of the Marine Corps

1. Stephen Crane, who accompanied the Marine landing at Guantanamo, Cuba, in 1898, and ended up an honorary second lieutenant.
2. Richard Harding Davis, who accompanied the Marines on a number of operations in the 1890s and early 1900s, and popularized the phrase "The Marines have landed and the situation is well in hand."
3. John Hershey, who was on Guadalcanal and a number of other Marine battlefields, and wrote *Into the Valley*.
4. Margueritte Higgins, who reported on the Marines in Korea and Vietnam.
5. J. Robert Moskin reported on Marine operations in Vietnam for *Look* magazine, and later wrote *The U. S. Marine Corps Story*.
6. Ernie Pyle, among the best of America's World War II war correspondents, who saw action in the ETO and then accompanied the Marines on several landings, before being killed in action on Ie Shima, while accompanying the 77th Infantry Division.
7. Joe Rosenthal, the AP photographer who despite being IV-F due to poor eyesight, accompanied the Marines on four invasions, and took the famous picture atop Mount Suribachi.
8. Robert Lee Sherrod, who accompanied the Marines at Tarawa and on several other operations and later wrote the authoritative *A History of Marine Aviation in World War II*.
9. Harry Smith, of UPI, who made the long walk out from the Chosin Reservoir, occasionally lending a hand with the fighting.
10. Richard Tregaskis, who reported on the Marines in three wars, and wrote *Guadalcanal Diary*.

A Dozen Prominent Americans Who Were Not Fond of the Marine Corps

1. Senator John Randolph, of Virginia, who called the Corps "an evil group" with praetorian tendencies.
2. President Andrew Jackson, who wished to abolish the Corps.
3. Henry David Thoreau, who said a Marine was "a man laid out alive and standing and already, as one might say, buried under arms with funeral accompaniments."
4. President Theodore Roosevelt, who wanted to make the Corps part of the Army.
5. General of the Army Douglas MacArthur, who could occasionally say nice things about the Marines, but in general made sure they received no publicity for their operations under his command.
6. General of the Army George C. Marshall, who seems to have wanted to abolish the Corps.
7. President Harry S Truman, who shared Marshall's opinion.
8. Secretary of Defense James Forrestal, who shared Marshall's opinion.
9. General J. Lawton Collins, USA, who definitely wanted to abolish the Corps.
10. Secretary of Defense Louis Johnson, who agreed with Collins.
11. President and General of the Army Dwight D. Eisenhower, who also agreed with Collins.
12. Walter Winchell, columnist, who adamantly sought the abolition of the Corps.

Three Traditional Names for the Marine Bulldog

1. "Sergeant Jiggs," used between the end of World War I and the 1930s
2. "Smedley," used for the Corps' bulldog from the 1930s into the 1950s
3. "Chesty," used for the Corps' bulldog since the 1950s.

One Famous Marine Duck

"Siwash" accompanied the 2nd Marine Division into action on Tarawa, Saipan, and Tinian, after which (in the meantime having become a mother), she was sent home to the U.S.

A Dozen Nicknames for Marines

1. "Leathernecks," from the heavy leather stocks—collars—issued Marines in the age of sail, to keep their heads erect, and, not incidentally, to prevent someone from cutting their throats in hand-to-hand combat.
2. "The Soldiers of the Sea," a traditional term for Marines dating back at least to the seventeenth century.
3. "Useless Sons Made Comfortable," popular in some circles during the late nineteenth century, in reference to certain officers who were commissioned through political influence. Refurbished in the late twentieth century as "Uncle Sam's Misguided Children."
4. "Gyrene," a term of uncertain origins which was applied to the Royal Marines as early as 1894, and to the U.S. Marines by about 1911.
5. "Seagoing Bell Hops," an early twentieth century term of derision among swabbies, apparently in reference to the pill box-type caps worn by Marines at the time.
6. "Jarheads," which some claim refers to the similarity between a Marine in dress blues, with his head above the collar, and a mason jar, but by some attributed to the often extreme haircuts customary in the Corps.
7. "Devil Dogs" (*Teufelhunden*), given by the Germans after Belleau Wood in World War I, in deference to the ferocity with which Marines fought.
8. "Harry's Police Force" had a brief vogue during the Korean Conflict, described by President Harry S Truman as a "police action."
9. "The President's Own," originally—and still—applied particularly to the Marine Band, but sometimes used to refer to the Corps as a whole.
10. "Yellow Legs," during the Korean War, from the canvas leggings that they wore.
11. "Tin Soldiers," a rude term used by sailors in the nineteenth century.
12. "State Department troops," used to describe the Corps in the 1920s, due to its use as an interventionist force in Latin America.

Some Notable Comments by Marines

1. "A few good men," Marine Captain William Jones, in the Corps' first recruiting advertisement, *The Providence Gazette*, 20 March 1779)
2. "Gone to Florida to fight Indians. Will be back when the war is over," pinned to his office door by CMC Archibald Henderson, 1836.
3. "We will do our best," CPT John T. Myers, commanding the Legation Guard at Peking, August 1900.

4. "Retreat Hell! We've just got here!" reportedly said by a Marine officer—variously COL Wendell Neville or CPT Floyd Williams of the 5th Marines—when he encountered French officers who urged him to advance in the wrong direction.

5. "Come on, you sons of bitches—do you want to live forever?" attributed to Gunnery Sergeant Daniel Daly, at Belleau Wood, in June 1918. *

6. "God damn it! Continue the advance!" said at Belleau Wood by CPT Randolph T. Zane, 6th Marines, when a lieutenant, reporting that his platoon was down to five men, asked what should he do.

7. "We kill or we get killed," said by an unknown Marine on 17 June 1918, when, as a prisoner of the Germans he was asked "What are you Americans doing here?"

8. "Few in number, though mighty," BG Albertus W. Catlin, 1919.

9. "Even Marines don't fight all the time," MG Smedley D. Butler, 1933.

10. "Soldiers trained in the ways of the sea," CMC Benjamin H. Fuller, c. 1934.

11. "The issue is in doubt," last message from Wake Island, 23 December 1941.

12. "Blood for Eleanor!" an unknown Marine on Guadalcanal, 1942, responding to taunts of "Blood for the Emperor" from Japanese troops.

13. "Goddam it, you'll never get the Purple Heart hiding in a foxhole! Follow me!" Captain Henry P. Crowe, Guadalcanal, 13 January 1943.

14. "Casualties many; Percentage of dead not known; Combat efficiency: We are winning," Colonel David M. Shoup, USMC, Tarawa, 21 November 1943

15. "Those poor bastards. They've got us right where we want them. We can shoot in every direction now," COL Lewis "Chesty" Puller, November 1950, when told that the 1st Marine Division was surrounded **

16. "Retreat Hell! We're just attacking in another direction," supposedly said by Major General Oliver P. Smith, USMC, Korea, November 1950.

17. "Wherever Marines assemble, they bring with them their past," COL Allen R. Millett, USMCR (Ret),1991.

*Some accounts have it that Daly said "Come on you crazy sons-of-bitches, do you want to live forever?" Daly himself denied having uttered any such vulgarity. When asked about the alleged statement, he told a reporter "You know a non-com would never use hard language. I said, For goodness sake, you chaps, let us advance against the foe." On another occasion, however, Daly said that his words were "For Christ's sake, do you want to live forever?" and on yet another occasion, claimed he'd said "Gracious, you chaps, do you want to live forever?" Whatever it was Daly said, the sentiment has certainly been expressed before. Holding the line at the Battle of Malvern Hill (1 June 1862), Nelson A. Miles (later a distinguished Indian fighter and Commanding General of the Army during the War with Spain) heard an unknown Confederate colonel lead an attack with the cry, "Come on! Come on! Do you want to live forever?"

** Alternatively reported as "They've got us surrounded. The bastards won't get away this time. "

A Baker's Dozen of Complimentary Comments About the Marines Made by Non-Marines

1. "The gallant corps," *The National Intelligencer*, 1837, commenting upon the role of the Marines in the Florida War.

2. "A gallant little band upon which rest the most widely extended duties at home and in every sea and clime," Secretary of the Navy Isaac Toucy, 1859.

3. "...At all times ready and prompt in the execution of any duty," COL Robert E. Lee, after the capture of John Brown, 1859.
4. "A ship without Marines is like a garment without buttons," Admiral David D. Porter, USN, 1863.
5. "With the help of God and a few Marines," a traditional phrase that originated in the late nineteenth century and has turned up frequently since.
6. "The Marines have landed and the situation is well in hand," sometimes found as "The Marines have landed and have the situation well in hand," has no known origin; it became common during the late nineteenth century, and was popularly associated with the famous war correspondent Richard Harding Davis.
7. "The Marines acquitted themselves nobly," Edwin N. Conger, U.S. Minister to China, concerning the defense of the Legations Quarter in Peking, during the Boxer Rebellion, 1900.
8. "You rushed into the fight as to a *fete*," French Major General Emanuel Mangin, 18 July 1918, after Belleau Wood.
9. "No one can ever say that the Marines have ever failed to do their work in handsome fashion," MG Johnson Hapgood, US Army, 1937.
10. "They are quite brave," unknown Japanese Staff Officer, in a report on the Battle for Guadalcanal, 4 March 1943, which considering Japanese expertise on the subject, and normal reticence, amounts to high praise.
11. "Among the men who fought on Iwo Jima, uncommon valor was a common virtue," Fleet Admiral Chester W. Nimitz, USN, 16 March 1945.
12. "Fortunately God loves the Marines," Samuel Eliot Morison, 1951, commenting on the good luck which seems to attend Marine operations.
13. "The Marines will be needed as long as America needs defending," J. Robert Moskin, 1992.

One Notable Comment About the 1st Marine Division

1. "The 1st Marine Division is the most efficient and courageous combat unit I have ever seen or heard of," MG Frank E. Lowe, US Army, 1950.

Ten Notable Comments About Individual Marines

1. "Contributed materially to the defeat and virtually the annihilation of a Japanese regiment," said by LTC Lewis "Chestry" Puller in his recommendation that the Medal of Honor be awarded to SGT John Basilone.
2. "In case of a national emergency, this officer should be given a division," comment on MAJ John A. Lejeune, by the Commandant, Army War College.
3. "One of [the Corps'] most distinguished and affectionately regarded officers," said by MG John A. Lejeune about MG Joseph Pendleton.
4. "Sometimes you love him, sometimes you hate him, but I'd rather fight with Red Mike than anyone else," said by a Marine Raider of LTC Merritt A. Edson, after the Battle of Edson's Ridge, Guadalcanal.
5. "The bravest man I have ever known," said by journalist Robert Sherrod of 1LT William Deane Hawkins, arguably the first Marine to land on Tarawa, who was posthumously awarded a Medal of Honor for heroism there on 20-21 November 1943.
6. "The fightingest Marine I ever knew," said by Smedley Butler of SGM Dan Daly.
7. "The finest soldier any captain could wish to have," said of Dan Daly by BG W. P. Upshur.

8. "The only man in any service who really likes to fight," said of COL Lewis "Chesty" Puller by the CMC, 1950.
9. "The outstanding Marine of all time," said of SGM Dan Daly by CMC John A. Lejeune.
10. "The tougher the action the louder Lou would yell," an unattributed comment about MGySGT Lou Diamond.

Eight Rude Things Said About Marines

1. "Tell it to the Marines! The sailors will never believe it!" King Charles II (Although Samuel Pepys wrote that the King actually said, "Henceforth whenever we cast doubt upon a tale that lacketh likelihood we will tell it to the Marines—if they believe it, it is safe to say it is true," because "from the very nature of their calling, no class of our subjects can have so wide a knowledge of the seas and lands.").
2. "Empty bottles," a traditional British comment about Marines.
3. "Undisciplined and ignorant of life at sea," John Adams.
4. "An evil group," Virginia anti-Federalist politician and Senator John Randolph.
5. "....a Marine—, a man laid out alive and standing and already, as one might say, buried under arms with funeral accompaniments," Henry David Thoreau, 1848.
6. "The two most useless things aboard ship, the mizzen royal and the Captain of Marines," an Old Navy saying.
7. "Tin soldiers," an Old Navy saying.
8. "They have a propaganda machine that is almost equal to Stalin's," said by President Harry S Truman in a letter dated 1 September 1950. When the letter became public, it caused a popular uproar, and the President apologized on 6 September. The letter was later sold to a collector for $2,500, an enormous sum in 1950.

## CHAPTER 12

Marine Aviation

The Marine Corps first became interested in aviation in 1911. By 1918 Marine aircraft were in action over Northern France and Belgium, while others conducted anti-submarine patrols in the Atlantic. Marine aviation has continued to grow since then, as a unique air-ground combat force.

Some Marine Aviation Firsts

First Marine Aviator, 1LT Alfred A. Cunningham, Naval Aviator No. 5.

First Marine Aviation Unit to Deploy Overseas, 1st Marine Aeronautic Company, landed, Punta Delgada, the Azores, 21 January 1918.

First Marine Corps Air Station, the Marine (formerly Curtis) Flying Field, Miami, FL, April 1918.

First Marine aerial resupply of a besieged garrison, Quilali, Nicaragua, 1-8 January 1928. *

First Marine combat aircraft, DeHaviland DH 4

First use of dive bombing in support of ground forces, Ocotal, Nicaragua, 16 July 1927.

First Marine to down seven enemy aircraft in one day, 1LT James E. Swett, 7 Apr 1943, off Guadalcanal. **

First Marine to make a carrier landing and take off, 1LT William Jennings Wallace

* In fact the first successful effective aerial resupply of a beleaguered garrison ever.

** And the first American to ever accomplish this feat.

Marine Aviators Who Earned the Medal of Honor

1. 2LT Ralph Talbot (#109), 8 & 14 Oct 1918, Pittham, Belgium
2. CySGT Robert G. Robinson (#109), 14 Oct 1918, Pittham, Belgium
3. 1LT Christian F. Schilt (#114), 6-8 Jan 1928, Quilali, Nicaragua
4. CPT Henry T. Elrod (#117), 8-23 Dec 1941, Wake Island *
5. LTC Harold W. Bauer (#118), 10 May-14 Nov 1942, SW Pacific & Guadalcanal
6. CPT Richard E. Fleming (#119), 4-5 Jun 1942, Midway
7. MAJ John L. Smith (#120), 1 Aug-30 Sep 1942, Guadalcanal
8. MAJ Robert E. Galer (#125), 1 Oct 1942, Guadalcanal
9. CPT Joseph J. Foss (#126), 9 Oct-19 Nov 1942 and 15 and 23 Jan 1943, Solomon Islands
10. CPT Jefferson J. DeBlanc (#130), 31 Jan 1943, Kolombangara
11. 1LT James E. Swett (#131), 7 Apr 1943, Solomons
12. 1LT Kenneth A. Walsh (#132), 15 & 30 Aug 1943, Vella LaVella
13. MAJ Gregory Boyington (#133), 12 Sep 1943-3 Jan 1944, Central Solomons
14. 1LT Robert M. Hanson (#134), 1 Nov 1943-1 Jan 1944, Bougainville **
15. CPT Stephen W. Pless (#258), 19 Aug 1967, Quang Nai, Vietnam
16. PFC Raymond M. Clausen, Jr. (#291), 31 Jan 1970, Vietnam

* Awarded for both air and ground combat.

** Killed in action, 3 February 1944, before learning he had been awarded the Medal of Honor.

Marine Aces of World War II

MC	Name	Score	US
1	Gregory Boyington	28	4-5
2	Joseph J. Foss	26	9
3	Robert M. Hanson	25	10
4	Kenneth A. Walsh	21	20-21
5	Donald N. Aldrich	20	23-25
6	John L. Smith	19	28-30
7-8	Marion E. Carl	18.5	31-33
	Wilbur J. Thomas	18.5	30-33
9	James E. Swett	15.5	
10	Harold L. Spears	15	
11	Archie G. Donahue	14	
12-15	James N. Cupp	13	
	Robert E. Galer	13	
	William P. Marontate	13	
	Edward O. Shaw	13	
16	Kenneth D. Frazier	12.5	
17-19	Loren D. Everton	12	
	Harold E. Segal	12	
	Eugene A. Trowbridge	12	
20	Philip C. DeLong	11.5	
21-22	Harold W. Bauer	11	
	Donald H. Sapp	11	
23	Jack E. Conger	10.5	
24	Herbert H. Long	10	
25-29	Jefferson J. DeBlanc	9	
	Christopher L. Magee	9	
	Thomas H. Mann	9	
	Edmund F. Overend	9	
	Franklin C. Thomas, Jr.	9	
30-32	Gregory K. Loeseh	8.5	
	John L. Morgan, Jr.	8.5	
	William N. Snider	8.5	
33-42	William N. Case	8	
	John F. Dobbin	8	
	Fred E. Gutt	8	
	Edwin J. Hernan, Jr	8	
	George L. Hollowell	8	
	Charles M. Kunz	8	
33-42	Joseph L. Narr	8	
	Nathan T. Post	8	
	Arthur T. Warner	8	
	Donald K. Yost	8	
43-57	Robert M. Baker	7	

MC	Name	Score	US
	William P. Brown	7	
	Dean Caswell	7	
	William E. Crowe	7	
	Roger A. Haberman	7	
	Henry B. Hamilton	7	
	Alvin J. Jensen	7	
	Robert W. McClurg	7	
	Jeremiah J. O'Keefe	7	
	Robert G. Owens, Jr.	7	
	Jack Pittman, Jr.	7	
	Joseph H. Reinburg	7	
	John W. Ruhsam	7	
	Robert Wade	7	
	Gerard M.H. Williams	7	
58	Paul A. Mullen	6.5	
59	Dewey F. Durnford	6.33	
60	Joseph V. Dillard	6.13	
61-84	George C. Axtell, Jr.	6	
	Robert Baird	6	
	John F. Bolt, Jr.	6	
	Creighton Chandler	6	
	Roger W. Conant	6	
	Eugene Dillow	6	
	Jefferson D. Dorroh	6	
	Frank C. Drury	6	
	Don H. Fisher	6	
	Robert B. Fraser	6	
	William B. Freeman	6	
	Sheldon B. Hall	6	
	John C. Hundley	6	
	Charles D. Jones	6	
	John McManus	6	
	Gilbert Percy	6	
61-84	Francis E. Pierce, Jr.	6	
	Zenneth A. Pond	6	
	Frank H. Presley	6	
	Perry L. Shuman	6	
	Robert F. Stout	6	
	Francis A. Terrill	6	
	Herbert J. Valentine	6	
	Milton N. Vedder	6	
85-89	Herman Hansen	5.5	
	William L. Hood	5.5	

MC	Name	Score	US		MC	Name	Score	US
	Floyd C. Kirkpatrick	5.5				Charles Kendrick	5	
	William M. Lundin	5.5				Wayne W. Laird	5	
	Frederick R. Payne, Jr.	5.5				Henry A. McCartney, Jr.	5	
90	Wallace E. Sigler	5.3				Selva E. McGinty	5	
91-	Stuart C. Alley, Jr.	5				Edwin L. Olander	5	
120	Frank B. Baldwin	5				Hyde Phillips	5	
	Richard L. Braun	5				George H. Poske	5	
	William A. Carlton	5				Ernest A. Powell	5	
	Leonard K. Davis	5				Orvin H. Ramlo	5	
	George E. Dawkins, Jr.	5				Hartwell V. Scarborough,	5	
	Cecil J. Doyle	5				Raymond Scherer	5	
	Charles W. Drake	5				Robert B. See	5	
91-	Hugh McJ. Elwood	5				Stanley Synar	5	
120	William Farrell	5				Gregory J. Weissenberger	5	
	Howard J. Finn	5				Albert P. Wells	5	
	Paul J. Fontana	5				Michael R. Yunck	5	
	Kenneth M. Ford	5						
	Albert C. Hacking	5						

Key: *MC* indicates the man's ranking in the series of Marine Corps Aces, with hyphenated numbers indicating a tie; *Score* is the number of aircraft with which he is credited, with decimals indicating a victory "shared" with other aircraft or anti-aircraft fire; *US*, for the first nine Marine Aces gives the man's rank among the top 33 U. S. aces of the World War II, with hyphenated numbers again indicating a tie.

The first Marine air victory of World War II occurred when 2LT David Kliewin shot down a two engined bomber in cooperation with ground fire off Wake Island on 9 December 1941. The last Marine air victory of the war occurred off Okinawa on 8 August 1945, when a Ki-61 "Tony" fighter was shot down by 2LT William Jennings. The first Marine to become an ace—that is to have shot down five or more enemy aircraft—was CPT Marion E. Carl of VMF-223 (*i.e.*, Marine Fighter Squadron 223), who eventually went on to shoot down 18.5 Japanese aircraft. Decimal figures indicate victories "shared" with other pilots or anti-aircraft fire. In the course of World War II USMC pilots shot down over 2,350 enemy aircraft. The 120 men listed above are officially credited with having downed slightly over 976 of them, about 41%. However, although this list is an official one, it is known to have errors. For example, George F. Dawkins, Jr. , listed as having five victories, observed that not only had he never shot down even a single enemy airplane, but he had in fact engaged in air combat on only one occasion during the war. Note that six of Gregory "Pappy" Boyington's victories occurred when he was a member of the American Volunteer Group ("The Flying Tigers") in China, although he apparently was only paid for 3.5 of them.

Some Marine Aircraft Carriers

From the late 1920s Marine aviation squadrons were commonly assigned to the Navy's carriers. During World War II, however, several escort carriers were assigned air groups that consisted entirely of Marine squadrons.

The "Special Escort Carrier Group, " March-April 1945

USS *Breton* (CVE-23)
USS *Hollandia* (CVE-97)
USS *Sitkoha Bay* (CVE-86)
USS *White Plains* (CVE-66)

These ships entered the Okinawa campaign equipped solely with aircraft of MAG-31 (COL J. C. Munn) and MAG-33 (COL W.E. Dickey). For the first three days of the campaign (1-3 April) these aircraft operated from the carriers. On 4 April the two air groups began conducting operations from land bases on Okinawa.

Escort Carriers with Operational Marine Air Groups

Carrier	MAG	Squadrons
USS *Block Island*(CVE-106)	MCVG 1	VMF 511 & VMTB 233
USS *Cape Gloucester* (CVE-109)	MCVG 4	VMF 351 & VMTB 132
USS *Gilbert Islands* (CVE-107)	MCVG 2	VMF 512 & VMTB 143
USS *Salerno Bay* (CVE-110)	MCVG 5	VMF 514 & VMTB 144
USS *Vella Gulf* (CVE-111)	MCVG 3	VMF 513 & VMTB 234
USS *Puget Sound* (CVE-113)	MCVG 6	VMF 321 & VMTB 459

The success of Marine squadrons operating from fleet carriers in early 1945 strengthened pressure on the Navy to provide some escort carriers with purely Marine Air Groups to support ground operations. The Navy agreed to equip eight escort carriers for this mission by the projected date for the invasion of Japan, 1 November 1945; each airgroup was to consist of one squadron of 18 Corsair fighters and one of 12 Avenger bombers. At the same time, the Navy began removing Marine squadrons from fleet carriers. The first of the 8 ships began entering the combat zone shortly after the end of the Okinawa Campaign. However, by then the war was "winding down," and 2 (*Block Island* and *Gilbert Islands*), reached the theater too late to take part in operations, while two others (*Vella Gulf* and *Cape Gloucester*) were still in training when the war ended.

Two Marines Who Became Aces in the Korean War

1. MAJ John F. Bolt, with six Japanese aircraft to his credit in World War II, shot down six MiG-15s while flying an Air Force F-86, thus becoming the Marine Corps's first, and only, jet Ace.
2. 1LT John W. Andre, who shot down one Yak-7 fighter, which, added to the four Japanese aircraft he had accounted for during the Second World War, placed him in the Ace category.

Altogether 21 Marine pilots accounted for some 35 enemy aircraft during the Korean War, many of them while on loan to USAF. Among them was the later astronaut, MAJ John H. Glenn, who downed three MiGs, tying with MAJ Alexander J. Gillis, for the second highest scoring Marine fighter pilot in the Korean War.

Grunt Ranking of the Quality of Close Air Support in Three Wars

1. Marine Aviation
2. Naval Aviation
3. The Air Force

Based on the opinions of both Marine and Army infantry veterans of World War II, Korea, and Vietnam.

A Chronological List of the Principal Combat Airplanes of the Marine Corps, 1918-1996

Years	Builder	Designation	Type	Wt	Crew	Arm	Ord	HP	SPD	Range	CV?
18-29	DeHaviland	DH4	Bmr	2.1	2	4 mg	.5	400	125	550	N
26-32	Boeing	FB1	Ftr	1.41	0	2 mg		435	159	371	N
27-31	Curtiss	F6C Hawk	Ftr	1.6	1	2 mg		410	155	360	Y
28-34	Curtiss	F8C Falcon	Ftr	2.1	1	3 mg	.05	431	144	650	Y
33-38	Boeing	F4B (P-12)	Ftr	1	41	2 mg		450	156	371	Y
34-40	Great Lakes	BG1	Bmr	3.2	2	2 mg	1.0	750	188	549	Y
37-42	Curtiss	SBC Helldiver	DBmr	3.8	2	2 mg	1.0	950	237	590	Y
38-41	Grumman	F3F	Ftr	2.4	1	2 mg		900	264	980	Y
40-42	Brewster	F2A Buffalo	Ftr	3.6	1	4 mg	-	1,200	321	965	Y
40-42	Vought	SB2U Vindicator	DBmr	4.7	2	2 mg	1.2	825	243	1,120	Y
40-43	Douglas	SBD Dauntless	DBmr	5.4	2	4 mg	2.2	1,200	245	1,100	Y
41-45	Grumman	F4F Wildcat	Ftr	4.1		6 mg	-	1,200	318	770	Y
42-45	Curtiss	SB2C Helldiver	DBmr	8.3	2	2 mg	2.0	1.900	295	1,165	Y
		2x20									
42-47	Grumman	TBF/TBM Avenger	Bmr	7.5	3	3 mg	1.6	1,700	217	1,215	Y
42-48	Grumman	F6F Hellcat	Ftr	7.2	1	6 mg	-	2,000	380	945	Y
42-50	Vought	F4U Corsair	Ftr	7.3	1	6 mg	2.0	2,100	416	1,005	Y
43-45	North American	PBJ Mitchell (B24)	MBmr	17.0	6	13 mg	4.0	3,400	275	1,560	N
45-50	Grumman	F7F Tigercat	Ftr	12.9	1	4 mg	3.0	4,200	435	1,200	Y
				4x20							
47-51	McDonnell	FD/FH Phantom	Ftr	25.0	1	4 mg	-	3,200	479	770	Y
48-70	Douglas	AD1 Skyraider	Bmr	9.1	1	2x20	8.0	2,700	321	915	Y
50-55	Grumman	F9F-2 Panther	Ftr	9.3	1	4x20	-	6,250	579	1,300	Y
50-62	McDonnell	F2H Banshee (F-2)	Ftr	11.1	1	4x20	1.0	6,500	532	1,475	Y
53-60	North American	FJ2 Fury (F-1)	Ftr	9.4	1	4x20	-	6,000	670	990	Y
54-70	Grumman	F9F-6 Cougar	Ftr	9.8	1	4x20	6.0	7,250	647	1,200	Y
55-65	North American	FJ4 Fury (F-1)	Ftr	12.9	1	4x20	3.0	7,700	680	2,020	Y
57-75	Vought	F-8 Crusader	Ftr	17.0	1	4x20	5.0	28,700	1,133	1,425	Y
61-83	McDonnell	F-4 Phantom II	Ftr	25.0	1	*	6.0	17,660	1,415	600	Y
64-86	Grumman	A2F Intruder (A-6)	Bmr	13.3	2	-	18.0	18,600	644	1,010	Y
66-89	McDonnell	A4D Skyhawk (A-4)	Bmr	12.3	1	2x20	9.21	1,200	670	390	Y
71-	McDonnell	AV8 Harrier	Ftr	9.5	1	*	12.0	24,500	661	553	Y
80-	McDonnell	F-18 Hornet	Ftr	18.4	1	*	-	32,000	1,190	460	Y
80-	McDonnell	A-18 Hornet	Bmr	24.6	1	*	17.0	32,000	1,190	660	Y

Note: Counting all types, the Marines have fought in, carried cargo in, trained in, or conducted experiments with well over 500 different models of airplanes. In many cases only a handful of a particular type were employed, often only one. It would be impossible to list them all. As a result, this list includes only the most commonly used fixed wing combat aircraft. Many of the airplanes shown went through several models. In most cases the differences were relatively minor. In others the differences can be enormous, and so in several instances different models of the same airplane have been listed separately.

Key: Years, those during which the indicated aircraft was in service; *Builder*, manufacturer; *Designation*, type designator and common name, with alternative designation in parentheses; *Type*, Bmr = bomber, DBmr = dive bomber, MBmr = medium bomber, Ftr = fighter, though since the 1960s most fighters can also double as attack bombers; *Weight* is in tons; *Crew*, number required to operate; *Arm*, air combat armament, indicating eight machine guns or 20mm guns, with an * indicating that the airplane can carry a variety of missiles or other weapons; *Ord*, weight of deliverable ordnance, in thousands of pounds; *HP*, horse power for piston engine aircraft, pounds of thrust for reaction engines; *SPD*, speed, in statute miles per hour; *Range*, range in statute miles; *CV?*, carrier capable, Y=yes, N=no.

## CHAPTER 13

Other Marines

Amphibious landings are the oldest form of naval warfare, followed by boarding. Both techniques require specially trained personnel. The earliest accounts of naval warfare come down to us from the Egyptians, who fought the "Sea Peoples" in ship-to-ship actions in the 10th Century B.C, Pharaoh's sailors being supplemented by his soldiers for the occasion. The first people to specifically train soldiers to serve as infantrymen aboard ship appear to have been the Ancient Greeks. This custom was taken up by other ancient seafaring peoples. But with the fall of Rome, the practice of distinguishing between the trade of sailor and that of marine died. Although sea battles were still fought, they were fought by the crews of the ships involved, sometimes supplemented by landlubber soldiers. The practice of having special troops trained and organized to fight as marines was not revived until the 16th century. Today 45 countries posses a marine corps, or at least a corps of naval infantry.

Although they usually perform similar duties, there is a critical difference between true Marines and Naval Infantry. Marines are recruited specifically for service as soldiers on the sea, use military rather than naval ranks, and wear military dress. Naval Infantry are usually recruited from naval officers and enlisted men, use naval ranks, and usually wear naval uniforms. In effect, to use the words of Cardinal Richelieu, naval infantry are "sailors who go ashore trained as infantry," while Marines are essentially soldiers trained to perform military duties (*e.g.*, man the guns, provide shipboard security, and make amphibious landings) in support of naval operations. Army personnel trained to make amphibious assaults (during World War II nearly a third of all personnel in the Army Ground Forces received such training) do not qualify as Marines, since their primary mission is land combat.

Marine and Naval Infantry Corps of the World, Ranked by Size, 1996

Rank	Service	Strength	Rank	Service	Strength
1	U.S.	174,639		Mexico	8,000
2	Republic of China	30,000		Romania	8,000
3	Vietnam	30,000	13	Spain	7,500
4	Korea	25,000	14	Britain	7,300
5	Thailand	20,000	15-16	China	5,000
6	Brazil	15,000		Venezuela	5,000
7	Indonesia	12,000	17	Argentina	4,000
8	Russia	12,000	18-21	Chile	3,000
9	Philippines	8,500		France	3,000
10-12	Colombia	8,000		Peru	3,000

Rank	Service	Strength	Rank	Service	Strength
	Turkey	3,000	34	Burma	800
22	Netherlands	2,930	35	Guatemala	700
23-24	Bolivia	2,000	36	Zaire	600
	India	2,000	37-38	Paraguay	500
	Iran	2,000		Uruguay	500
26	Portugal	1,880	39	Bulgaria	450
27-30	Ecuador	1,500	40	Honduras	400
	Italy	1,500	41	Israel	300
	Morocco	1,500	42	Dominican Republic	200
	Saudi Arabia	1,500	43	El Salvador	120
31	Pakistan	1,200	44	Madagascar	100
32	Croatia	1,000	45	Togo	50
33	Yugoslavia	900			

This list includes all countries with an active marine corps or a distinct naval infantry branch of service. Some figures have been estimated. Note that in the case of France only the *Fusiliers-Marins*, a part of the naval service, have been included. France also has the *Troupes de marine* (c. 18,000), who are part of the army, providing garrison and intervention forces for present and former colonial possessions, and not at all analogous to the USMC.

The Dozen Oldest Existing Marine Corps

Seniority	Country	Founded
1	Spain	1537
2	Portugal	1585
3	France	1622
4	Britain	1664
5	Netherlands	1665
6	Russia	1705
7	Italy	1713
8	U.S.	1775
9	Argentina	1807
10	Brazil	1808 *
11	Chile	1818
12	Venezuela	1822

This list makes allowance for occasional short lapses in continuity, such as occurred in the case of the USMC between 1783 and 1798. Note that the date for the creation of the Spanish *Infanteria de Marina* could be put back as early as 1528, which in any case would not alter its status as the senior marine corps in the world.

* The Brazilian Marine Corps traces its origins to a brigade of Portuguese Marines which arrived in Rio de Janeiro with the Royal Family in 1808. One battalion of this brigade remained in Brazil when the King returned to Portugal in 1821, becoming the nucleus of the Marine Corps of an independent Brazil in 1822. If one discounts the 1808 date, then the 10th oldest Marine Corps is that of Chile, founded in 1818, with Brazil tied with Venezuela for 11th place.

Two Landlocked Countries that Have a Marine Corps

1. Bolivia
2. Paraguay

Since the primary mission of these forces is in operations on rivers and other inland waters, a more appropriate title for these troops would be Fluvials (from the Latin for "riverine"). In fact Paraguay does precisely that, terming its Marine Corps, the *Cuerpo de defensa fluvial.*

Foreign Marine Corps that Were Created with the Help of the USMC

1. Republic of Korea Marine Corps
2. Republic of Vietnam Marine Corps
3. Republic of the Philippines Marine Corps

The Mottoes of Nine Foreign Marine Corps

1. Argentina's *Infanteria de Marina,* "*Patriae semper vigiles*—Always watchful for the Fatherland."
2. Brazil's *Fuzileiros Navais,* "*Adsumus*—We are here"
3. Britain's Royal Marines, "*Per mare per terram*—By sea and by land."
4. Denmark's *Marineregiment* (1670-1692), "*Nec temere, ne timide*—Neither rashly nor timidly."
5. Ecuador's *Infanteria de Marina,* "*Vencer o morir*—Conquer or Die!"
6. Italy's *Reggimento San Marco,* "*Pax tibi Marce, evangelista meus*—Peace to you Mark, my evangelist," from the coat of arms of Venice, adopted as the regimental insignia in 1919. However, during World War I "*Per mare per terram*" was used, after the motto of the Royal Navy.
7. Netherlands' *Korps Mariniers,* "*Qua patet orbis*—In any part of the globe."
8. Spain's *Infanteria de Marina,* "*Valientes por tierra y por mar*—Courageous by land and by sea," a modification of the original motto, "*Por tierra y por mar*—By Sea and By Land" in Spanish.
9. Republic of Vietnam's Marine Corps, "*Danh-Du-To-Quoc*—Honor and Country."

Six Foreign Marine Corps that Have Served Alongside the USMC

1. The Royal Marines, on numerous occasions
2. Brazil's *Fuzilieros Navais,* in the Dominican Republic, 1965
3. Italy's *Reggimento San Marco,* in Lebanon, 1983, and Somalia, 1990-1991
4. Netherlands's *Korps Mariniers,* during Operation Provide Comfort
5. Republic of Korea Marine Corps, in Korea, 1950-1953, and in Vietnam 1966-1970
6. Republic of Vietnam Marine Corps, in Vietnam, 1964-1972

Arguably the Three Most Famous Marines Ever

1. Miguel de Cervantes, author of *Don Quixote*, served in the *Infanteria de Marina* at the Battle of Lepanto, 7 October 1571, during which he was severely wounded.
2. John Churchill served in the Marines 1672-1683 before passing into the Army and becoming the hero of the War of the Spanish Succession, for which he was created Duke of Marlborough; also happens to have been an ancestor of Winston Churchill.
3. Jose de San Martin, "The Liberator" of Argentina and Chile, served a short tour as a junior officer in the *Infanteria de Marina*, before passing into the Spanish Army during the early part of the Napoleonic Wars.

Four Marine Corps that Have Organized Parachute Battalions

1. France's *Fusiliers-Marins* formed a parachute commando in Britain during World War II, which took part in the Normandy Invasion with the British 6th Airborne Division.
2. Italy's *Reggimento San Marco* fielded a parachute battalion during World War II. Actually, it was composed of "swimmer parachutists," organized for special operations. Small detachments from this battalion conducted sabotage missions and raids behind Allied lines in North Africa and, after Italy switched sides, behind German lines in Italy.
3. Japan's Special Naval Landing Forces fielded at least two parachute battalions during World War II, which made several successful combat drops in the early months of the war in the Pacific, most notably at Medon on Celebes and Palembang on Sumatra, in the Dutch East Indies, in February 1942.
4. The USMC fielded four parachute battalions during World War II, none of which made a combat air drop, but three of them accumulated distinguished combat records.

Four World Marine Corps Musical Oddities

1. The Brazilian *Fuzilieros Navais* has a pipe band, complete with kilted pipers, created in the nineteenth century because it seemed like a good idea at the time.
2. The Netherlands *Korps Mariniers* has a steel drum band, a heritage of its long ties with the Caribbean.
3. The Hymn of the Royal Thai Marine Corps was written by King Bhumibol Adukyadej, who is an accomplished musician and composer.
4. The USMC's band is the oldest musical organization in the United States.

Six Modern Marine Corps that No Longer Exist

1. Imperial and Royal Austro-Hungarian Marine Corps, 1856 -1918
2. Gran Colombian Marine Corps, 1811-1845
3. Royal Danish Marine Corps, 1670-1692 *
4. Imperial German Marine Corps, 1850-1918**
5. Imperial Japanese Special Naval Landing Forces, 1927-1945
6. Republic of Vietnam Marine Corps, 1954-1975

* The *Marineregiment*, a battalion of the Danish Army stationed on Bornholm Island is descended from this force, but is not actually a marine corps.

** The Royal Prussian Marine Corps was created in 1850, becoming the Imperial German Marine Corps in 1871.

The Royal Marines

Six Nicknames of the Royal Marines

1. "Her Majesty's Jollies" or "The Jollies," because they are ever cheerful
2. "Leathernecks," from those infamous stocks Marines used to wear
3. "Lobsters," from their red coats
4. "Porgies," because they are little fish
5. "Reds and Blues," from their uniforms
6. "Real Marines," which they use when they wish to annoy US Marines

The Fourteen Most Notable Dates in the History of the Royal Marines

1. Organization of the Royal Marines, 28 October 1664
2. Capture of Gibraltar, 24 July 1704 *
3. Battle of Belle Isle, 7 June 1781
4. Battle of Bunker Hill, 17 June 1775
5. Battle of Cape St. Vincent, 14 February 1797
6. Battle of Camperdown, 11 October 1797
7. Battle of the Nile, 1 August 1798
8. Battle of Copenhagen, 3 April 1801
9. Battle of Trafalgar, 21 October 1805
10. The Gallipoli Landings, 25 April 1915
11. Battle of Jutland, 31 May-1 June 1916
12. The Zeebrugge Raid, 22-23 April 1918
13. Capture of Mons, 10-11 November 1918
14. The Walchern Operation, 1 November 1944

* In company with the Netherlands *Korps Mariniers*

Battle Honors Carried on the Colors of the Royal Marines

1. Gibraltar

The Royal Marines have been involved in so many actions, usually with considerable distinction, that it was decided only their most glorious day, the capture of Gibraltar on 24 July 1704, should be emblazoned on their colors.

British Army Regiments that Have Served as Marines

1. The Royal Artillery, on numerous occasions.
2. 17/21st Lancers, the West Indies, 1796 (now incorporated in the Queen's Royal Lancers).
3. Grenadier Guards, the Second Dutch War, 1665-1667.
4. 2nd, "The Glorious First of June," 1794 (later incorporated in the Queen's Regiment).
5. 25th, "The Glorious First of June," 1794 (King's Own Scottish Borderers).

6. 1ˢᵗ Battalion, 69ᵗʰ, "The Glorious First of June," 1794
7. 2ⁿᵈ Battalion, 69ᵗʰ, the Battle of the Saintes, 1782, and "The Glorious First of June," 1794 (69ᵗʰ later incorporated in the Welsh Regiment now part of the Royal Regiment of Wales).

The Most Important Royal Marine in American History

1. MAJ John Pitcairn, the man who said "Disperse ye rebels," on Lexington Common, 19 April 1775, shortly before the firing of "The shot heard 'round the world."

Occasions on Which the USMC and the RM Have Fought Against Each Other in Ground Combat*

1. The Penobscot Expedition, 26 July-13 August 1779
2. The Siege of Charleston, 1 April-12 May 1780
3. Battle of New Orleans, 8 January 1815

* Omitting numerous ship-to-ship actions between 1775 and 1815.

Fourteen Occasions on Which the USMC and RM Have Served Side-by-Side

1. Defense of Curacao, Netherlands Antilles, 10-24 September 1800.
2. Occupation of Callao & Lima, Peru, 10 December 1835-24 January 1836.
3. Occupation of Buenos Aires, Argentina, 3-12 February 1852.
4. Occupation of Buenos Aires, Argentina, 17 September 1852-c. 15 April 1853.
5. Occupation of Shanghai, China, 4 April 1854.
6. Occupation of Canton, China, 3-5 August 1855.
7. Occupation of China Ports, 20 October -23 November 1856.
8. Raid on slaver stations, Kisembo, Portuguese Angola, 1-4 March 1860.
9. Occupation of Montevideo, Uruguay, 7-27 February 1868.
10. Occupation of Alexandria, Egypt, 14-24 July 1882.
11. China Relief Expedition, 24 May-28 September 1900.
12. Occupation of Port-au-Prince, Haiti, 29 January-9 February 1914.
13. The Korean War, 1950-1951 (41 Commando, RM).
14. Operation Provide Comfort, Iraq, 1991-date.

One Occasion on Which the Royal Marines and the U. S. Marines Served in the Same Ship

1. September 1800: A detail of Royal Marines from HMS *Nereid* was assigned to the USS *Sally,* to assist in the defense of Curacao, in the Netherlands Antilles, against a French assault.

One Occasion on Which the Royal Marines Provided CAS for the US Marines

Okinawa, 1 April-2 July 1945, when Royal Marine aircraft operating from Royal Navy carriers supported the III Marine Amphibious Corps.

Royal Marines Who Were Awarded the Victoria Cross

1. LT George D. Dowell, RMA, Viborg, Russia, 13 July 1855.
2. CPL John Prettyjohn, RM, Battle of Inkerman, 5 November 1854.
3. Bombardier Thomas Wikinson, RMA, Assault on Sebastapol, 7 June 1855.
4. CPT Lewis S. T. Halliday, RMLI, China Relief Expedition, 24 June 1900.
5. MAJ Frederick J. M. Harvey, RMLI, Battle of Jutland, 31 May-1 June 1916, posthumous.
6. MAJ Frederick William Lumsden, RMA, 1915, posthumous.
7. LCPL Walter R. Parker, RMLI, Royal Navy Division, France, 30 April-1 May 1915.
8. CPT Edward Bamford, RMLI, Zeebrugge Raid. 22-23 April 1918.
9. SGT Norman A. Finch, RMA, Zeebrugge Raid, 22-23 April 1918.
10. CPL Thomas P. Hunter, RM, 43 Commando, Italy, 1945.

Note: In 1858 the Royal Marines were reorganized into the Royal Marine Artillery (RMA) and the Royal Marine Light Infantry (RMLI), a division that remained in force until 1923, when the two forces were again merged to form the Royal Marines.

The First Woman Royal Marine

1. Hannah Snell (1723-????).

A rather reliable tradition has it that, disguised as a man, Snell had already seen service in the British Army when she enlisted in the Royal Marines in 1745, serving undetected until honorably discharged in 1749, afterwards confessing her deception to her erstwhile comrades. She subsequently opened a pub, at which her former brothers-in-arms were ever welcome.

Peak Strength of the Royal Marines during Its Principal Wars

War	Years	Strength
The Seven Years' War *	1756-1763	18,355
War of the American Revolution	1775-1783	25,000
The French Wars	1793-1815	30,000
World War I	1914-1918	55,000
World War II	1939-1945	78,000

* In the U.S. this is more generally known as the French and Indian War.

Principal Active Units of the Royal Marines

3 Commando Brigade, Royal Marines
    40 Commando
    42 Commando

45	Commando Group
	Comacchio Group
	Commando Logistic Regiment
	Signal Squadron
847	Naval Air Squadron
539	Assault Squadron
29	Commando, Royal Artillery
	Special Boat Service
	Commando Company
	Landing Craft and Amphibious Training Wing
	Amphibious Trials and Training Unit Royal Marines

Number 847 Naval Air Squadron is actually a part of the Fleet Air Arm, and 29 Commando is a battalion of the Royal Artillery, a part of the Army. The independent Commando Company has the duty of protecting the North Sea oil fields from terrorist attack. With the Netherlands *1 Mariniers Bataljon* (1st Marine Battalion), No. 3 Commando Brigade, RM, forms the UK/Netherlands Amphibious Force.

Spain, Infanteria de Marina Española

A Dozen Notable Actions in the History of the *Infanteria de Marina*

1. Battle of Lepanto, 7 October 1571
2. Capture of Tunis, August 1572
3. The Spanish Armada, 19-28 July 1588
4. Defense of Gibraltar, 23-24 July 1704
5. Capture and Defense of Sicily, 15 October 1718-29 October 1719
6. Capture of Oran, 30 June 1723
7. Defense of Havana, 20 June-10 August 1762
8. Capture of Menorca, 6 January 1782
9. Defense of Toulon, 7 September-19 December 1793
10. Liberation of Buenos Aires, 12 August 1806
11. Battle of Callao, 2 August 1866
12. Alhucemas Landing, Morocco, 8-9 September 1925

One Spanish Marine Who Earned the *Cruz Laureada de San Fernando*

1. Marine Manuel Lois Garcia died of burns after having prevented an explosion aboard the heavy cruiser *Baleares*, following her torpedoing on 7 September 1937, during the Spanish Civil War.

One Notable Thing Said by a Spanish Marine

1. "The Marines die, but never surrender," CPT Antonio Suarez, when called upon to surrender at El Ferrol on 21 July 1936, at the onset of the Spanish Civil War.

Unique Distinctions of the Spanish *Infanteria de Marina*

1. Sergeants wear gold braid on their caps to honor the courage of the *Infanteria de Marina* at Havana in 1762.
2. Corporal's stripes are outlined in gold, for the same reason.

Daily Ration of Spanish Marines, 1580

26 ounces of hard tack
12 ounces of fresh beef, pork, or fish (when in port) or 6 ounces of salt (when at sea)
c. 1 liter each of wine and oil
salt and vinegar

Principal Active Units of the Spanish Marine Corps

Tercio de Armada, San Fernando
Tercio Norte, El Ferrol
Tercio Sur, San Fernando
Tercio de Levante, Cartagena
Agrupacion de Madrid, Madrid
Agrupacion de Canarias, Las Palmas de Gran Canaria
Compañia Mar Oceano de la Guardia Real, Madrid
Seccion Martin Alvarez, V/STOL Carrier *Principe de Asturias*

The *Tercio de Armada* is an amphibious assault brigade. The units stationed at El Ferrol, San Fernando, Cartagena, Madrid, and Las Palmas are security details of regiment and battalion size. The *Compañia Mar Oceano* provides security for the Royal Family.

Republic of Korea Marine Corps

A Dozen Notable Actions of the ROK Marines

1. The Inchon Landings, 15-16 September 1950
2. Liberation of Seoul, 20-30 September 1950
3. Defense of Wonsan, 2-10 December 1950
4. Capture of Hill 975, Operation Ripper, 20-3 March 1951
5. Capture of Hill 509, Chinese "Fifth Phase Offensive, " 22-23 April 1951
6. Battle for Hill 1316, 4-9 June 1951
7. Battle for Hills 937 and 1026, Taeam-Son Offensive ("The Punchbowl"), 27 August-3 September 1951
8. Defense of the Imjin River (Jamestown Line), 1-14 August 1952

9. Operation Van Buren, Vietnam, 19 January-21February 1966
10. Operation John Paul Jones, Vietnam, 21 July -5 Aug 1966
11. Operation Daring Rebel, Vietnam, 5-20 May 1969
12. Battle of Hoi An, Vietnam 7-19 September 1969

For most of the Korean War, the ROK Marine Corps, founded in 1949, operated as a fourth regiment of the 1st Marine Division. The only important occasion on which this arrangement was not in force was during the advance to and wihtdrawl from the Chosin Reservoir. During the Vietnam War the 2nd Brigade of ROK Marines ("Blue Dragons"), occasionally operated in conjunction with the USMC or the Vietnamese Marine Corps.

The Five Tenets of the Korean Marine Corps

1. Loyalty to the Nation
2. Ever Victorious
3. United as Family
4. Honor before Life
5. Love of Fellow Countrymen

France, Fusiliers-Marins

Two French Marine Regiments Important in U. S. History

Regiment Walsh-Serrant, an Irish regiment that provided many of the Marines aboard John Paul Jones' *Bon Homme Richard* in 1770.

Le Regiment Royal de Marine, which, landing from the French fleet, supported the investment of Yorktown in 1781.

Four Famous Names in the History of the *Fusiliers-Marins*

1. Cardinal Armand Jean de Plessis Richelieu, who founded the *Fusiliers-Marins* in 1622.
2. RAdm Pierre Alexis Ronarc'h, commander of the *Brigade de fusiliers marins* in 1914.
2. VAdmde la Ronciere Le Noury, commander of *Fusiliers marins*, Paris 1870-1871
4. *Capitain de Corvette* Philippe Kiefer, who led the *Commandos francais* at Ouistreham, 6 June 1944.

The Ten Most Notable Actions by French Marines

1. Battle of the Plains of Abraham, Quebec, 13 September 1759
2. Battle of Trafalgar, 21 October 1805
3. Storming of the Sambre River Bridge at Charleroi, 15 June 1815
4. Defense of Paris, 20 September 1870-28 January 1871
5. Combat of Douars during the Battle of Amiens, 27 November 1870
6. Battle of Le Mans, 10-12 January 1871
7. Defense of Dixmude and Nieuport, 7 October-10 November 1914
8. Defense of Bir Hacheim, 1-11 June 1942

9. Normandy Airdrop, 6 June 1944
10. Normandy Landings and Capture of Ouistreham, France, 6 June 1944

The Finest Compliment Ever Paid to the French Marines

"You are my best infantrymen," Joseph Jacques Cesaire Joffre, *Marechal de France*, Supreme Commander, the French Armies, 1914.

Principal Active Units of the *Fusiliers-Marins*

> Commando Jaubert
> Commando Monfort
> Commando Trepel
> Commando DePenfentenyo
> Commando Hubert

Each commando is a small battalion-sized special warfare force analogous to the SEALS. *Commando Hubert* specializes in underwater operations. The *Fusiliers-Marins* also provide security details for naval installations and vessels.

Italy, Reggimento San Marco

A Dozen Notable Actions by the *Reggimento San Marco*

1. Battle of the Sile, 15-19 December 1917
2. Defense of the Cortelazzo Bridgehead, 19-20 December 1917
3. Battle of the Piave, 15-19 June 1918
4. Battle of Vittorio Veneto, 24 October-4 November 1918
5. Capture of Addis Abeba, Ethiopia, 5 May 1936
6. Raid on the Alexandria-Alamein Railroad, 29 August 1942
7. Defense of Tobruk, 13-14 September 1942
8. Defense of Teboura, Tunisia, 5 December 1942
9. Capture of the Heights of Dabus, Tunisia, 21-22 Janaury 1943
10. Battle for Cassino, 18 March 1944
11. Battle of Belvedre Ostrense, 21 July 1944
12. Storming of Tossignano, 12 April 1945

One Notable Comment about the *San Marco*

1. "*Il piu forte!*— The Strongest," by Gabrielle d'Annunzio, about the regiment's defense of the Cortelazzo Bridgehead.

Four Italian Marines who Earned the *Medaglia d'Oro* for Valor

1. CDR Andrea Bafile, at Cortellazzo on 12 March 1918, posthumous *
2. 2LT Baldassare Mazzuchelli, at Mussana, 3-4 November 1918 **, posthumous

3. LCDR Anselmo Marchi da Lucca, at Belvedere Ostrense, 21 July 1944, posthumous
4. 2LT Alfonso Casati, at Corinaldo, 6 August 1944, posthumous *******

* The *San Marco* uses naval ranks, Bafile was *Tenete de Vascello*.

** An Army Engineer serving with what was then known as the *Brigata Marina*, the designation *Reggimento San Marco* not being conferred until 17 March 1919.

*** Count Casati, the only son of the Italian War Minister, was an army *sottotenente*, on loan to the San Marco.

One Unknown Hero of the *San Marco*

1. On 3 January 1941 a marine of the *San Marco* was killed when he refused to lower the Italian flag at Bardia, which had just been captured by the 6th Australian Division.

Unique Distinctions of the *San Marco*

1. Battalions of the *San Marco* bear names, rather than numbers, in memory of notable heroes or actions of the regiment.
2. The regiment has the oddest motto of any military force in the world, *Pax tibi Marce, evangelista meus* ("Peace to you Mark, my evangelist"), from the coat of arms of the city of Venice, adopted as the regimental insignia in 1919.
3. The regiment once included a battalion of "Swimmer Parachutists," for special operations.

The Netherlands, Korps Mariniers

Founders of the *Korps Mariniers*

1. Michiel DeRuyter, the finest admiral of the seventeenth century
2. John de Witt, notable Dutch admiral

The Nine Most Notable Actions by the *Korps Marniers*

1. DeRuyter's Raid in the Medway, England, June 1667
2. Battle of Sole Bay, 28 May 1672
3. Battle of the Texel, 11 August 1673
5. The Capture of Gibraltar, 24 July 1704 *
5. Battle of Malaga, 13 August 1704
6. Battle of the Dogger Bank, 5 August 1781
7. Capture of Toeloe Cetopang, Malacca, 18 June 1784
8. Algerian Expedition, August 1816 *
9. Defense of Zealand, 10-17 May 1940

* In company with the Royal Marines.

The Most Notable Dutch Marine

Joseph van Ghent, first colonel of the *Regiment Scheepsoldaten* of 1665.

Unique Distinctions of the *Korps Mariniers*

1. The entire *Korps Mariniers* was awarded the *Militaire Willems Orde*, the Netherlands' highest decoration, 10 December 1946, for outstanding performance of its duty since 1665, but specifically for the Defence of Zealand in 1940.
2. The *Korps Mariniers* is the only marine corps in the world with a steel drum band, a symbol of its Caribbean ties.
3. The *Korps Mariniers* wears naval insignia of rank, but uses military terminology.

Occasions on Which the *Korps Mariniers* and the Royal Marines Have Operated Together

1. Capture of Gibraltar, 24 July 1704
2. Algerian Expedition, August 1816

Principal Active Units of the *Korps Mariniers*

1 Mariniers Bataljon
2 Mariniers Bataljon
3 Mariniers Bataljon
4 Mariniers Bataljon
Gevechssteun Bataljon
Bijzondere Bijstands Eenheid

The 1st Battalion is integrated in the Royal Marine's 3 Commando Brigade, forming the United Kingdom/Netherlands Amphibious Force, and has attached to it an amphibious reconnaissance platoon, a boat company, and a 120-mm mortar company. The 2nd Battalion forms part of the NATO Allied Mobile Force-Land. The 3rd Battalion is in standby status, formable on orders. The 4th forms the garrison of the Netherlands Antilles. The *Bijzondere Bijstands Eenheid* consists of two platoons specialized for anti-terrorist actions. The *Gevechssteun Bataljon* is a combat support battalion, comprising two 120 mm mortar companies, a detachment of 105 mm light field guns, and anti-air craft platoon, and a platoon of combat engineers, a logistical support battalion, and an amphibious landing craft command. There are marine barracks at several naval bases, and marines are also stationed on several of the ships of the Royal Netherlands Navy

Russia, Morskaya pekhota

Notable Actions of the Russian Naval Infantry

1. Battle of Chesme, 7-8 July 1770
2. Defense of Sebastapol, 28 September 1854-9 September 1855
3. Defense of the Peking Legations, 20 June-14 August 1900
4. Defense of Port Arthur, 1 June 1904-2 January 1905
5. Defense of Odessa, 13 August-16 October 1941
6. Recapture of the Kerch Peninsula, 25 December 1941-2 January 1942
7. Stanichki-Myshako Landings, 4-10 February 1943

8. Golubin Operation, 10 September 1943
9. Lake Ladoga Operation, 23-24 June 1944
10. Capture of Vormsi Island, the Gulf of Finland, 27 September 1944

A Notable Nickname for Russia's Naval Infantry

"*Schwarz tod*—black death", given by German soldiers during World War II, from the black uniforms which the Soviet Naval Infantry wore in combat.

Venezuela, Infanteria de Marina

Principal Units of the Venezuelan Marine Corps

Nº 1 Comando Anfibio, Puerto Cabello, Carabobo *
Nº 2 Comando Anfibio Carúpano, Estado Sucre *
Nº 1 Comando Fluvial Fronterizo, Puerto Ayacucho, Amasonas
Nº 2 Comando Fluvial Fronterizo, El Amparo, Estado Apure
Comando de Operaciones Especiales, Punto Fijo, Falcón
Batallón de Ingenieros de Construcción

* Each consisits of two battalions of infantry, an artillery group, a combat engineer unit, an amphibious vehicles unit, and a communications unit. The *commandos fluviales* are smaller versions of these groups, organized and equipped for riverine operations. As with many Latin American and European Marine Corps, battalions of the Venezuelan Marines bear names honoring various heroes or notable actions.

Argentina, Infanteria de Marina

Some Argentine Marine Heroes

1. *Teniente de Navio* Candido de Lasala, mortally wounded 5 June 1807, in the defense of Buenos Aires. *
2. SGM Ricardo Baxter, who led the Marines in capturing Martin Garcia Island from the Spanish.
3. *Capitain de Fregata* Pedro Edgardo Giachino, died of wounds during the capture of the Falkland Islands, 2 April 1982.

* The Argentine Marine Corps—which has been disbanded and reactivated a surprising number of times—uses naval ranks for officers.

Six Notable Actions of the Argentine Marine Corps

1. Defense of Buenos Aires, 4-7 July 1807.
2. Capture of Martin Garcia Island, 15 March 1814
3. Battle of Colonia, 1-2 March 1826
4. Capture of Islas Ratas, 29 April 1843
5. *Correo* vs *Merced*, 17 February 1853

6. Falkland Islands Campaign, 1 April- 14 June 1982

Principal Units of the Argentine Marine Corps

Superior Commands
>   *Brigada de Infanteria de Marina No. 1*
>> *Fuerza de Infanteria de Marina No. 1*
>> *Fuerza de Apoyo Anfibio*

Operational Forccs
>> *Batallón de Infanteria de Marina No. 1*
>> *Batallón de Infanteria de Marina No. 2 "Don Pedro Edgardo Giachino"*
>> *Batallón de Infanteria de Marina No. 3 "Almirante Eleazar Videla"*
>> *Batallón de Infanteria de Marina No. 4*
>> *Batallón de Infanteria de Marina No. 5*
>   *Batallón de Artilleria de Campaña No. 1*
>   *Batallón de Communicaciones No. 1*
>   *Batallón Antiaereo*
>   *Compañia de Inengieros Anfibios*
>   *Compañia de Exploracion*
>> *Compañia Antitanque*
>> *Agrupacion Commandos Anfinbios*
>   *Batallón de Vehiculas Anifibios*

There are also two command and logistical battalions, one for each of the two principal superior commands.

Vietnam Marine Corps

The Eleven Most Notable Actions of the Vietnamese Marines

1. Hai Dong San, 25 November 1963
2. An Thai, April 1965 *
3. Bong San, 7-8 April 1965
4. Hai An, 9 March 1965
5. Rach Ruong, 3-4 December 1967
6. Bien Hoa, March 1969 **
7. Operation Tran Hung Dao IX, 9-11 May 1970
8. Hill 147, Chaeu Kech, 14-15 May 1970
9. Pre Veng, Cambodia, 28 May-4 June 1970
10. Task Force Tango, 26-31 January 1973 ***
11. Long Binh, April 1975

* On this occasion a U. S. Presidential Unit Citation was awarded to the 2nd Battalion.

** On this occasion a U. S. Meritorious Unit Citation was awarded to the 5th Battalion

*** On this occasion the U.S. Valorous Unit Award was granted to the Vietnamese Marine Division, including the 2nd, 4th, and 9th Marine Battalions, elements of the 2nd and 3rd Marine Artillery Battalions, and several attached ARVN units.

Principal Units of the Vietnamese Marine Corps

Battalion	Emblem
1st Infantry	Wild Bird
2nd Infantry	Crazy Buffalo
3rd Infantry	Sea Wolf
4th Infantry	Killer Shark
5th Infantry	Black Dragon
6th Infantry	Sacred Bird
7th Infantry	Black Tiger
8th Infantry	Sea Eagle
9th Infantry	Mighty Tiger
1st Artillery	Lightning Fire
2nd Artillery	Sacred Arrow
3rd Artillery	Sacred Bow

The first Vietnamese Marine battalions were formed in 1956, when the Marine Infantry Corps of the Vietnamese Navy (formed in 1954) was redesignated as the Vietnam Marine Corps. By 1966 there were six battalions of infantry and three of artillery. Three additional battalions were raised by 1970, and the entire Marine Corps was organized as a division of three brigades. Between 1970 and 1975 an additional nine battalions were created, but most of the later ones were barely formed before the fall of Saigon.

Battalions were organized into brigades which took their numbers from the component battalions: the 147th Brigade included the 1st, 4th, and 7th Battalions, the 258th Brigade comprised the 2nd, 5th, and 8th Battalions, and the 369th Brigade included the 3rd, 6th, and 9th Battalions.

It was not unusual for battalions to be nicknamed after their emblem, so that the 1st Battalion was often known as the "Wild Birds. "

Japan, Rikusentai (Special Naval Landing Force)

Branches of the SNLF

1. Kure SNLF
2. Maizuru SNLF
3. Sasebo SNLF
4. Yokosuka SNLF

In 1927 each of the four principal bases of the Imperial Navy were ordered to raise detachments of naval infantry. For the balance of its existence, SNLF battalions were named and numbered for their home stations, thus there was a "Sasebo 1st SNLF," a "Kure 1st SNLF," a "Maizuru 1st SNLF," and a "Yokosuka 1st SNLF" At the onset of World War II there were about a dozen SNLF battalions, including two of parachutists. Total SNLF strength seems to have peaked at about three dozen battalions.

Ten Notable Operations of the SNLF not involving the USMC

1. Landings at Shanghai, 28 January 1932
2. Landings at Shanghai, 25 October 1937
3. Landings at Legaspi, Luzon, Philippines, 12 December 1942
4. Capture of Jolo, Philippines, 24 December 1942
5. Capture of Medon, Celebes, 11 January 1942, by an airborne assault.
6. Capture of Amboina, 30 January-4 February 1942
7. Capture of Palembang, Sumatra, 14-16 February 1942, by an airborne assault.
8. Capture of Java, 28 February-8 March 1942
9. Capture of Rabaul, 23 January 1942
10. Defense of Kwajelein Island, 1- 4 February 1944 *

* The SNLF troops on Kwajelein Island were at the southern end of the atoll, which was attacked by Army units, but none facing the Marines on Rio and Namur Islands, on the northern side of the atoll.

Six Occasions on which the USMC Fought with the SNLF

1. Guam, 10 December 1941, a provisional group of the SNLF *vs* the Marine garrison
2. Wake Island, 20-23 December 1941, the Maizuru 2nd SNLF *vs* the 1st Defense Battalion
3. Guadalcanal, 19 August 1942-8 February 1943: the Yokosuka 5th SNLF *vs* the 1st Marine Division
4. Tarawa, 20-22 November 1943: the Sasebo 7th SNLF and Yokosuka 6th SNLF *vs* the 2nd Marine Division
5. New Georgia, 5-20 July 1943, the Kure 6th SNLF *vs* the 1st and 4th Raider Battalions
6. Saipan, 11 June-10 July 1944: the Yokosuka 1st SNLF *vs* the 2nd and 4th Marine Divisions

There were several occasions on which Marines encountered Japanese Navy ground troops who were not from the SNLF, the Imperial Navy having a number of security, pioneer, base defense, and construction units that were often pressed into service as combat troops. Although they were neither properly trained nor properly equipped for combat, these units often gave a good account of themselves, particularly since some were created from former SNLF personnel.

## CHAPTER 14

Marines and the Muses

Marines may be soldiers—and sailors, too—but they also have an artistic side, write a great deal, dabble in science, and do well in sports. They also turn up in a lot of motion pictures and even television programs. And we had to put the bibliography somewhere.

The Marine Band

Directors of the Marine Band

1.	William Farr	21 Jun 1799-22 Nov 1804
2.	Charles Ashworth	24 Nov 1804-16 Oct 1816
3.	Venerando Pulizzi	17 Oct 1816- 9 Dec 1816
4.	John Dowley	10 Dec 1816-18 Feb 1818
5.	Venerando Pulizzi	19 Feb 1818- 3 Sep 1827
6.	John B. Cuvillier	3 Sep 1827-16 Jun 1829
7.	Joseph Cuvillier	16 Jun 1829-25 Feb 1835
8.	Francis Schenig	26 Feb 1835- 9 Dec 1836
9.	Raphael R. Triay	10 Dec 1836-22 May 1843
10.	Antonio Pons	22 May 1843- 1 May 1844
11.	Joseph Lucchesi	1 May 1844-31 Jul 1846
	Vacancy	31 Jul 1846-26 Oct 1846
12.	Antonio Pons	26 Oct 1846- 7 Jul 1848
13.	Raphael R. Triay	8 Jul 1848- 9 Sep 1855
14.	Francis Scala	9 Sep 1855-13 Dec 1871
15.	Henry Fries	14 Dec 1871-27 Aug 1873
	Vacancy	27 Aug 1873- 2 Sep 1873
16.	Louis Schneider	2 Sep 1873- 1 Oct 1880
17.	John Philip Sousa	1 Oct 1880-30 Jul 1892
	Vacancy	30 Jul 1892- 1 Nov 1892
18.	Francesco Fanciulli	1 Nov 1892-31 Oct 1897
	Vacancy	31 Oct 1897- 3 Mar 1898
19.	William H. Santelmann	3 Mar 1898- 1 May 1927
20.	Taylor Branson	2 May 1927- 1 Apr 1940
	Vacancy	1 Apr 1940- 3 Apr 1940
21.	William F. Santelmann	3 Apr 1940-30 Apr 1955
22.	Albert F. Schoepper	1 May 1955-28 Apr 1974
23.	Dale Harpham	28 Apr 1974-31 Oct 1974

24. Jack T. Kline   1 Nov 1974-31 May 1979
25. John R. Bourgeois   31 May 1979-11 Jul 1996
26. Timothy W. Foley   11 July 1996-

Unusual Honors and Distinctions of the Marine Band

1. The Marine Band is the oldest musical organization in the United States.
2. Since 1869, the Marine Band has serenaded the CMC at his quarters on the morning of 1 January, after which they are invited in for a some hot buttered rum and breakfast.
3. The Marine Band has played at every Presidential Inauguration since 1801, and is known as "The President's Own."

A President Who Never Had the Pleasure of Hearing the Marine Band Play

1. George Washington, 1789-1797.

Presidential Inaugurations at Which the Marine Band Did Not Play

1. George Washington, 1789
2. George Washington, 1793
3. John Adams, 1797

One Ballet Company Managed by Marine Corps Veterans

1. The Bossov Ballet Theater, Waterville, Maine
     Executive Director: Col. Michael Wyly, USMC (Ret)
     Board Members: PFC Arthur J. Bredhoft, USMC (Ret)
                    CPT Charles A. Leader, USMC (Ret)
                    Col. G. I. Wilson, USMCR

One Notable Work of Art Guarded by Marines

1. Leonardo da Vinci's *Mona Lisa*, which had a Marine security detail assigned when on exhibit in Washington in January 1963.

Scientific Marines

Seven Pioneering Scientific Expeditions that Included Marines

1. CPT John Wilkes's "United States Exploring Expedition," 1838-1842
2. Alaska Exploration Expedition, 1867
3. Darien Exploration Expedition, 1870
4. Arctic Expedition, 1881

5. Arctic Expedition, 1883
6. RAdm Richard E. Byrd's First Antarctic Expedition, 1928-1929
7. RAdm Richard E. Byrd's Second Antarctic Expedition, 1933-1935

Marines in Space

Some Marine Space Firsts

First Marine in Space, LTC John H. Glenn, 1962. *
First Marine to the Moon, LTC Walter Cunningham, Apollo 7.
First Marine Chief of Astronauts, COL Robert Cabana, 1996.
First Marine Space Shuttle Commander, COL Jack Lousma, *Columbia*, 1982.

* And the first American in Orbit.

Eight Marine Astronauts

1. Vance D. Brand
2. Robert Cabana
3. Gerlad P. Carr
4. Walter Cunningham
5. John H. Glenn
6. Fred Haise
7. Jack Lousma
8. Story Musgrave *

* A former Marine

The Marines Corps Marathon

Winners of the Marine Corps Marathon

Men

Year	Time	Name	Home
1976	2: 21: 14	Kenneth Moore	Eugene, Or
1977	2: 19: 36	Kevin McDonald	Greenville, SC
1978	2: 18: 08	Scott Eden	Richmond, Va
1979	2: 19: 35	Phil Camp	Pensacola, Fl
1980	2: 18: 31	Michael Ward	Great Britain
1981	2: 16: 31	Dean Matthews	Atlanta. Ga
1982	2: 21: 29	Jeff Smith	Cumberland, Md
1983	2: 17: 46	Farley Simon	Alea, Hi
1984	2: 19: 40	Brad Ingram	Mansfield, Oh
1985	2: 19: 16	Thomas Bernard	Hayes, Va

1986	2: 23: 13	Brad Ingram	Mansfield, Oh
1987	2: 14: 01	Jeff Scuffins	Hagerstown, Md*
1988	2: 21: 59	Jim Hage	Lanham, Md
1989	2: 20: 23	Jim Hage	Lanham, Md
1990	2: 21: 32	Matthew Waight	New Britain, Pa
1991	2: 17: 54	Carlos Rivas	Mexico City, Mexico
1992	2: 24: 09	Rene Guerrero	Mexico City, Mexico
1993	2: 23: 56	Dominique Bariod	Morez, France
1994	2: 22: 51	Graciano Gonzales	Mexico City, Mexico
1995	2: 16: 34	Darrell General	Mitchellville, Md
1996	2: 15: 09	Isaac Garcia	Mexico City, Mexico

* Marine Corps Marathon record holder.

Women

Year	Time	Name	Home
1976	2: 56: 33	Susan Mallery	Columbus, Oh
1977	2: 54: 04	Susan Mallery	Columbus, Oh
1978	3: 03: 34	Jane Killion	New York, NY
1979	2: 58: 14	Joanna Martin	Quantico, Va
1980	2: 41: 48	Jan Yerkes	Buckingham, Pa
1981	2: 50: 33	Cynthia Lorenzoni	Charlottesville, Va
1982	2: 44: 57	Cynthia Lorenzoni	Charlottesville, Va
1983	2: 45: 55	Suzanne Carden	Stroudsburg, Pa
1984	2: 43: 20	Pamela Briscoe	Chevy Chase, Md
1985	2: 44: 42	Natalie Updegrove	Richmond, Va
1986	2: 42: 59	Kathy Champagne	Plattsburgh, NY
1987	2: 44: 36	Mary Robertson	Richmond, Va
1988	2: 51: 26	Lori Lawson	Philadelphia, Pa
1989	2: 45: 16	Laura Dewald	Grand Rapids, Mi
1990	2: 37: 00	Olga Markova	Leningrad. USSR*
1991	2: 44: 27	Amy Kattwinkel	Charlotte, NC
1992	2: 47: 58	Judy Mercon	Clearwater, Fl
1993	2: 48: 41	Holly Ebert	Ogden, Ut
1994	2: 39: 34	Susan Molloy	Charlottesville, Va
1995	2: 49: 21	Claudia Kasen	Williamsburg, Va
1996	2: 48: 34	Emma Cabrera	Mexico City, Mexico

* Marine Corps Marathon record holder

Winners of the Annual "Challenge Cup" Marathon

Year	Winner
1978	USMC
1979	USMC
1980	RN/RM
1981	USMC
1982	USMC

1983	USMC
1984	RN/RM
1985	RN/RM
1986	RN/RM
1987	RN/RM
1988	RN/RM
1989	USMC
1990	RN/RM
1991	RN/RM
1992	RN/RM
1993	RN/RM
1994	RN/RM
1995	USMC
1996	RN/RM

Since 1978 the "Challenge Cup" has been a part of the annual Marine Marathon, pitting a team from the USMC against a combined one from the Royal Navy and the Royal Marines. Since 1978 the combined Royal Navy/Royal Marine team has won a dozen times, and the USMC only seven. Moreover, not since 1983 has the Marine Corps team won twice in succession.

Participants in the Marine Corps Marathon

Year	Runners
1976	1,174
1977	2,655
1978	5,883
1979	7,622
1980	7,800
1981	8,205
1982	11,525
1983	11,761
1984	12,000
1985	10,939
1986	11,255
1987	12,091
1988	12,198
1989	12,798
1990	13,771
1991	14,515
1992	14,330
1993	14,922
1994	16,211
1995	18,397
1996	c. 19,700

A Marine Bookshelf

Eleven Useful Older Books About the Marines

1. *History of the United States Marine Corps*, by M. Almy Aldrich (Boston: 1870)
2. *History of the United States Marine Corps*, by Richard S. Collum (Philadelphia: 1890) *
3. *The Records of Living Officers of the U.S. Navy and Marine Corps*, by Lewis Hamersly (Philadelphia: 1890)
4. *List of the Officers of the Navy of the United States and of the Marine Corps, from 1775 to 1900*, by Edward W. Callahan (New York: 1901)
5. *Soldiers of the Sea*, by Willis J. Abbot (New York: 1919)
6. *"With the Help of God and a Few Marines,"* by A.W. Catlin (New York: 1919)
7. *The United States Marine Corps in the World War* (Washington: 1920)
8. *A History of the United States Marine Corps*, by C.H. Metcalf (New York: 1939)
9. *Famous American Marines*, by Charles L. Lewis (Boston: 1950)
10. *Heroes: USMC, 1861-1955*, by Jane Blakeney (Washington: 1957)
11. *The Marine Corps Biographical Dictionary*, by Karl Schoun (New York: 1963)

* Although Aldrich's book predates Collum's first edition by 15 years, it was in fact largely plagiarized from memoranda and essays that Collum had prepared for Marine Corps internal use.

A Baker's Dozen of Very Good Books About the Marine Corps, by Year of Publication

1. *Guadalcanal Diary*, by Richard Tregaskis (New York: 1943)
2. *The Old Breed*, by George McMillen (Washington: 1949)
3. *The U. S. Marines and Amphibious Warfare*, by Peter A. Isely and Philip A. Crowl (Princeton: 1951)
4. *The Compact History of the United States Marine Corps*, by Philip N. Pierre and Frank O. Hough (New York: 1960)
5. *Soldiers of the Sea: The United States Marine Corps, 1775-1962*, by Robert D. Heinl (Annapolis: 1962)
6. *Strong Men Armed: The U.S.M.C. Against Japan*, by Robert Leckie (New York: 1962)
7. *The United States Marine Corps in World War II*, edited by S. E. Smith (New York: 1967)
8. *The Story of the U.S. Marine Corps*, by J. Robert Moskin (New York: 1977)
9. *Semper Fidelis: The History of the United States Marine Corps*, by Allan Millett (New York: 1980)
10. *The Marine Corps' Search for a Mission, 1880-1898*, by Jack Shulimson (Lawrence, KS: 1993).
11. *Our War Was Different: Marine Combined Action Platoons in Vietnam*, by Albert Hemingway (Annapolis: 1994)
12. *The Marine Book: A Portrait of America's Military Elite*, by Chuck Lawliss (2nd edition, New York: 1992)
13. *Marine: A Guided Tour of a Marine Expeditionary Unit*, by Tom Clancy (New York: 1996)

Ten Important Books About Marines that Have Not Yet Been Written

1. *The United States Marine Corps in the "Banana Wars."*
2. *A History of the Japanese Special Naval Landing Forces*
3. *A History of the Vietnamese Marine Corps*
4. *A History of the San Marco Regiment*
5. *A History of the Korean Marine Corps*
6. *The Marine Corps in the Florida War*
7. *The China Marines*
8. *The Marines in the War with Mexico*
9. *The Marine Corps Lineage Book*
10. *Historical Dictionary of the Marine Corps*

One could actually readily add to this list, since there are no histories of many naval operations in which the Marine Corps served aboard ship, such as the various scientific expeditions, the anti-piracy campaigns (in the Caribbean, the Gulf of Mexico, and the Aegean Sea), and the many years spent on anti-slavery patrol, and so forth.

One Very Strange Book About the Marine Corps

1. *American Samurai: Myth, Imagination, and the Conduct of Battle in the 1st Marine Division, 1941-1945*, by Craig M. Camberon (Cambridge: 1994)

Six Good Books About Marine Aviation

1. *Cavalry of the Sky*, by Lynn Montross (New York: 1954)
2. *Devilbirds: The Story of United States Marine Corps Aviation in World War II*, by John A. DeChant (New York: 1947)
3. *Ground Attack—Vietnam: The Marines Who Controlled the Skies*, by J. M. Moriarty (New York: 1993)
4. *History of Marine Corps Aviation in World War II*, by Robert L. Sherrod (2nd edition, San Rafael, CA: 1980)
5. *Marine Air: First to Fight*, by John Trotti (Novato, CA: 1977)
6. *Marine Corps Aviation, 1912 to the Present*, by Peter B. Mersky (Annapolis: 1983)

One Excellent Book in German About the USMC

1. *Ledernecken: Das U. S. Marine Corps*, by Hartmut Schauer (Stuttgart: 1993)

Five Notable Books by Marines That Are Not Specifically About Marines

1. *The Adventures of General Marbot*, edited by John W. Thomason, Jr. (New York: 1935)
2. *The Art of War*, by Sun Tzu, translated by S.B. Griffith (New York: 1981)
3. *The Doughboys: The Story of the AEF, 1917-1918*, by Laurence Stallings (New York: 1963)
4. *The Military Staff: Its History and Development*, by James D. Hittle (Harrisburg, Pa: 1944)
5. *Written in Blood: The Story of the Haitian People*, by Robert D. Heinl (Boston: 1978)

Eleven Notable Memoirs by Marines

1. *The Reminiscences of a Marine*, by John A. Lejeune (Philadelphia: 1930)
2. *Old Gimlet Eye: The Adventures of Smedley D. Butler*, as told to Lowell Thomas (New York: 1933)
3. *Coral Comes High*, by George P. Hunt (New York: 1946)
4. *Once a Marine: The Memoirs of a General*, by Alexander A. Vandegrift, with R. B. Asprey (New York: 1964)
5. *Coral and Brass*, Holland M. Smith (New York: 1949)
6. *The White King of Gonave*, by Faustin E. Wirkus, with Taney Dudley (Garden City, NY: 1931)
7. *A Marine Tells It to You*, by Frederic M. Wise (New York: 1929)
8. *D-Plus Forever*, by Dave Davenport (New York: 1993)
9. *Suddenly We Didn't Want to Die: Memoirs of a World War I Marine*, by Elton E. Mackin (Novato, CA: 1993)
10. *Colder than Hell: A Marine Rifle Company at Chosin Recersoir*, by Joseph R. Owen (Annapolis: 1996)
11. *The Fortunate Son: The Autobiography of Lewis B. Puller, Jr.*, by Lewis B. Puller, Jr. (New York: 1991)

Two Good Novels About the Marines in World War I

1. *Company K*, by William E. March (New York: 1933)
2. *Through the White*, by Thomas Boyd (New York: 1923)

One Very Good Play About the Marines in World War I

1. *What Price Glory?*, by Max Anderson and Laurence Stallings (New York: 1926)

Four Books by MG Smedley D. Butler

1. *Walter Garvin in Mexico*, with Arthur J. Banks (Philadelphia: 1927)
2. *Old Gimlet Eye: The Adventures of Smedley D. Butler*, as told to Lowell Thomas (New York: 1933)
3. *War Is a Racket* (New York: 1935)
4. *General Smedley D. Butler, the Letters of a Leatherneck*, edited by Anne Cipriano Venzon (Westport, CT: 1992)

The Books of COL John W. Thomason

1. *Fix Bayonets* (New York: 1926)
2. *Red Pants and Other Stories* (New York: 1927)
3. *Marines and Others* (New York: 1929)
4. *Jeb Stuart* (New York: 1930)
5. *Salt Winds and Gobi Dust* (New York: 1934)
6. *The Adventures of Davy Crockett*, edited and with an introduction by John W. Thomason (New York: 1934)
7. *Davy Crockett and his Adventures in Texas*, edited and with an introduction by John W. Thomason (New York: 1934)

8. *The Adventures of General Marbot*, translated and edited with an introduction by John W. Thomason (New York: 1935)
9. *Gone to Texas* (New York: 1937)
10. *Lone Star Preacher* (New York: 1941)
11. *...and a Few Marines* (New York: 1943)

COL Thomason, nicknamed "The Kipling of the Corps," was also the author of nearly 70 articles, essays, reviews, and short stories, which appeared in publications as diverse as *The Saturday Evening Post, The New Yorker, Harper's* and the *Marine Corps Gazette*, as well as being anthologized in over 20 books. A talented illustrator, he also contributed sketches and paintings to over 30 books, and was one of the creators of the Marine Corps' combat art program during World War II. He died of natural causes while on active duty during the war.

The Books of COL Robert D. Heinl, Jr

1. *The Marines at Midway* (Washington: 1944)
2. *The Defense of Wake* (Washington: 1947)
3. *The Marshalls: Increasing the Tempo* (Washington: 1947)
4. *A Dictionary of Military and Naval Quotations* (Annapolis: 1966)
5. *Soldiers of the Sea: The United States Marine Corps, 1775-1962* (Annapolis: 1962)
6. *Victory at High Tide: The Inchon-Seoul campaign* (Philadelphia: 1968)
7. *Handbook for Marine NCOs* (Annapolis: 1970),with collaborators
8. *The Marine Officer's Guide,* (Annapolis: 1977), with collaborators
9. *Written in Blood: The Story of the Haitian People* (Boston: 1978)

COL Heinl, one of the most flamboyant officers in the history of the Marine Corps, also wrote numerous newspapers and magazine articles, introductions, essays, and a variety of other literary works. Many of his books are still in print.

Nine Excellent Biographies of Marines

1. *Guadalcanal General: The Story of Alexander A. Vandegrift, USMC*, by John T. Foster (New York, 1966)
2. *In Many a Strife: General Gerald C. Thomas and the U. S. Marine Corps*, by Alan Millett 1917-1956 (Annapolis: 1993)
3. *Pete Ellis: An Amphibious Warfare Prophet, 1880-1925*, by Dirk Anthony Ballendors and Merrill L. Bartlett (Annapolis: 1996)
4. *Ira Hayes: Pima Marine*, by Albert Hemingway (Lanhan, Md: 1988)
5. *Lejeune: A Marine's Life, 1867-1942*, by Merrill L. Bartlett (Annapolis: 1996)
6. *Marine! The Life of General Lewis B. (Chesty) Puller, USMC (Ret)*, by Burke Davis (Boston: 1962)
7. *Maverick Marine: General Smedley D. Butler and the Contradictions of American Military History*, by Hans Schmidt (Lexington, KY: 1987)
8. *Once a Legend: "Red Mike" Edson of the Marine Corps*, by Jon T. Hoffman (Novato: 1994)
9. *The World of COL John W. Thomason, USMC*, by Martha Anne Turney (Austin: 1984)

One Book that Explains a Lot of Fuss

1. *"Howlin' Mad" vs the Army: Conflict in Command, Saipan, 1944*, by Harry A. Gailey (Novato, CA: 1986)

Two Amusing Books About the Marine Corps

1. *101 Things You Should Never Ask a Marine to Do*, by Edward Temple (New York: 1978)
2. *Short Timers' Guidebook*, by Edward Temple (New York: n.d.)

Two Good Photographic Collections About the Marine Corps

1. *The Marines*, by Anthony Edgeworth and John de St. Jorre (Garden City, NY: 1989)
2. *Warriors: The United States Marines*, by Agostino von Hassell (n.p.: 1988)

One Book About the CMC's House

1. *The Commandant's House*, by Karl Schuon (Washington: 1966)

Four Valuable Studies of the Confederate Marines

1. *Biographical Sketches of the Commissioned Officers of the Confederate States Marine Corps* (1973)
2. *The History of the Confederate States Marine Corps* (1976)
3. *Service Records of Confederate Enlisted Marines* (1979)
4. *The Rebel Leathernecks: The Confederate States Marine Corps* (Shippensburg, PA: 1989)

These are all by Ralph Donnelly. Mr. Donnelly died shortly before the publication of *The Rebel Leathernecks*. A revised edition of the original three volumes, prepared by David Sullivan, will be published in the near future by White Mane Publishing, Shippensburg, Pennsylvania.

Nine Useful Books About Other Marine Corps

1. *Britain's Sea Soldiers*, by Cyril Field (Liverpool: 1924)
2. *Corsairs en Berets Vert: Commandos Marin*, by Rene Bail (Paris: 1976)
3. *De Nederlandse Marniers*, by P. M. Bossche (Bossum: 1966)
4. *Historia de la Infanteria de Marina Española*, by Jose Enrique Rivas Fabal (Madrid: 1970)
5. *Il Reggimento 'San Marco,'* by Antonio Giordani (Milano: 1920)
6. *Infanteria Marina Argentina* (Buenos Aires: 1987)
7. *Marine Badges and Insignia of the World*, by Bert L. Campbell and Ron Reynolds (Poole, Dorset: 1983)
8. *Naval and Marine Badges of World War 2*, by Guido Rosignoli (Poole, Dorset: 1980)
9. *Per mare per terram: A History of the Royal Marines*, by Peter Smith (St. Ives, Hunts: 1979)

Seven Periodicals for Marines

1. *Fortitudine*, an official journal for Marine historians.
2. *Leatherneck*, published by the Leatherneck Association
3. *Manpower Quarterly*, an official journal of personnel concerns
4. *Marines*, the official magazine of the USMC
5. *The Marine Corps Gazette*, published by the Marine Corps League

6. *The Navy Times*, Marine Corps edition, a service-oriented newspaper tailored for Marines
7. *Semper Fidelis,* for retired Marines.

Marine Corps-Related Organizations

1st Marine Aircraft Wing Association, Box 7240, Freeport, NY, 11520
1st Marine Division Association, Inc., Box 220840, Chantilly, VA, 22022
2d Marine Division Association, Inc., Box 8180, MCB Camp Lejeune, NC, 28542
3d Marine Division Association, Inc., Box 297, Dumfries, VA, 22026-0297
4th Marine Division Association, Inc., Box 595, Ft. Laurel, FL, 34272
5th Marine Division Association, Inc., 260 Norwinden Dr, Springfield, PA, 19064-3517
6th Marine Division Association, Inc., Route 4, Box 338-A, Neosho, MO, 64850
A.A. Cunningham Air Museum Foundation, 207 West Main St., Suite 100, Havelock, NC, 28532
Association of Survivors—WWII Marine/Navy Parachute Units, Box 1972, La Jolla, CA, 92038
China Marine Association, 28 Mcrequoit Dr, Brunswick, ME, 04011-7612
Edson's Raiders Association, Box 3195, Oakton, VA, 22124-9195
Marine Corps Association, Building 715, MCB, Quantico, VA, 22134
Marine Corps Aviation Association, Inc., Box 296, Quantico, VA, 22134
Marine Corps Combat Correspondents Association, Inc., 304 Glen Rock La, Conroe, TX, 77385
Marine Corps Command and Staff College Foundation, Inc., Box 112, Quantico, VA, 22134
Marine Corps Drill Instructors Association, 4085 Pacific Highway, San Diego, CA, 92111
Marine Corps Engineer Association, Box 566, Jacksonville, NC, 28541
Marine Corps Historical Foundation, Box 420, Quantico, VA, 22134-0240
Marine Corps League, Box 3070, Merrifield, VA, 22116-3070
Marine Corps Musician Association, 1209 Huntley Pl, Alexandria, VA, 22307
Marine Corps Mustang Association, Inc., Box 1314, Delran, NJ, 08075-0142
Marine Corps Reserve Officers Association, 11 North Royal, Suite 406, Alexandria, VA, 22314
Marine Corps Scholarship Foundation, Inc., Box 3008, Princeton, NJ, 08543
Marine Corps Tankers Association National Headquarters, Box 2029, Oceanside, CA, 92051
Marine Executive Association, Box 9372, McLean, VA, 22102-0372
Marine Night Fighter Association, 26 Merry Rd., Newark, DE 19713-2515
Montford Point Marine Association, 11509 Chantilly La, Mitchellville, MD, 20721
The Chosin Few, 100 Mountain Spring Rd, Waynesville, NC, 28786
United States Marine Raider Association, HQ, 4711 Del Monte Ave., San Diego, CA, 92107
Women Marines Association, 36 South Broadway (6B), Nyack, NY, 10960
Young Marines of the Marine Corps League, Box 70735 SW Station,Washington,DC,20024-0735

Marines and the Moving Image

The Ten Best Motion Pictures About Marines

1. *What Price Glory?* (1926), with Victor McLaglen, Edmund Lowe, and Delores Del Rio, based on the play by Maxwell Anderson and Laurence Stallings, but with less of an anti-war message and more patriotic ardor.
2. *Tell It to the Marines* (1926), starring Lon Chaney, William Haines, and Eleanor Boardes, plus thousands of Marines and sailors serving as extras, through the courtesy of the Department of the Navy.
3. *Wake Island* (1942). An heroic, exciting, but very unrealistic film about the defense of the island outpost, highly rated at the time, with William Bendix, Brian Donlevy, Robert Preston, and others
4. *Guadalcanal Diary* (1943). Film version of Richard Tregaskis' classic book, with Preston Foster, Lloyd Nolan, William Bendix, Richard Conte, and Anthony Quinn.
5. *Sands of Iwo Jima* (1949), starring John Wayne (who was IV-F), as well as Forrest Tucker, among others, and lots of original footage.
6. *Halls of Montezuma* (1950).Marines in the Pacific, with Richard Widmark, Jack Palance, Robert Wagner, Jack Webb, and Karl Malden, among others.
7. *Battle Cry* (1955), based on the novel by Leon Uris, with Van Heflin, James Whitmore, Aldo Ray, and many others, about the "Fighting 6th Marines" in training and in the Marianas.
8. *The D.I.* (1957), with Jack Webb as the archtypical D.I.
9. *The Great Santini* (1979), with Robert Duvall, Michael O'Keefe, and more, about a "warrior without a war."
10. *Full Metal Jacket* (1987), by Stanley Kubrick, with Matthew Modine, Adam Baldwin, and Vincent D'Onofrio, about Marines during the Vietnam War, from Boot Camp to combat.

Two Musicals About the Marine Corps

1. *The Singing Marine* (1937), with Dick Powell, Dorris Weston, and Lee Dixon, and musical numbers choreographed by Busby Berkeley, a China Marine and a fancy dame.
2. *Iceland* (1942), with Sonja Henie, John Payne, and Jack Oakie, among others, and lots of ice-skating in Iceland.

Eight Television Shows Featuring the Marines

1. *Baa-Baa Black Sheep,* later renamed *Black Sheep Squadron* (1976-1978), with Robert Conrad and James Whitmore, about the adventures of MAJ Gregory "Pappy" Boyington and his squadron during World War II.
2. *Gomer Pyle, USMC* (1964-1970), with Jim Nabors, a service comedy.
3. *JAG* (1995-date), David James Elliot, Tracey Needham, and Andrea Thompson play Navy JAG officers, one of them a Marine, who pursue miscreants in and out of uniform.
4. *The Lieutenant* (1963-1964) was an exploration of the life and experiences of a young Marine officer, created by Gene Roddenberry, who went on to do *Star Trek*, and featuring Gary Lockwood in the title role, serving as a platoon leader in CPT Robert Vaughn's company.

5. *Major Dad* (1989-1991), with Gerald McRaney, was a surprisingly realistic service sit-com with some serious overtones.
6. *Navy Log* (1955-1958) was devoted to dramatic portrayals of historic episodes in the history of the Navy, with occasional programs about the Marine Corps.
7. *Supercarrier* (mid-1980s) was a short-lived series about the mythic USS *Georgetown*, which featured several Marines in various capacities.
8. *Space: Above and Beyond* (early 1990s), science fictional Marines in an intergalactic war a century or two hence. Not very well done.

Marines in Cyberspace

Two Important Official USMC Websites

1. Marine Corps Home Page: http: //www.usmc.mil/
2. *Marines Magazine Online*, http: //www.usmc.mil/marines/default.htm

Actually, the Marine Corps Home Page provides links to scores of official Marine Corps pages, and many, many other unofficial ones as well.

Nine Good Unofficial USMC Websites

1. The Marine Corps League: http: //www.mcleague.org/
2. Psybernaut's Cyber Spot: http: //www.cris.com/~Psyber0/
3. Brian's Marine Corps Page: http: //www.sover.nct/%7Ebrjl/
4. Uncle Sam's Misguided Children: http: //www.nwlink.com/~park/marines/devildoggz.html
5. USMC: http: //www.umiacs.umd.edu/~jicore/usmc/
6. Semper Fi, Mac!: http: //cpcug.org/user/gyrene/
7. Fortitudine: http: //dubhe.cc.nps.navy.mil/~bkandber/
8. Marine 1's Home Page: http: //www.cris.com/%7Emarine1/
9. Marine Corps Edition of *NavyTimes*: http: //www.armytimes.com/nmhome.html

Some Websites for Foreign Marine Corps

1. Britain, Royal Marines: http: //www.royal-navy mod.uk/today/marines.htm
2. Brazil, *Fuzileiros Navais*: http: //www.mar.br/~cnb/gptfnb.htm
3. The Netherlands, *Korps Mariniers*: http: //www.mindef.nl/marine/kamarns.htm
4. The Netherlands, *Korps Mariniers*: http: //www.cybercomm.nl/~manning/
5. Peru, *Infanteria de Marina:* http: //www.marina.mil.pe/fuerzas/fuerzas_navales.html
6. Spain, *Infanteria de Marina:* http: //www.redestb.es/personal/esz/im.htm
7. Venezuela, *Infanteria de Marina:* http: //dubhe.cc.nps.navy.mil/~vamichel/cim.html

Appendix: A Short Marine Vocabulary

Aboard	On base, on analogy with "aboard ship"
Adrift	Loose from towline or moorings; scattered about; not properly stowed
Abaft	Toward the rear of a vessel, vehicle, or aircraft
Aft	Referring to or toward the stern (rear) of a vessel, vehicle, or aircraft
Airdale	An aviator, particularly a naval aviator
ALICE	"All-purpose, Lightweight, Individual Carrying Equipment, " who everyone else calls a backpack
All Hands	Everyone
As you were	An imperative meaning "Resume your former activity."
Ashore	Not on base, an aircraft, or a ship.
Aye, Aye, Sir	Acknowledgment that an order has been received, understood, and will be carried out; not the equivalent of "Yes"
BAM	"Broad Assed Marine," World War II slang for a Woman Marine
BCD	Bad Conduct Discharge
BDR	Basic Daily Routine
Belay	To make fast or to secure, as in "belay that line," or, figuratively, an order or instruction to disregard something just said.
Below	Downstairs, from shipboard usage
Billet	Assignment, job, or duty
Blouse	Military for uniform jacket
Blues	Full dress uniform.
Boondockers	Field boots, for operating in the boondocks
Boondocks	The wilderness
Boot	A recruit, who goes to "Boot Camp"
Bow	The front of a vessel, vehicle, or aircraft
Breakout	To make something ready for use, to unpack
Brig	What the Army calls the "Stockade"
Brown bagger	A married man
Bulkhead	A wall, from shipboard usage
Buttkit	An ashtray.
C.P.	Command Post
Camies	Camouflage uniform
Catch a hit	Being "chewed out."
Carry on	The order to resume previous activity
Chewed	Scolded, as in "Chewed out"
Chit	Documentation, as a receipt
Chow	Food
Chow Down	Eat

Chow Hound	One who enjoys his food immensely, in volume
CMC	Commandant of the Marine Corps
Colors	The flag, also the ceremonial raising and lowering thereof
Corpsman	A U.S. Navy medical aidman attached to a Marine unit
Cover	A cap or hat
Cruise	An enlistment
Deck	From shipbarod usage, the floor
Deuce Gear	Basic equipment, as outlined in the legendary "Regulation 782"
DI	Drill Instructor, a godlike being to Boots
Ditty Bag	A carryall, often restricted to one containing toiletries
Ditty Box	A place to store things
Doggies	Army guys
EST	Essential Subject Test, annual examination for lower ranking enlisted personnel
Fantail	The main deck on the after part of a ship.
Field day	Barracks cleanup.
Field scarf	Regulation neck tie, which is never worn in the field
Forecastle	The upperdeck at the bow of a ship
Forward	Towards the front end of a ship, aircraft, or vehicle
Galley	Ashore or afloat, the kitchen
Gangway	An imperative, meaning "Clear a path!"
Gator	An amphibious ship, and by extension the sailors who serve in it, from "alligator"
Gear	Equipment, particularly one's own
Geedunk	An place where ice cream, candy, and other toothsome goodies are available aboard ship, "Gedunk Bar" during World War II
Goat Lockers	Senior NCO quarters
God Box	The Chapel
Green Weanie	"Getting screwed"
Grunt	Infantryman, Vietnam era
Gunny	A gunnery sergeant
Hashmarks	Longevity stripes, found on the sleeves of senior enlisted personnel
Hatch	A door or doorway, from shipboard usage
Head	What the Army calls a latrine
High and Tight	Extreme Marine haircut
Hooch	One's quarters, even if only a shelter half
Hump	March
Ladder	Stairs, from shipboard usages
Leave	A long holiday; a vacation
Liberty	A short holiday; a pass
Mount Out	To load for movement, particularly by sea
Mustang	An officer who started out as an enlisted man
Old Salt	A long service Marine
Overhead	The ceiling, from shipboard usages
Passegeway	A corridor, from shipboard usage
Payback	Revenge
Piece	A weapon, particularly one's own
Pogey Ropes	Derisive reference to the French *fourragere* worn by the 5th and 6th Marincs, for their services in France during World War I

Police	To straighten or tidy up
Port	Left in relation to the layout of a ship, vehicle, aircraft, as determined by standing on deck and facing its bow
Rack	A bed, hence "rack out" for "go to bed"
Sack	Also a bed
Scrambled Eggs	Gold decoration on the visor of dress caps for officers from major on up; once referred to as "Chicken Guts"
Scuttlebutt	A water fountain, and, by extension, gossip and rumor, which are most conveniently spread while taking water at a scuttlebutt
Seabag	What the Army calls a "duffle bag," for storing clothing and other belongings
Secure	To cease an activity, to store something, to tie something down
Sick Bay	Hospital or infirmary, from shipboard usage
Ship Over	What the Army calls "re-upping"; also "shipping over"
Skipper	Commanding Officer
Skivvies	Underwear
Skylark	To goof-off; to loiter
Smoking lamp	Controls smoking; when it is "lit" smoking is authorized
Sound Off	To shout, or to complain
Square Away	To straighten out, literally or figuratively
Starboard	Right in relation to the layout of a ship, vehicle, or aircraft, as determined by standing on deck and facing its bow
Stern	The back end of a vessel, vehicle, or aircraft
Swab	A mop.
Swabbie	A Navy guy, who has been known to wield a swab
Topside	Upstairs or the upper deck, from shipboard usage
Turn to	To get started, to begin
Wardroom	Officer's lounge and dining area aboard ship, also used figuratively to mean officers in general
Word ("The Word")	Accurate information
Yardbird	A loafer